The Drama of Redemption

Walking with Jesus Through The Prophets

A Resource Book for Teachers

By

Sarah Fallis

HOPKINS publishing inc.

PO Box 3687
Cleburne, TX 76033
HopkinsPublishing.com

Discover Other Titles by Hopkins Publishing:
HopkinsPublishing.com

The Drama
of
Redemption

Dedicated to
Tonya and Paden,
who helped me see the Bible anew
through the eyes of a child.
"Behold, children are a heritage from the LORD,
The fruit of the womb is a reward" (Ps. 127:3).

In loving memory of
Granddaddy
George Thomas (Tom) Howard
1899-1980
"Then I heard a voice from heaven saying to me, 'Write:
"Blessed are the dead who die in the Lord from now on."'
'Yes,' says the Spirit,
'that they may rest from their labors,
and their works follow them'" (Rev. 14:13).

Contents

Illustrations

Chapter 9

Chapter 10

Chapter 11

Chapter 12

Chapter 13

Chapter 14

Chapter 15

Chapter 16

Chapter 17

Chapter 18

Chapter 19

Chapter 20

Chapter 21

Chapter 22

Chapter 23

Chapter 24

Appendix

Endorsements

In this book Sarah Fallis has given us an Illustrated Commentary of Old Testament Prophets (Major and Minor), containing ample and appropriate New Testament Messianic Fulfillment; supplying Material and Methods by which Bible Class Teachers (for varied age groups) could develop clear and commendable lessons from the Divine Decrees God so beautifully unfolded over 4 millenniums.

Her writing helps to "clear the air" as to true fulfilment of prophecy in contrast to both confused scribes (teachers of the Law) and modern day theologians (Note Isaiah's survey of Messianic suffering as covered by Isaiah (52:13-53:12 in Chapter 14).

As chapters of the book unfold, key points of previous chapters are inserted and applied to give a grasp of God's plan and grandeur unfolding (cf. Chapter 16, where Isaiah 61 is related to 60, 59, 53, and 4, plus Isaiah 60:6 is related to I Peter 2:5; Revelation 1:6).

The harmony of Scripture is presented as a golden thread throughout the book: Prophecy and Fulfillment; Harmony of the righteous, both Jew and Gentile; God's purpose and plan culminated in Christ (cf. Chapter 18).

Application material is made easy by the use of graphics, pictures, etc. (cf. Racing Horses from Jeremiah 12, lesson 3, in Chapter 18).

Summary material occurs along the way, supplying a clear focus as to: biblical harmony; true interpretation; God's unfolding plan, etc. (cf. Chapter 23, which is a beautiful blending of material from Zechariah, Isaiah, Jeremiah, Ezekiel, the Psalms, etc., with prophetic utterances about Jesus as Messiah [Priest & King], in the New Testament fulfillment [as covered by Matthew, John, Peter, Paul, the Hebrew writer, etc.].

If a Teacher carefully studies and utilizes the multiple methods and materials contained in this book, he/she will be, at the end, a better Teacher!

— **Dayton Keesee,** author, preacher in Indiana, Louisiana, Texas, and Oklahoma, instructor at the Sunset International Bible Institute, teacher and missionary in Nigeria, Canada, Ukraine, India, S. Africa, Trinidad, and Russia.

God's Old Testament prophets are some of the most fascinating, courageous and interesting men of the Old Testament. I've taught the prophetic books for over 40 years and, on a few occasions, have even attempted to teach some of their stories to children. They loved learning about these prophets! The great events and lessons found in these books are for all people, and children are no exception. Sarah Fallis has done a superb job of providing teaching materials for both teachers and children on the writing prophets. If you teach children, you need to get this book. If you've been afraid that they will not understand the material, you need to get this book. It is done in a practical way with descriptions and illustrations, and most importantly is scripturally sound.

– **Denny Petrillo**, president, Bear Valley Bible Institute, Denver, CO.

Sarah has made a major contribution toward accomplishing our God-given purpose of communication of His word, and in this case engaging the minds of those whom many dismiss – children. I was impressed with the "simple" way she presents the sweeping scope of God's eternal purpose. It reminded me of Paul's teaching method of "opening" and "placing before" as he reasoned from the Scriptures (Acts 17:2-3). Being aware of, enthralled by, and thoroughly convinced of the reality and power of fulfilled prophecy, is not only a powerful evidence of the inspiration of Scripture, but is a major factor that will keep Christians craving the pure milk of God's word (I Pet.2:2) and ensuring that we "retain the standard of sound words" (II Tim.1:13).

– **Ed McGeachy**, preacher, Bridgewood Church of Christ, Fort Worth, TX.

The books of Prophecy in the Old Testament can often be a confusing and sticky subject to teach for adults, let alone young children. However Sarah has given us a resource that will gently guide us through the Prophets's actions, their prophecies, and most importantly their anticipation of our Savior. Whether you have spent a lot of time studying this section of scripture or not, this book will give you the necessary tools to understand and teach this vital, but often overlooked section of the Bible. I have enjoyed teaching from The Drama of Redemption: Walking with Jesus from Creation to Canaan with my own children, and cannot wait to use this book next!

– **Christa Bryant**, preacher's wife, speaker for women's programs, author, instructor in wives' program, Southwest School of Bible Studies, Austin, TX.

Having taught children's Bible classes for many years, this holistic approach on the prophets which Sarah Fallis has presented here, as well as in her book, The Drama of Redemption: Walking with Jesus from Creation to Canaan, has brought even greater excitement and joy to the privilege of teaching God's word. Where most teachers might shy away, Sarah boldly shines the light on God's prophesies through the prophets of the Old Testament to bring out for children the incredibly multifaceted beauty of God's redemption of sinful man. The word pictures, memorable illustrations, thoughtful questions, and practical teaching tips and tools instill confidence and enthusiasm in teachers to courageously study the often forgotten prophets with their students. Focusing on God's great plan to bring man back to Him, this material encourages tremendous awe and appreciation for Him, lays a strong foundation, and stirs up deeper motivation for seeking His will more diligently in children and adults alike.

– **Cheri Deaver**, preacher's wife, Bible class teacher, Denton, TX.

The first time I heard Sarah Fallis speak, she mentioned her ideas for teaching children the writing prophets. I was thrilled with the idea because I always found our brotherhood's curriculum choices lacking in this wonderful area of the Old Testament.

This book has fulfilled my expectations and then some! In the first chapter, she makes a solid and well-researched case for teaching our children about the writing prophets.

This would also be an excellent study for adults; we need this kind of faith-building material!

I like the side-by-side layouts of the Old Testament prophecies with their New Testament fulfillments.

For teachers, Sarah offers great lesson-presentation ideas, and gives application ideas for different grade levels. The illustrations are not cartoonish and are very illustrative of sometimes-hard concepts. There are helpful worksheets to use as well. She brings God and faith in Him into clear focus.

Thank you Sarah, for giving us some great faith-building lessons that will ground our children in ways no other curriculum I have seen can do.

– **Luann Rogers**, preacher's wife, speaker for women's programs, children's Bible teacher, Atlanta, GA.

Acknowledgments

My grandfather, Tom Howard, gave me a valuable gift—a love for the fascinating preachers in the Old Testament, the ones we call "the prophets." And, God has given me the opportunities to share that gift with others, especially with children. I must first express my gratitude to Him for those blessings, because it has been a joy to share my love for these great men of God with others. God has also blessed me with the education and ability to study, teach, and write so I can give this valuable gift to others whom I may never meet personally. To Him be the glory both now and forever.

When I think of those who have impacted my life and encouraged me to write this book, I must express appreciation to the children in my third and fourth grade classes at the Brown Trail Church of Christ in Bedford, Texas. This is the group where I had the time to finally teach all of these lessons, develop the materials, and work up puzzles and simple drawings to illustrate the prophets' messages. It was also with this group that I began to see more fully the importance of what my grandfather had taught me. I'm indebted to their parents, especially Sheri Miller and Linda Griffin, for encouraging me to write these lessons for others. I'm also indebted to co-teachers like Sandi Smith and Kim Chapman who saw the importance of holistic teaching of the unifying message of the Bible.

The Ladies' Bible Class at the Bridgewood Church of Christ in Fort Worth, Texas, deserves my sincere gratitude. They listened to many of these lessons, offered insight, and encouraged me through their love and interest in God's Word and work. However, there is one person from that class that I could not have done without, and that is Jeane Coffey. She helped me significantly on the first book, proof-reading, formatting, and helping me choose the best wording of some of the concepts. On this book, she has been invaluable! She has read and reread the manuscript for grammar and typos and has proofed all of the illustrations. Many of my older puzzle sheets were a combination of computer work and hand drawings. Jeane took those and put them all into computer generated work that is very professional looking. Teachers are the beneficiaries of her expertise in that area. Her encouragement, love, and friendship are blessings I treasure.

I am also grateful to Jodie Boren for the use of his artwork. He graciously did the drawings for some of these lessons when I was teaching the children at Brown Trail Church of Christ, and he gave me permission to use them in this publication. Roy Johnson, who did the artwork for my first book, has provided the other illustrations. Everyone who has read this work has commented on the quality of his art! All I had to do was email Roy and ask him to read a certain section and illustrate it. He always exceeded my expectations! He is also responsible for the cover design. I could not have written this without his artistic talent and willingness to work with me on it.

There is one person who has gone on to his reward who deserves my sincere gratitude, and that is Homer Hailey. For three or four years, I corresponded with him about the prophets. In fact, Gary liked to tease me about my "ninety-year-old pen-pal!" In the summer of 1998, we had the pleasure of meeting him and visiting with him at his son's ranch in Abilene, Texas. I took the material I was teaching the children and enjoyed showing him the notebook they prepared with drawings, scripture sheets, puzzles and story sheets. He was fascinated with what I was doing with children and encouraged me to continue my study and write this book. You will see his influence throughout.

Several Bible class teachers have been interested in this project and have encouraged me to complete it. Almost every time I saw Luann Rogers after we first met, she asked me if I was still working on it! I'm thankful for her gently pushing me to the finish line, and I'm also thankful for her reading some of the material and writing a recommendation. Cheri Deaver has also been gently pushing me to complete this, especially since she was using my first book in her Bible class and would be ready for the prophets in the fall of 2015. Christa Bryant, a teacher and writer with whom I share a special bond since both our husbands teach in schools of preaching, has also taken time to read the manuscript. Pam Harris has made valuable suggestions and helped me with age-appropriate vocabulary, especially in Isaiah 53. Dayton Keesee read all the manuscript as Jeane and I were completing the corrections, and he was gracious to write a review. I'm also thankful to Denny Petrillo and Ed McGeachy for their time and scholarship in their comments.

Gary Fallis, my husband of fifty-one years, has encouraged me almost daily since I began to envision this book years ago. He has added his knowledge and expertise in the Bible, but most importantly, he has lifted me up when I was discouraged and helped me see there really is a need for this book when I doubted.

> The righteous shall flourish like a palm tree,
>
> he shall grow like a cedar in Lebanon.
>
> Those who are planted in the house of the LORD
>
> shall flourish in the courts of our God.
>
> They shall still bear fruit in old age;
>
> they shall be fresh and flourishing,
>
> to declare that the LORD is upright;
>
> He is my rock, and there is no unrighteousness in Him (Psalm 92:12-15).

Introduction

This book is a natural follow-up to <u>The Drama of Redemption: Walking with Jesus from Creation to Canaan</u>. However, the organization and presentation is different. In the first volume, I focused on the shadow of Jesus as seen in Genesis through Joshua and how we can teach that to children of various ages. I've been humbled by the response to that work. Many good teachers are using the book as a resource to supplement their curriculum; others are using it as the main curriculum for their classes. It has been a joy to have teachers show me their bulletin boards with the shadow of Jesus encompassing it and to have them share how the children are interested in seeing Jesus in those familiar Bible stories of the Old Testament.

The writing prophets kept the Messianic hope alive throughout the history of Israel and Judah. Their pictures of the Messiah and His kingdom provide a rich treasure chest for teachers willing to open those books and bring those treasures into their classrooms. I heard Tim LaHaye of the "Left Behind" series say, "Fulfilled prophecy is the unsung message of the church!" To which I have to say, "Amen!" However, he is singing a different song from what Jesus and the apostles sang. And, because we have neglected the prophets in our teaching of both children and adults, the premillennial doctrine touted by LaHaye, John Hagee, David Jeremiah, and countless others has taken root in the fertile soil of biblical ignorance among many in the world of Christendom. I don't want that to happen to our children!

Have you thought about the fact that the premillennial doctrine is a uniquely American doctrine? Let me illustrate: A few years ago, I was in Ukraine teaching women some of my favorite lessons from the prophets. At one point, I mentioned that before the break-up of the Soviet Union, many preachers in America were teaching that the bear in Daniel chapter 7 is Russia. They laughed! That doctrine just did not make sense to them. When they read Daniel 7, they didn't get that idea at all. And, neither would anyone in America who is knowledgeable in the Word, but false doctrine always takes root in the soil of ignorance. Once it has taken root, it is very difficult for the truth to grow and thrive in that heart. This incident also illustrates the fact that if a Bible doctrine is true, it is true and makes sense in any culture.

There is also a bit of a "cult-like" intellectualism among those who study and teach the prophets. I'm the first to admit that it takes time, effort, and diligence to mine the treasures of these books, but there are many wonderful lessons that even a child can learn. There may be some who will think that if I can help children actually understand the prophets, I either don't know them myself because they are much too difficult for children, or I have ruined their scholarly position by making the prophets accessible. I certainly hope not. I would like to think that every teacher from kindergarten through doctoral work would want children to know as much of the Bible's message as possible, including these fascinating pictures in the prophets. I've heard it said that the Bible is deep enough to drown an elephant and shallow enough for a child to wade in. I think that's definitely true of the prophets. I want the children to have the experience I did with my grandfather as I note in Chapter 1 so they will not be afraid to study these fascinating messages later in greater depth.

This book is not a commentary on the prophets. It is, rather, a collection of my favorite lessons from the prophets. I don't deal with all the prophets; some like Obadiah, have messages that are not suited to the purpose of this book. Others, like Jonah, are rather straight forward, and children are usually familiar with them. However, I think it is very important to show children how Jesus used Jonah as a sign of His death and resurrection, so that will be included in this book in the appendix. I do not deal with Daniel in the lion's den, Isaiah and the sun dial, or Jeremiah being put in stocks and in the dungeon. These are the action type lessons that are most often taught to children in a regular curriculum. I do not deal with the kings and many of the specific events in Israel's history, since my purpose is to illuminate the messages of the prophets.

I also do not deal in detail with each prophet. My purpose is to focus on the Messianic prophecies that are vivid pictures of Jesus and the kingdom that children can relate to. A second purpose is what we learn about God from the prophets. And, a third purpose is to highlight some life lessons from colorful word pictures of the prophets. Some of these will be intertwined into one lesson. Others will be separate, individual lessons.

Resources: When we think about holistic Bible study/teaching, especially as it relates to the prophets, we may think it is too advanced for children or too difficult for teachers. Admittedly, many of the resources on the prophets are scholarly and can be intimidating. There are 3 books by Homer Hailey that I've found extremely helpful:

1. From Creation to the Day of Eternity – this book, in the author's own words "... sets forth the divine plan in simple language, beginning with God and the creation, tracing the plan to its consummation in 'the day of eternity.'" The primary focus is the historical development of God's purpose. It will help you make good choices and keep Jesus in your lessons as you teach the historical events of the Old Testament.

2. Hailey's Comments Vol. 1 – this book has a brief Old Testament Survey of about 65 pages; almost all the rest of it is devoted to the topic, "Studying the Prophets." Hailey gives a summary of the main message of each of the writing prophets with particular emphasis on the Messianic hope. If your knowledge of the prophets is lacking, this volume will give you a nice, comfortable introduction to each of these men and their messages.

3. The Messiah of Prophecy to the Messiah on the Throne – this is my favorite of all of Homer Hailey's books! I feel like I'm sitting with Granddaddy, looking anew and with childlike wonder into the pictures of Jesus these preachers paint for us. Your Bible knowledge will be enriched and your teaching energized by reading this book.

Another book I have found helpful is Preaching from the Prophets by Kyle M. Yates. He deals more with the social, moral and religious evils than with the Messianic hope. Probably the most helpful section of the book is at the end of the discussion of each prophet where he lists "Practical Lessons of Permanent Value." This section will stimulate your thinking as you teach some of the life lessons from the prophets. Yates also has a good, concise summary of the historical background of each prophet. This will give you a good sense of what was going on in the social and political world and the events that affected Israel's future. Don't become overwhelmed with the world history, wars, and pagan kings. When teaching children, this is only vaguely important. This information is definitely helpful, though, if you are teaching junior high, high school, or adults.

Another excellent resource for the prophets is The Prophet Motive by Kenny Barfield. He has taught Christian evidences to high school, college age, and adults. This book approaches the prophets from that perspective—fulfilled prophecy as an evidence of the inspiration of the Bible. He deals with the specific prophecies about the ancient nations, verifying the fulfillment with historical accounts. He also deals with the questions regarding the dating of the prophets that teachers need to be prepared to answer. One excellent section compares the ancient "prophets" like Nostradamus and Zoroaster with the prophets of God. He does the same with modern-day prophets. This will give you a wealth of material to include if you are teaching fifth grade and above; it will also strengthen your faith. One thing you will appreciate about this book is that it is well-researched. Barfield leaves no "loose ends" for the atheist, agnostic, or liberal scholar to pick to pieces.

For deeper, richer study, there are other good commentaries available. Homer Hailey has an excellent book on Isaiah and one on The Minor Prophets; and Burton Coffman has a series of four volumes on The Minor Prophets. I can recommend any works by Furman Kearley and Rex Turner. (My husband, Gary, studied under Dr. Kearley at Lubbock Christian University and did graduate work under him at Abilene Christian. I was also privileged to sit in many of his classes at lectureships and workshops. His scholarly and humble presentation of the work of the prophets has influenced us both in content and attitude.) Don Simpson's commentary on Daniel is concise, scholarly, and easy to read; I found it especially helpful on the latter part of Daniel, dealing with the seventy weeks prophecy. I also found Jim McGuiggan's work on both Daniel and Ezekiel helpful. The commentary set Truth for Today contains scholarly and well-written volumes on the various prophets. However, for teaching children the Old Testament prophets the ones I listed earlier will be sufficient. I guarantee, though, you will get "hooked" by the prophets and desire to learn more about these fascinating men and their messages!

Important concepts to keep before the children: The prophets speak in figurative language about both the goodness and severity of God, and that can sometimes be overwhelming to children. Therefore, it is vital to stress the **purpose of God's discipline** of both His people and the nations. "For when your judgments are in the earth, the inhabitants of the world will learn righteousness" (Isa. 26:9). God's judgments, even when they involved extreme punishment, were not executed capriciously, but were for the greater purpose of instructing in righteousness. Also, in relation to Israel, His discipline was to purify, protect and prepare them for the coming of the Messiah. This is the reason God commissioned the prophets. Six times in the book of Jeremiah, God says something similar to this: "I have also sent to you all My servants the prophets, rising up early and sending them, saying, 'Turn now everyone from his evil way, amend your doings, and do not go after other gods to serve them; then you will dwell in the land which I have given you and your fathers.' But you have not inclined your ear, nor obeyed Me" (Jer. 35:15). Notice that God said He rose up early to send His prophets. This is God's way of saying that sending His prophets to instruct and warn was vitally important.

Related to this concept is the recurring theme of the **remnant**. The word is found 86 times in the NKJV; only 7 times does the word refer to some "remnant" other than of Israel. The message of the prophets was that God would preserve a believing remnant; the remnant would return to the land; and the remnant would be saved through the work of Jesus Christ, the Messiah of prophecy. The prophets were God's instruments to instruct the remnant, to give them hope, and to prepare them for the coming of Christ. At the close of the Old Testament, we might think the prophets had failed, but when we open the New Testament, we meet members of the faithful remnant—Zacharias and Elizabeth, Mary and Joseph, Simeon, Anna, the shepherds, Nicodemus, the twelve, etc. The prophets had been faithful with a difficult task, and we are the beneficiaries of their work.

Some "How To…" Suggestions: Many of these suggestions are in my first book, so I will be brief here. I always have the children make a notebook that they leave in the classroom; they only take it home on special occasions, and they must bring it back. We collect the scripture sheets, puzzles, question sheets and illustrations in the notebook. For the lessons from the prophets, I use the side-by-side scripture sheets for almost every lesson. I will include several in this book, but I strongly suggest you prepare your own; it is good review/study. I have about three different colors of highlighters for the students. I instruct them to highlight the words, phrases or "picture language" in the prophets' statement in the Old Testament and the corresponding fulfillment in the New Testament in the same color. This keeps the prophecy/fulfillment concept in focus for every lesson.

The "follow the stars" concept that I describe in my first book is excellent for the prophets. It is helpful to place stars on or above the timeline in the classroom with a keyword that will remind the students of the specific prophecy. You may also want to include a smaller star on the illustration page in their notebook.

I thoroughly enjoy teaching the prophets to children! My most recent experience with children was with third and fourth grades I was teaching on Wednesday evening. When they studied Old Testament on Sunday morning, I taught special lessons I called "Life Lessons from the Prophets"—what the prophets tell us about God, about worship, about obedience. I usually had a lesson about the prophets in general and why God sent the prophets to His people—what their responsibility and purpose was. Then, when the children were studying the life of Jesus in the Sunday morning class, I would teach about Jesus from the Old Testament—mainly from the prophets, but I would always begin with the lessons in Genesis.

You can use these lessons in the "teach it forward" and "teach it backward" method I noted in my first book. When you are teaching the Old Testament, teach it forward, pointing to Jesus. Then, when you are teaching the New Testament, do like Matthew and link back to "that it might be fulfilled…" It is amazing how many times Old Testament references are in the New Testament. Also, when you teach the book of Acts, don't just teach the events—teach the sermons! Note that the apostles preached Old Testament prophecy has been fulfilled. What they did is important because they left us with good, encouraging and courageous examples of faith. However, what they preached is important because this is the message that saves, the message of hope, the message our children need! We may tell children the two oft repeated slogans: "What the Old Testament prophets wrote, the New Testament apostles quote." And, "The Old Testament is the New Testament concealed and the New Testament is the Old Testament revealed." However, these truths are much more powerful and memorable if we show them—if this is evident in our teaching.

I found this picture on this website: http://lavistachurchofchrist.org/Picture.htm. It perfectly illustrates Isaiah 55:8-9: "'For My thoughts are not your thoughts, nor are your ways My ways,' says the LORD. 'For as the heavens are higher than the earth, so are My ways higher than your ways, and My thoughts than your thoughts.'" This was also one of Granddaddy's favorite verses, so I had to include it at the beginning of this book.

Chapter 1
WHY TEACH CHILDREN THE PROPHETS

The writing prophets are the most neglected books in our Bible class curriculum, both for children and adults. I have researched several Bible class curricula for children, and I have found a huge gap relating to the prophets. Usually, there are two or three lessons about Isaiah since he is prominent in the latter part of 2 Kings and Chronicles in his interaction with King Hezekiah. I've found a few lessons on Jeremiah, but these usually relate to his being persecuted by the king—put in a dungeon, having his message torn apart, and being the "weeping prophet." Of course, Jonah is an easy one to teach about because his account involves action and has what most teachers consider a good application about obedience. Then, there is Daniel—Daniel and his friends make good choices, the fiery furnace, the lion's den, the handwriting on the wall, and perhaps Nebuchadnezzar's dream in chapter two. Some materials I've perused have one or two lessons from Ezekiel—usually the valley of dry bones, but the application that's suggested is something like "prophecies will come true" or "you can trust what God says." Sometimes I've found one lesson at the end of the Old Testament that suggests the teacher pick some of the Messianic prophecies to teach before teaching the birth of Jesus. I was excited to find one curriculum that had a quarter devoted to the main Messianic prophecies, but I found the approach more like an art gallery director lecturing on his collection of paintings instead of giving us a tour of the gallery. I suppose it's because of my experience as a child with the prophets, but I still find their pictures wonderfully fascinating!

In my research of children's Bible curricula, I did a little mathematical analysis. The accounts of the prophets Elijah and Elisha make up less than 3% of the Old Testament, but most children's materials spend about 8-10% of the time with these two prophets. I'm assuming it is because their work is action-oriented, and simple applications can be made. That is, these accounts are easy to teach. Sadly, I did not find any curriculum that mentioned Elijah as the type or shadow of John the Baptist. By contrast, the writing prophets take up about 8% of most of the curricula, but they comprise almost 30% of the Old Testament. This did not surprise me, but I'd like you to think of it this way: We are ignoring about one-third of God's message in the Old Testament! That concerns me, and that is the reason for this book.

Why don't we teach the writing prophets to children? The most common objection I've heard is that **children can't understand the prophets** and therefore we shouldn't bother. I'm glad my grandfather didn't know that! My grandfather loved the Old Testament prophets, and he shared his knowledge and love with me. Some of my fondest memories are sitting in his lap with him reading his well-worn Bible. He would read from the prophets, then turn to the New Testament and say, "Did you know that prophecy made hundreds of years before Christ was fulfilled when He…." You get the idea—he was showing me Messianic prophecy and how it is fulfilled in Christ and His Church. Also, I remember coming to his home after school, telling him about some interesting film we saw, and he'd respond, "Oh, you think you saw something grand? You didn't see what Daniel (or Ezekiel or Zechariah, etc.) saw." Then he'd read about the Son of Man before the Ancient of Days in Daniel 7 or about the glory of the Lord, the wheel within the wheel and the "four living creatures" from Ezekiel 1. Through his eyes I became fascinated with the prophets. Their visions captured my youthful imagination.

As I grew in my understanding of the Word Granddaddy was opening to me, I became more and more intrigued by the prophets and their messages. Where can you meet more interesting, dynamic and dramatic preachers? Who can forget Ezekiel cutting his hair and beard, scattering some, burning some, and placing a small portion safely in his cloak? Or what about Amos and the basket of summer (over-ripe) fruit or the plumb line? What better way to portray the folly of not giving to God than Haggai's "bag with holes?" Where can you find a more passionate expression of love for His wayward children than God's cry through Hosea, "How can I give you up, Ephraim? How can I hand you over, Israel? My heart churns within me!"

When I've spoken with friends who are also Bible teachers, one of the most common objections I've heard is **children need to have the chronology of the Old Testament firmly in their minds before they can understand the prophets.** My grandfather proved that to be false, and my experience with children has also. Even very young children can understand the concept of time and distinguish among time frames relating to the past, present and future. All we need to do is key into that knowledge with examples they can relate to. For instance, asking if they know exactly what will happen tomorrow. Or, we can talk about time before they were born and time before their parents, etc. I've found that putting the names of the prophets on my timeline in the classroom helps children associate each prophet with some major event or person in the Old Testament. However, I think all that is really necessary is to let them know God was telling the prophets things that would happen hundreds of years after they died.

Another objection is that **children can't understand figurative language.** Don't underestimate them! You can relate to figures of speech they have heard or use. I usually give them a few examples and then ask them to supply some. Children can understand figurative language, and they use it, too. They may not know the difference between a metaphor and simile, but they read, hear and use figures of speech regularly. However, the power of the prophets with children is children love pictures! The problem for us as teachers is there aren't many good pictures and illustrations of the prophets' messages. I'm working on solving that problem with this publication.

Still another objection is **children can't relate to the prophets' messages; they need lessons that apply to their lives.** Children need both—it is not either/or, but both/and. Children need to see God—to know God. They need to know God communicated in the Old Testament in a variety of ways, but now communicates to us through His Son (Heb. 1:1-2). And, they need to see that God performed exactly what He said He would—that He fulfilled His promise in Jesus. Jesus is not just the "next main character" in a long list of main characters of the Bible; He is not the "super hero" of the Bible, like Superman or Batman. Jesus is The One to whom all the other main characters pointed and for whom all their stories are recorded.

I think you will see, though, that there is tremendous, eternal value in teaching the writing prophets to children. First, **the prophets' messages read like they were "ripped from the headlines" of today's newspapers.** They address all the sins we see in our society – sexual immorality, infidelity, divorce, greed, oppression of the poor, materialism, idolatry, etc. And, they take a strong stand against hypocrisy, worship without the heart, token sacrifices, unspiritual leadership, and willful ignorance of God's Word. Human nature has not changed, and God's attitude toward sin has not changed. Their messages are timely!

Second, **children need to learn about God, and the prophets give us a very "up close and personal" view of God.** One lesson that has stood out to me as I have been studying the prophets is a lesson we don't stress like the prophets did. Yes, the prophets condemned the moral and social sins of the people. However, they got to the root sin—idolatry. Homer Hailey states: "There are some who believe that a decaying moral and social order brings about a decline in religion… the very opposite is true. The social, moral, and political conditions follow the religious condition. If a nation goes into religious apostasy, it is certain that their morals will disintegrate, and the whole social order of the nation will decline" (Hailey 1985, 54). Henry H. Halley adds: "Modern books on the prophets lay great emphasis on their social message, their denunciation of the political corruption, oppression and moral rottenness of the nation. However, the thing that bothered the prophets most was the IDOLATRY of the nation. **It is surprising how largely this is overlooked by modern writers**" (emphasis, mine, SEF) (Halley 1965, 282 -- first copyright, 1927).

Third, one of the main lessons we learn from the prophets and one that I will be stressing throughout this series is this: **We become like the God (or gods) that we worship** (Ps. 115:4-8; 135:15-18; Jer. 10:14). Stated another way, our concept of self, sin, purpose, life and death is directly related to our concept of God. The Bible stresses over and over the "obedience of faith"—not just "obedience," but "obedience of faith"—obedience that flows out of faith. The prophets show us God—His holiness, righteousness, goodness and severity. He rides on the clouds, holds the oceans in the palm of His hands, weighs the mountains in scales, and stretches out the heavens as a tent to dwell in (Is. 40:9-24). He is also one who cares for His creation as a father does his children (Ps. 103:13), and He gives strength to those who fear Him (Is. 40:28-31). One of the sins of Israel is stated in Psalm 50:21 – "You thought that I was altogether like you…" The wrong concept of God, whether it is of one who is condemning and severe or whether it is of one who is our cosmic Santa Claus, manifests itself in various ways in life—abandoning God, seeking to appease His anger, thinking His desire is mainly for my success and happiness, approaching Him with "worship" that is entertaining and self-centered, and so forth.

Fourth, **the prophets also strengthen our faith.** What they saw dimly—the King and His Kingdom—we see clearly. The blessings they anticipated, we now fully enjoy. The salvation in Christ they "inquired and searched diligently" for, we have received! Truly, they were ministers not just "for themselves, but for us" (1 Pet. 1:9-12). The first preaching in Acts resounded with, "All the prophets… have told of these days." And, fulfilled prophecy is the strongest proof of the inspiration of the Bible (2 Pet. 1:16-21).

The modern and liberal scholars among us have minimized the predictive nature of the Old Testament prophets. They use phrases like, "On the Day of Pentecost, Peter was trying to convince the Jews that Jesus was the Christ, so he quoted Nathan's words to David in 2 Samuel 7 and **applied** it to Christ." I have noticed these ideas have crept into our thinking and have caused us to shrink back from boldly emphasizing the message that the prophets never lost sight of—One is coming who will redeem God's people and will rule all nations on David's throne, which is God's throne—"at the right hand of God, exalted" (Acts 2: 33). Henry H. Halley addresses this issue: "And in the Prophets, though they themselves may not have understood the full import of some of their words, and though some of their predictions are cloudily blurred with historic events of their own day, yet the whole Story of Christ and the Spread of Christianity over the earth is pictured beforehand, in outline and in detail, in language that cannot refer to anything else in history" (Halley 1965, 282).

At the risk of being too personal, I'd like to use another example from my background. I've already told you how my grandfather taught me the prophets. When I was in late high school and in college, the theory of evolution was making major advances in textbooks and college biology classes. Also, the Bible teacher at the church I attended in college was a theistic evolutionist. I wanted to be an "A-student." I wanted to be well-educated. The "wisdom of this world" was inviting. I searched for answers. I read. I questioned. At that time I did not have readily available the numerous materials on the scientific evidences of the Bible that we have now. There were many times my questions led me to the edge of unbelief.

What pulled me back? Fulfilled prophecy! The prophecies Granddaddy had shared with me—the Old Testament/New Testament unity, the harmony and beauty of a message written over hundreds of years by various writers—brought me back to a stronger belief in God and in the Bible as the Word of God. At this point, I'm reminded of what Paul told Timothy in 2 Tim. 3:12-15: "Yes, and all who desire to live godly in Christ Jesus will suffer persecution. But evil men and impostors will grow worse and worse, deceiving and being deceived. But you must continue in the things which you have learned and been assured of, knowing from whom you have learned them, and **that from childhood you have known the Holy Scriptures**, which are able to make you wise for salvation through faith which is in Christ Jesus." The only scriptures Timothy knew as a child were those Old Testament writings. Surely, he was aware of the Messianic promises of the prophets and that what Paul and the other apostles preached fulfilled their words.

It is my conviction that the strongest proof that the Bible is from God is fulfilled prophecy. As I noted earlier, children are being taught the myths and fables of pagan and other religions as equal to Christianity. They are told other religions have a "resurrection myth" and a "god becoming man myth." What makes Christianity different? How can we know we haven't followed fables? Children MUST know the Old Testament prophets!

Fifth, **the prophets show us that Jehovah is different from the other gods men worship.** They show us a God who is intimately involved with His people; a God who cares; a God who desires the best for them. I'm reminded of Isaiah 48:18: "Oh, that you had heeded My commandments! / Then your peace would have been like a river, / And your righteousness like the waves of the sea." Without the prophets, we would not have a record of the loving kindness and patience of Jehovah as He dealt with His chosen people when they continued to disregard His commandments. "The fact that we know the time of the prophets is more important than we realize. It tells us that God entered into the actual life of men in the Old Testament. There is no way of dating the work of the gods in Hindu scriptures. Their actions seldom interfaced with real human history" (Olbricht 1980, 165). Do you see the connection? Fulfilled prophecy gives us evidence that Jehovah is, and the dates when they ministered gives us evidence that He is unique among all so-called "gods." Take time to read Isaiah 40:21-31 and chapters 44 through 46. You will see both of these great evidences woven together. We see not only Jehovah's concern for the nation, but His concern for the individual.

Let me illustrate: Several years ago in preparing for a lecture on witchcraft, I interviewed a woman who was a high priestess in Wicca. She was intelligent and well-educated. As I drove home, I thought, "This woman is basing all her life on myths and fables..." Then, I thought, "But someone might say I'm doing the same thing. After all, the resurrection of Jesus is the foundation of my life." It was then I remembered, "Somewhere the Bible says, 'We have not followed fables...'" As soon as I arrived home, I ran to my office and grabbed my Cruden's. And, there it was!

For we did not follow cunningly devised fables when we made known to you the power and coming of our Lord Jesus Christ, but were eyewitnesses of His majesty. For He received from God the Father honor and glory when such a voice came to Him from the Excellent Glory: "This is My beloved Son, in whom I am well pleased." And we heard this voice which came from heaven when we were with Him on the holy mountain.

And so we have the prophetic word confirmed, which you do well to heed as a light that shines in a dark place, until the day dawns and the morning star rises in your hearts; knowing this first, that no prophecy of Scripture is of any private interpretation, for prophecy never came by the will of man, but holy men of God spoke as they were moved by the Holy Spirit (2 Pet. 1:16-21).

The point Peter is making is obvious. Even a child can see Peter is saying we can know we haven't followed fables because of the two-fold proof: (1) apostolic eyewitness "...eyewitnesses of His majesty...we heard..." and (2) fulfilled prophecy "... And so we have the prophetic word confirmed... holy men of God spoke as they were moved by the Holy Spirit."

As I researched this, I found that Albert Barnes in his <u>Notes on the Bible</u> has a good summary of the main scholarly views of what is meant by "prophetic word confirmed" or "more sure word of prophecy." If you are interested in pursuing that further, Barnes' Notes is a good place to begin. Raymond Kelsey's comment is consistent with the apostolic preaching in Acts: "He (Peter) regards prophecy which has been authenticated by historical fulfillment as being made more sure than was the prophecy before it was so authenticated" (Kelsey 1972, 132). However, Homer Hailey states the obvious meaning: "The prophecies spoken by the prophets over a period of hundreds of years, in diverse places, and under varied conditions, all find their fulfillment in the person of Jesus. These offer stronger evidence than the eye and ear testimony. In this skeptical age all Biblical evidence needs to be clearly and forcefully set forth" (Hailey 1995, x). The children in our Bible classes stand in the place of Theophilus to whom Luke wrote and in the place of those "who have not seen and yet have believed" whom Jesus called "blessed" (John 20:29). Let's not overlook the strongest evidence that Jesus is the Messiah of Old Testament prophecy who came to buy us back from Satan's power through sin and death.

The following incident will illustrate the simple truth of Peter's words: At that same time of the above mentioned interview with the high priestess of Wicca, I was teaching a class of third and fourth graders on Wednesday evenings; we had been studying the prophets' pictures of Jesus. I shared this experience with them and read them Peter's words. The light came on immediately! Their eyes sparkled with an understanding of a grand truth. When I asked what Peter was telling us, all hands went up immediately! I didn't have to explain those verses—they knew that fulfilled prophecy is one of the greatest proofs that we have not believed fables and myths. One of the girls from that class asked her mother if she could miss school the morning I spoke on witchcraft. Lauren was in that lecture, and when I came to this point, I said, "Lauren is here from my Wednesday night class, and she knows exactly where I'm going with this!" Yes, children must know and can know Old Testament prophecy to insulate them against the myths and fables of false world religions that are being paraded today as equal to Christianity.

Chapter 2
LET'S BEGIN TEACHING THE PROPHETS

*S*ince the prophets enlarge on God's plan He announced in the garden, when you begin teaching from the writing prophets, I think it is important to review God's plan and purpose. The world does not understand why Jesus came, suffered and died, and children must begin to understand that grand truth because they are being challenged by worldly thought at a very early age. In fact, I have several quotes from militant atheists that say things like, "Supposedly, God and Jesus are one, so God sacrificed himself on the cross to save us from himself." This makes it sound like God is our enemy, not Satan. Sometimes we may inadvertently give children that idea if we stress God driving Adam and Eve from the garden as punishment for their sin but fail to stress sufficiently the promise and provision from Genesis 3:15 & 21. "Genesis 3:15 is the dawning ray of light and hope for a sin-darkened world, the first hint that the old serpent, the murderer of the human family, and the one whose food was death, would himself some day be cast into the lake of fire and brimstone which is the second and final death. Truly, the 'all things …which are written in the Law of Moses…concerning me' and fulfilled in Christ (Luke 24:44), had their beginning in Genesis 3:15" (Hailey 1995, 18).

I like to get the children involved and discover what they know about the prophets; I usually begin by asking what they know about the prophets in general. For instance, can they name some prophets, and when they do, I ask for them to tell me something about that prophet. Sometimes, I will tell them something interesting or different about the one they name. For older children, you may want to use some of the questions I've included at the end of this chapter. Some of these questions can be rephrased for younger children, or you can use them as interesting facts about these men. This little activity raises their level of curiosity, and they are more excited about learning something new in Bible class.

My favorite scripture to use in the beginning is 1 Peter 1:9-12:

> …receiving the end of your faith -- the salvation of your souls. Of this salvation the prophets have inquired and searched carefully, who prophesied of the grace that would come to you, searching what, or what manner of time, the Spirit of Christ who was in them was indicating when He testified beforehand the sufferings of Christ and the glories that would follow. To them it was revealed that, not to themselves, but to

us they were ministering the things which now have been reported to you through those who have preached the gospel to you by the Holy Spirit sent from heaven -- things which angels desire to look into.

I illustrate this passage with a chart in pictures which I have included in this chapter (figure 2.1). This lays the foundation for all the lessons in the prophets. You can make a larger picture/chart like figure 2.1 and place it in the room or on the bulletin board to help keep this idea before the children. If you don't have room for that, just a picture of an open Bible and an arrow pointing to a figure representing Jesus and the Church will suffice. I have used the Betty Lukens "Bible in Felt" figures for a chart like this to illustrate the passage as I teach.

As I discuss 1 Peter 1, I tell the children the prophets knew God planned to bless all nations through the seed (or the One Special Person) of Abraham. They knew this Special Person would be from David's family; they knew God was telling them about this One and His kingdom. They wanted to learn all they possibly could, so they searched the things God had revealed to them. "By prayer, by close study, by meditation, by the exercise of all their mental faculties they sought to learn the significance of the matters which had occasioned their prophecies" (Woods 1953, 32). To put it more simply for children, these prophets were asking questions like: What will it be like when the Messiah comes? What will He be like? What will His kingdom be like? When will He come? Then, I ask them, "If you and I had lived then, wouldn't we want to know the same thing?"

God answered the prophets' questions. However, God answered those questions in shadow ways, using things they could relate to. He answered with figurative language, in visions and pictures. That's what makes His answers so interesting! Don't we all like to see pictures? We also remember pictures longer than we remember what we are told or what we read. And, now, since we know about Jesus and His Church, as we look backward at the pictures, we can see them more clearly than the prophets did. We can also know for certain that God kept His promises to the Jews and to all people. Here is another place to reflect back to the shadow illustration in my first book.

A good theme scripture to use as a memory verse and as the foundation and purpose of this study is Isaiah 46:9-10 –"Remember the former things of old, For I am God, and there is no other; I am God, and there is none like Me, Declaring the end from the beginning, And from ancient times things that are not yet done, Saying, 'My counsel shall stand, And I will do all My pleasure...'" I like to explain this scripture the way Granddaddy explained it to me. I stand to one side and say, "God, in the past time, looked into the future and said, 'This or that is going to happen.'" Then, I move a bit toward the other side and say, "God stepped into the present and made that event happen exactly the way He said it would." I step farther down and say, "God stepped into the future after the event had happened and said, 'I told you I would do it, and I did!'" (Granddaddy would sometimes say, "God said, 'I told you so!'") This is simple, but it gets across the idea that Isaiah was teaching the people then and that children need to know now—God is the only god, and the proof is that He, alone, can fulfill prophecy.

Sometimes children ask, "Why did God answer in those ways? If He knew He was going to send Jesus to die on the cross, why didn't He just say so directly?" I have studied with adults who have also asked that question. One obvious reason is that Satan also wanted to know all the details of God's plan so he could thwart His purpose and keep man in his domain. This is alluded to in 1 Cor. 2:6-8. So, God revealed His plan in a way that the faithful and diligent student could anticipate and recognize its fulfillment. It is interesting to look through Old Testament history and see how many times Satan tries to thwart God's plan—in the garden, death of Abel, the flood, slavery in Egypt, etc. This is a dynamic way to do a summary of the Old Testament account, especially for older students.

"Why?" questions about God and His plan and purpose can sometimes be daunting for us to answer with children. We don't want to give them the wrong answer, and we also don't want to act as if their questions are trivial or unimportant. Here, again, is where I'm thankful for my grandfather! I remember asking him questions like that and many others as well. When it seemed like I was trying to figure out God, to bring Him down to my level and put Him under my microscope, I remember with a smile Granddaddy's response. He would say something like, "Well, let's see now, can you pass the test God gave Job? Can you figure out the answers to all those questions?" Then, he would turn and read Job 38 and 39 and lovingly tell me when I could answer all those questions correctly then I still would not know all about God! So, I tell the children that I've asked those same questions of my grandfather, and I share with them how he answered me. They always respond well to that—I let them know their questions are important and that God is beyond our complete knowledge. Job's friend Zophar asked the question, "Can you search out the deep things of God? Can you find out the limits of the almighty?" (Job 11:7). The KJV renders it this way, "Canst thou by searching find out God? Canst thou find out the Almighty unto perfection?" We can know God—this is what He desires for us. However, we cannot know Him perfectly as God's encounter with Job suggests. I do remind children that Jesus came to show us God (John 14:9), and that He is the "the brightness of His (*God's*) glory and the express image of His person…" (Heb. 1:3). Thus, we can know God better than Job could, but we still cannot answer all the "why" questions about God.

Other supporting scriptures you may want to use for older children or for your own background study are:

Romans 1:1-5 – Paul clearly states that the gospel was "promised before through His prophets in the Holy Scriptures."

Romans 16:25-26 – The gospel was "kept secret since the world began, but now made manifest, and by the prophetic Scriptures made known to all nations…" You may relate the idea of "kept secret" to the concept of being revealed in those shadowy pictures, and promises to the prophets.

Ephesians 1:3-14 – The gospel is God's eternal purpose to redeem us; it was prepared in eternity before He made the world, and it will be fully realized in eternity when we who are redeemed are with Him forever.

I have included the questions about the prophets on a separate page. You may want to use them as I've already suggested, or you may want to make copies for the students to keep in their notebooks and answer those questions as you study the different prophets.

The chart (figure 2.1) may seem a bit cluttered with all the arrows. I've tried to think of ways to make it less so, but the arrows are important to illustrate the truth Peter is teaching in this passage. I have included another chart (figure 2.2) that is exactly the same, but without the arrows. You may want to use this for the children, and as you teach this lesson, have the children draw the appropriate arrows on their charts, using different colors for each arrow (concept). You might also have them highlight the phrases "not for them" and "but for us" in the same color. Use these charts in any way to help your children understand the concept that God was revealing to the Old Testament prophets things that would involve us and our salvation in Christ. This is an extremely important concept. In many of our Christian colleges, scholarly professors are teaching that the Old Testament does not prophesy of Christ in any indisputable fashion (Willis, 2009, 66). We must arm our children with the positive truth of Isaiah 46:9-10 which is confirmed by Peter in this passage.

WHAT DO YOU KNOW ABOUT THE PROPHETS?

Which prophet saw:

1. God's throne? (More than one prophet)
2. The Lord with a plumb line in His hand?
3. Four chariots drawn by red, black, white and grizzled & bay horses?
4. Four living creatures (cherubim) and a wheel within a wheel?
5. The Lord standing upon the altar?
6. A roll of a book and was told to eat it?
7. Seraphim with 6 wings?
8. A man measuring the temple, the altar and the priests?
9. A lion, bear, leopard and a beast having 10 horns?
10. A basket of summer (ripe) fruit?
11. The Son of Man coming before the "Ancient of Days" and receiving a kingdom?
12. Two women lifting up an ephah between heaven and earth?
13. Gabriel, who told him about a 70 week time frame for the return of the people to Israel?
14. The Lord's house exalted above the hills and all nations flowing into it?
15. The high priest dressed in filthy clothing and Satan accusing him?
16. A ram with 2 horns fighting with a goat?
17. A man dressed in linen marking some of the people with a writer's ink horn?
18. A candlestick of gold with 7 lamps and 2 olive trees beside it?
19. Four horns and four carpenters?
20. A valley of dry bones and was told to preach to them?
21. A great city with gates named after the 12 tribes of Israel and whose name is "The Lord is there?"

Which prophet:

1. Called the women of Israel cows (kine)?
2. Saw God as a great woodcutter, using an axe and saw to cut down the trees of Lebanon?
3. Told the parable of wild grapes?
4. Told a parable of a boiling pot?
5. Preached to the mountains?
6. Preached to the wind?
7. Built a miniature city with battering rams and "played war" with it?
8. Had an unfaithful wife?
9. Said that God hated Israel's sacrifices, worship and holy days?

10. Shaved his head and beard; burned a third, threw away a third, and placed a third in his cloak?

11. Was lifted up by his hair and taken to Jerusalem in a vision?

12. Complained that God had deceived him?

13. Told of a time when the stars would fall from heaven, the sun be darkened, etc.?

14. Packed his bags and dug a hole through the wall and moved out of the city?

15. Was challenged to race horses?

16. Put a girdle in the cleft of rocks and left it there until it rotted?

17. Bought his wife from a slave auction?

18. Put a crown on the high priest?

19. Name means "Who is a God like thee?"

20. Had two staves named "Beauty" and "Bands."

21. Pouted because God forgave the people to whom he preached?

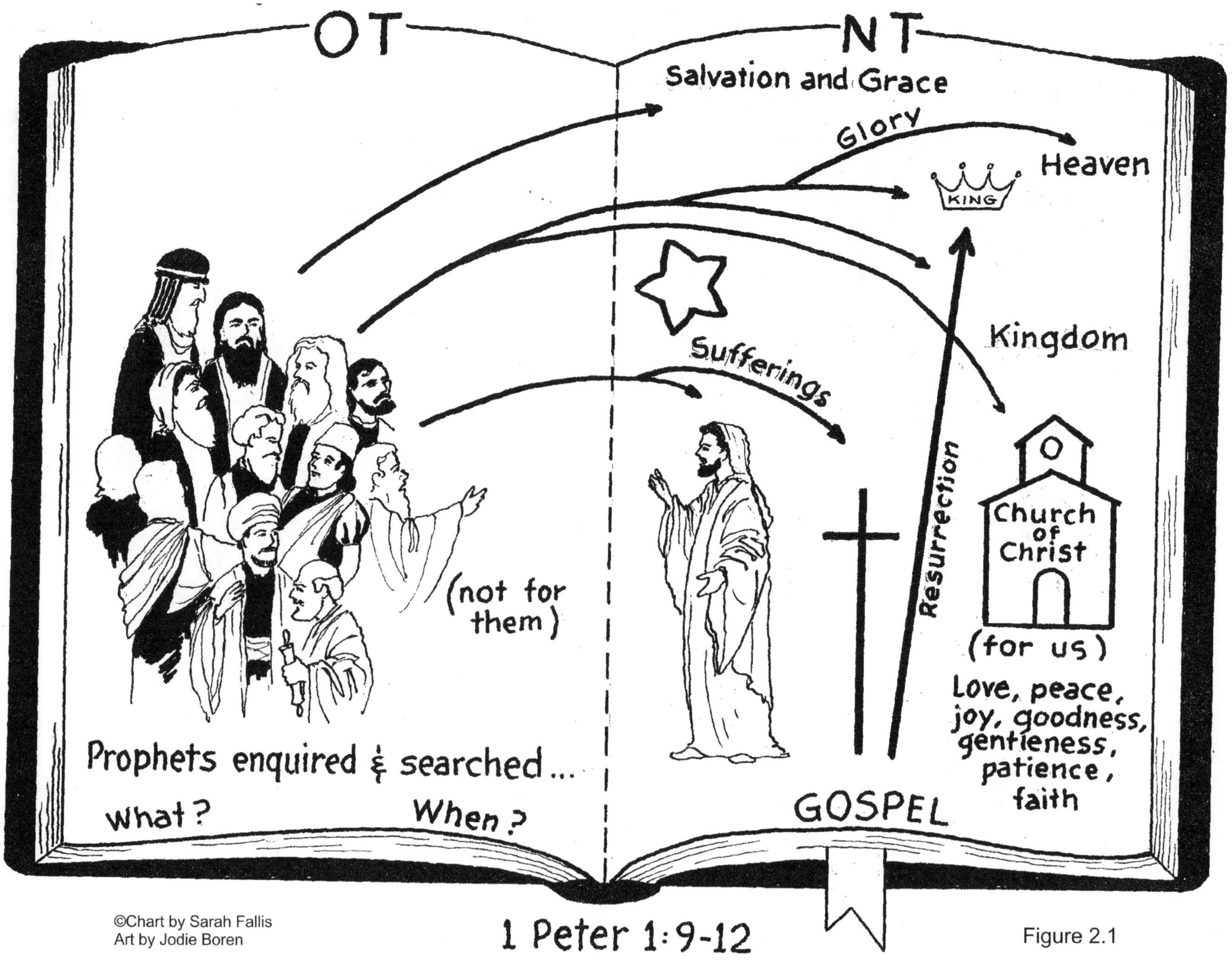

©Chart by Sarah Fallis
Art by Jodie Boren

Prophets enquired & searched ...

what?

When?

1 Peter 1:9-12

(not for them)

OT

NT

Salvation and Grace

Sufferings

Glory

Heaven

Resurrection

GOSPEL

(for us)

Love, peace, joy, goodness, gentleness, patience, faith

Church of Christ

Kingdom

KING

Figure 2.1

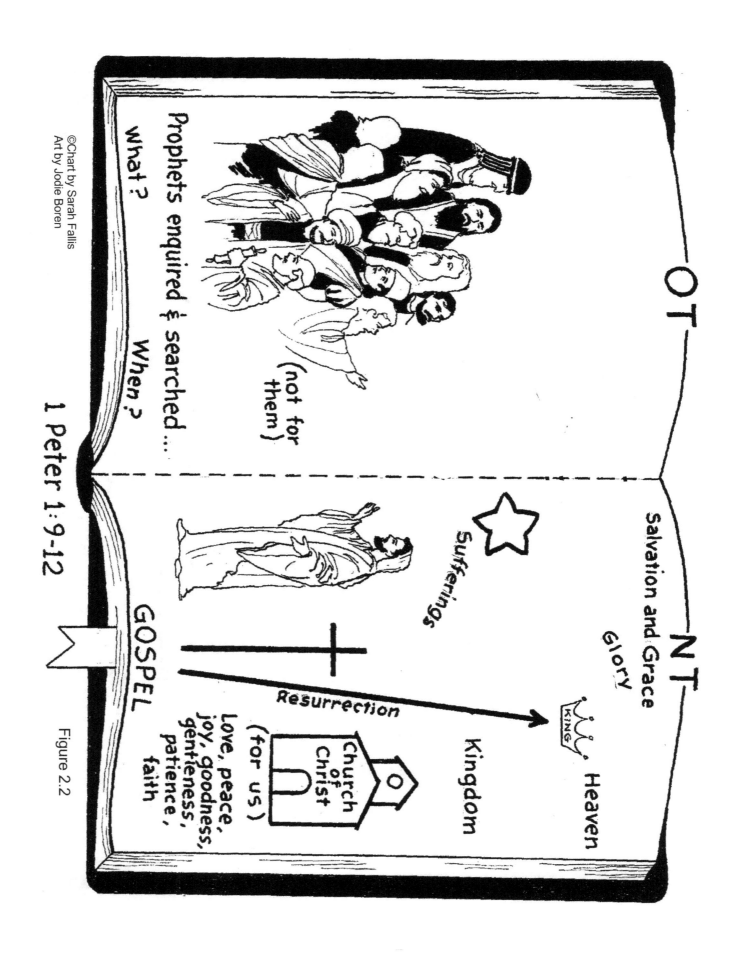

Prophets enquired & searched ...

What?   When?

(not for them)

OT

NT

Salvation and Grace

Glory

Sufferings

GOSPEL

Resurrection

KING

Heaven

Kingdom

Church of Christ

(for us)

Love, peace, joy, goodness, gentleness, patience, faith

1 Peter 1:9-12

Figure 2.2

 Have you ever seen figure skating on television? Maybe you have skated before, on ice or with roller blades. The sport is called figure skating because the athletes skate in special shapes, or figures.

A figure is a shape or drawing. When we use a figure of speech, we try to make someone see a picture in their minds from the words we choose. A figure of speech can make things easier to understand.

When a person uses a figure of speech, he usually does not mean exactly what he says. Here is an example: "Your room is a pig sty!"

If I told you that your room was a pig sty, I wouldn't mean that it had mud and pigs in it! Pigs live in a very messy place, and I would mean that your room is a very messy place, too. My figure of speech would help you understand how messy your room is by comparing it to another very messy thing.

In Matthew 19:23-24, Jesus tells his disciples something in a figure of speech.

> 23 Then Jesus said to his disciples, "I tell you the truth, it is hard for a rich man to enter the kingdom of heaven.
> 24 Again I tell you, it is easier for a camel to go through the eye of a needle than for a rich man to enter the kingdom of God."

Jesus says that it is a difficult thing for a rich person to get into heaven. Then, he talks about a huge camel and a tiny needle. He helps the disciples "see" how hard it would be by talking about something else that would be very difficult.

Write down what these figures of speech mean, and then try to think of some more.

Figure of speech: What we mean when we say it:

I think I could eat a horse.   _____

The monster in that movie scared me
To death!   _____

She was heartbroken when her dog
ran away.   _____

_____   _____

_____   _____

By Amy Franchina, 1997

Figure 2.3

Brief History of Isaiah & Micah

Isaiah & Micah prophesied in Jerusalem and Judea during the reigns of Uzziah, Jotham, Ahaz and Hezekiah, from about 740 to 700 B. C. Assyria was the major world power, with ruthless kings Tiglath Pileser, Shalmanezer and Sargon II; it was Sargon II who completed the capture of Samaria and took the Northern Kingdom into Assyrian captivity. Sennacherib invaded Judah and conquered most of the cities except Jerusalem. King Hezekiah's faithfulness to God and his prayer for Jerusalem's deliverance resulted in a miraculous defeat of the Assyrian army as described in 2 Kings 19. This is one of the outstanding events in the history of God's people, and it also demonstrates God working all things according to His purpose to fulfill the covenant He had made with David that One of his descendants would sit on His (God's) throne forever. Shortly after returning to Nineveh, Sennacherib is killed by two sons, and Esarhaddon ruled in Assyria. The Southern Kingdom was spared, but soon forgot their deliverance and returned to worship idols. God raised up Nebuchadnezzar of Babylon to destroy Jerusalem and the temple and take the people into Babylon for seventy years. The prophets Jeremiah, Daniel and Ezekiel belong to this period.

Figure 3.0

Chapter 3
THE MOUNTAIN OF THE LORD'S HOUSE

*I*saiah and Micah both prophesied during the same time in Judah and Jerusalem. They address similar themes, and this is one picture of the Lord's house they each record: Micah, in chapter 4:1-5 and Isaiah, in chapter 2:1-4. There are many truths and applications that come from this scene, so I would not just limit this account to one class period for children, especially for fifth grade and older.

The word that Isaiah the son of Amoz saw concerning Judah and Jerusalem.

Now it shall come to pass in the latter days That the mountain of the LORD's house Shall be established on the top of the mountains, And shall be exalted above the hills; And all nations shall flow to it. Many people shall come and say, "Come, and let us go up to the mountain of the LORD, To the house of the God of Jacob; He will teach us His ways, And we shall walk in His paths." For out of Zion shall go forth the law, And the word of the LORD from Jerusalem. He shall judge between the nations, And rebuke many people; They shall beat their swords into plowshares, And their spears into pruning hooks; Nation shall not lift up sword against nation, Neither shall they learn war anymore (Isa. 2:1-4).

Micah states this prophecy in the same way, but adds an additional explanation of the peace that both he and Isaiah note among nations. "But everyone shall sit under his vine and under his fig tree, and no one shall make them afraid; for the mouth of the LORD of hosts has spoken. For all people walk each in the name of his god, but we will walk in the name of the LORD our God forever and ever" (Mic. 4:4-5). Micah brings the picture of peace down to a personal and individual level. Note "everyone" and "no one shall be afraid"—why? God has spoken! And, "we will walk in the name of the Lord…"

The illustration in figure 3.1 will help the children see what Isaiah and Micah are describing. You will want to point out that the prophets use the terms like mountains and hills to refer to various nations. Also, note that Isaiah is painting a picture of a future time "in the last days" when a new and wonderful event will take place. He states that this event will involve both

Zion and Jerusalem. Jerusalem is the physical city in Judah. Zion, however, refers to the idealized spiritual kingdom (Heb. 12:22-24) where God dwells, which is the Church. Isaiah describes the beginning of the Lord's house, which Paul tells us is the "church of the living God, the pillar and ground of the truth" (1 Tim. 3:15). All of this demands a fulfillment in the New Testament. Let's see how, when and where.

From Isaiah 2, turn to and read or summarize Acts 2. You may need to fill in some of the basic events of the life, death and resurrection of Jesus, pointing out that the Day of Pentecost was 50 days after the Passover and the resurrection of Jesus. Also, remind the children that it was the first day of the week and the commemoration of the giving of the Law at Sinai. You may want to proceed with questions like a news reporter:

<u>Where are you, Peter</u>? I'm in the city of Jerusalem with my fellow apostles as Jesus commanded us.

<u>What are you doing</u>? I've received the power from the Holy Spirit as Jesus promised, and I'm preaching the gospel for the first time.

<u>What is the essential content of the gospel</u>? I'm preaching that the sacrifice of Jesus was foreknown by God and promised through the prophets. Jesus has been raised from the dead, and the proof of that is in the fulfillment of Nathan's promise to David in 2 Samuel 7:11-17, in the pouring out of the Holy Spirit, and in the fact that we (the apostles) saw Him after his resurrection. Also, because He has been raised, Jesus is by God's right hand, exalted.

<u>Who are you preaching to</u>? Jews and proselytes, devout men from every nation under heaven.

<u>What is the result of your preaching</u>? Today, more than 3,000 people believed our message and were baptized for the remission of their sins.

<u>Peter, is this the establishing of the Lord's house that Isaiah spoke about in chapter 2</u>? Yes, indeed! We are the right people, in the right place, doing the right thing, at the right time, and with the right power. Also, God plans to call many others from near and far away to be a part of His house.

The biblical conclusion is clear. Isaiah's prophecy is fulfilled when "the word of the Lord" goes forth from Jerusalem. However, there is another dimension to this prophecy. Notice that in the latter part of verse 3, Isaiah says, "for out of Zion shall go forth the law..." I have already noted Heb. 12:22-27 where the writer tells us that we have come to "Mount Zion...the city of the living God, the general assembly and Church of the Firstborn..." Do you see this powerful connection? In its immediate fulfillment, the word goes forth from physical Jerusalem in 33 A.D. In its greater fulfillment, the word or law of God is sounded forth from Zion—the Church is charged with making known the gospel to all the world. This is part of what Paul meant when he said the church is the "pillar and ground (*support*) of the truth" (1 Tim. 3:15). I'm reminded also of Phil. 2:15 that Christians shine as lights in the world as we hold forth the Word. Paul commended the Thessalonians for sounding out the word throughout the world (1 Thess. 1:8). Each generation has a part in the greater fulfillment of Isaiah's prophecy as we preach and teach the gospel to the lost.

There is much more we can learn about the "mountain of the Lord's house" from Isaiah's picture. I like to tell the children that this is not a family portrait with everyone sitting still, hands folded, and a sweet smile on each face. Rather, this is a video—a DVD, a motion picture of the action in Zion or God's holy mountain. Listed below are some other things we learn about the church from this picture in Isaiah. You can choose how detailed you want to present these, depending on the age and Bible knowledge of the children.

1. <u>God's house is exalted above all earthly kingdoms</u>. His kingdom is more important than any nation on the earth. The "gates of Hades" or powers of death would not overpower Jesus' church (Matt. 16:16-20); the Old Testament faithful desired a heavenly city, and God has prepared something better for us (Heb. 11:16 & 40). We also have a dual citizenship—our most precious citizenship is the heavenly one (Phil. 3:20). Practical application: The value of the church, of being faithful to Christ even when friends may laugh at us and not value the church the way God does.

2. <u>All nations are a part of God's house</u>. This was not a new Old Testament concept, because the promise of Gen. 3:15 embodied all Adam and Eve's posterity, and the promise to Abraham definitely stated that God would bless all nations. However, the Jews had become self-centered and needed to be reminded of God's desire for all people to be saved. Practical application: "God shows no partiality" (Acts 10:34), and neither should we (James 2:1-9).

3. <u>People come into this kingdom because they are taught by God</u>—"He will teach us His ways…" In Isaiah 54:13, the prophet states, "All your children shall be taught by the LORD, and great shall be the peace of your children." When Jeremiah spoke of the new covenant God would make with His people, God says, "I will put My law in their minds…" God will be the teacher. As we turn to the New Testament, we hear Jesus saying "my doctrine is not mine, but His who sent me" (John 7:16). He told the apostles that He would send the Comforter, the Holy Spirit, who would guide them in all truth (John 16:5-15). Through His anointed (the Christ) and the apostles whom He had chosen, God did the teaching. God's message comes to us through the word these inspired men wrote (Eph. 3:1-3). Practical application: It is important to know God's Word and obey Him. Some of your students may be old enough to be considering baptism. This is a good time to discuss the "obedience to the faith" (Rom. 16:26).

4. <u>The citizens in God's house live according to His teaching</u>. Isaiah sees beyond the rebellious people of His day to a time when men and women would desire to live as God directs them. Practical application: The Christian life is the best way to live. As the teacher, you can make various applications here depending on the maturity of your students.

5. <u>Those in God's house are also involved in evangelism</u>. This might be easy to overlook, but notice verse 3: "Many people shall come and say, 'Come and let us go up to the mountain of the Lord…'" Those enjoying the blessings in the mountain of God desire for others to do so, too. This reminds us of what Jesus said to the apostles in Acts 1:8, "…and you shall be witnesses to Me in Jerusalem, and in all Judea and Samaria, and to the end of the earth." This is a good time to plant the seeds of world

evangelism in the hearts of the children. We are commissioned as were the apostles to take the message of hope to all the world (Matt. 28:18-20; Mark 16:15-16). Practical application: The purpose of the church is to make known God's wisdom (Eph. 3:10). You may want your class to have a special contribution to a missionary supported by your congregation or one the children know personally. There are many other ways to involve them in both foreign and local missions. Also, remind them of the simple act of bringing a friend to Bible class or to Vacation Bible School.

6. <u>There is peace in God's holy mountain.</u> Though the words of verse 4 are inscribed at the United Nations building in New York City, the peace Isaiah speaks of has nothing to do with physical nations and carnal warfare. The ones living in peace and making peace are citizens of this new spiritual kingdom. Those who have come into God's house have peace with God, but through that relationship, must make and maintain peace with one another. Angels announced Jesus' birth with "peace on earth, good will to men" (Luke 2:14-17), and He claimed to give a peace that is different from the world's peace (John 14:27). For young children, you may want to stress only the beatitude from Matt. 5 – "Blessed are the peacemakers..." For older children, Eph. 2:14-17 comes to mind – Christ is our peace, He made peace, and He preached peace. Also, stress Eph. 4:3 – we are to work diligently to have "the unity of the spirit in the bond of peace." Peace is also a fruit of the spirit (Gal. 5:22). The illustrations (figures 3.2 and 3.3) show the picture Isaiah is painting that Jews of his day would understand—making instruments of war into instruments of peace, and people sitting joyfully, without fear in their gardens. Practical application: "Bullying" has always been a problem that children face—not just since it has become popular to talk about it because of the LGBT agenda. You can help children know how to deal with this and other actions/words that may hurt them or their friends.

Concluding Comments:

When I teach this and many of the other pictures of the kingdom, I like to ask the children, "Are you in the picture?" This helps make these prophecies personal and applicable. On figure 3.1, you may want the children to write their names or to draw a stick-figure of themselves in the picture. If you want to make pictures of each child, print them out on regular paper, and have them available for the children to glue on this picture, that would be great. Technology helps us do many good things to help our children learn God's Word. With younger children, I make the application that they are now going to the mountain of the Lord's house with their parents, holding their parents' hand. However, there will come a time when they will want to make the decision for themselves and go to the Lord's house, not because their parents want them to, but because they want to enjoy these blessings.

This chapter may seem a bit overwhelming with all the suggested applications. Let me share how I have used it: With children in first and second grades, I have stressed mainly that God fulfilled His promise in this prophecy when the church was established, and that we can trust God to fulfill His promises to us. When I taught third and fourth grades, I highlighted some of the facts we learn about the church that I have listed, dealing with the ones I thought were more understandable and applicable to them. I've also taught this to adults, stressing all the things we learn about the nature of the kingdom and making various applications. Good teachers will know their students and their needs and make the proper applications. The most important lesson is that God has given us evidence in the Bible that He is the only God and the Bible is trustworthy!

The Mountain of the Lord's House

Figure 3.1

Peace in God's Holy Mountain

Figure 3.2

Old Testament

Isaiah 2:2-4

2 Now it shall come to pass in the latter days that the mountain of the LORD's house shall be established on the top of the mountains, and shall be exalted above the hills; and all nations shall flow to it. 3 Many people shall come and say,"Come, and let us go up to the mountain of the LORD, to the house of the God of Jacob; He will teach us His ways, and we shall walk in His paths."For out of Zion shall go forth the law, and the word of the LORD from Jerusalem. 4 He shall judge between the nations, and rebuke many people; they shall beat their swords into plowshares, and their spears into pruning hooks; nation shall not lift up sword against nation, neither shall they learn war anymore.

New Testament

Acts 2:2-6; 22-24; 36-39

2 "And there were dwelling in Jerusalem Jews, devout men, from every nation under heaven. 6 And when this sound occurred, the multitude came together, ... But Peter, standing up with the eleven, raised his voice and said to them, 'Men of Judea and all who dwell in Jerusalem, let this be known to you, and heed my words...'"

22 "Men of Israel, hear these words: Jesus of Nazareth, a Man attested by God to you by miracles, wonders, and signs which God did through Him in your midst, as you yourselves also know -- 23 Him, being delivered by the determined purpose and foreknowledge of God, you have taken by lawless hands, have crucified, and put to death; 24 whom God raised up, having loosed the pains of death, because it was not possible that He should be held by it..."

36 "Therefore let all the house of Israel know assuredly that God has made this Jesus, whom you crucified, both Lord and Christ." 37 Now when they heard this, they were cut to the heart, and said to Peter and the rest of the apostles, "Men and brethren, what shall we do?"
38 Then Peter said to them,"Repent, and let every one of you be baptized in the name of Jesus Christ for the remission of sins; and you shall receive the gift of the Holy Spirit. 39 For the promise is to you and to your children, and to all who are afar off, as many as the Lord our God will call."

Figure 3.3

Chapter 4
JUDGMENT AND "THE BRANCH OF JEHOVAH"

*I*saiah chapters 1 and 3 – 4:1 deal with God's judgment on Jerusalem and Judah because of their sin and rebellion. Though the prophet lists several sins, it is worthy of note that the root sin was idolatry (2:20). Chapter 4:2-6 is another picture of what it will be like when Jesus comes. However, in chapter 3, Isaiah tells why judgment must come—"For they have brought evil upon themselves" (3:9b). I like to read the description of the women in 3:16-24 and "act out" just a bit the way they are described. Children really remember that!

Judgment must come, but there is the promise of God from the very beginning of time, and Isaiah pulls back the curtain again on the future glory of Zion:

In that day the Branch of the LORD shall be beautiful and glorious;

And the fruit of the earth shall be excellent and appealing

For those of Israel who have escaped.

And it shall come to pass that he who is left in Zion and remains in Jerusalem will be called holy -- everyone who is recorded among the living in Jerusalem. When the Lord has washed away the filth of the daughters of Zion, and purged the blood of Jerusalem from her midst, by the spirit of judgment and by the spirit of burning, then the LORD will create above every dwelling place of Mount Zion, and above her assemblies, a cloud and smoke by day and the shining of a flaming fire by night. For over all the glory there will be a covering. And there will be a tabernacle for shade in the daytime from the heat, for a place of refuge, and for a shelter from storm and rain (Isa. 4:2-6).

Isaiah introduces a new description of the Messiah—He will be "the Branch of Jehovah." It is important to explain this concept to children because Isaiah will use it again in chapter 11, and Jeremiah and Zechariah use the term in passages that are definitely Messianic. So, we will meet "the Branch" again as we continue to walk with Jesus through the prophets. Hailey gives a good argument on the identity of the Branch from word studies and other passages (Hailey 1995, 96). However, I like to make things simple for children. I just ask them to think about a tree; I may even bring pictures of several kinds of trees. Then, I ask something like, "Is a branch on the oak tree an oak branch or a pine branch?" Of course, it is an oak branch! The branch possesses the same qualities as the tree. In the same way, "the Branch of Jehovah" is describing the Messiah as having the same qualities as Jehovah. This is exactly what John said in chapter 1: "In the beginning was the Word, and the Word was with God, and the Word was God… And the Word became flesh and dwelt among us…" (John 1:1, 14). John is introducing Jesus to us as "the Branch of Jehovah" though he doesn't use those exact words, but he is telling us that Jesus has the same qualities as God, which is what the prophets said in the figurative term "the Branch."

What will it be like when Jesus comes? Isaiah said those in Zion will be called holy (v.3). Peter calls Christians a "holy priesthood" and "a holy nation" (1 Peter 2:5, 9). All those in Zion will be washed and clean (v.4); this cleansing or purging refers historically to the cleansing of the people through Babylonian captivity. However, all those in the spiritual Zion to which Isaiah points are to be clean. We are made clean from our sins when we are baptized into Christ (Rom. 6:3-6).

This is one of those prophecies that is intertwined with Israel's history so much that we may not see the full import of what Isaiah is saying, and some may think I'm pressing the context for the application in the previous paragraph. I refer back to an example I used in my first book. Don Simpson who taught at the Brown Trail School of Preaching in Bedford, Texas, from 1975 – 2000 explained the shadow/prophecy concept this way: The prophets were standing in their own time, shining a light down through the future, in the foreground was the tabernacle, then the temple, but in the background they saw the church as the true dwelling of God and the true temple of God. This prophecy perfectly illustrates Don's point: Isaiah sees in the foreground the return from Babylonian captivity and the purging of their sin through that experience. However, in the background is true Zion pictured in Heb. 12:18-24 and the blessings associated with coming into the Church. The joyful return from Babylon was only a shadow of the great joy of being free from sin and from the power of Satan through death in the spiritual Mount Zion. Figure 4.1 will help you illustrate this to children.

Isaiah not only looks forward to Mount Zion, but he looks backward to the protection God gave His people in the wilderness when they were on their way to the promised land. You remember that God covered them with a cloud by day to shelter from the sun's glaring heat in the desert and with fire by night to give them warmth when the sun went down. The cloud and fire also served to lead them and protect them from their enemies. We who have come to Mount Zion have God's richest spiritual blessings (Eph. 1:3), His protection from our enemies (1 Cor. 10:13), His guidance in our lives (2 Pet. 1:3), and the assurance of eternal rest with Him (Rev. 2:10). All these promises are based on our continued faithfulness and trust in God (1 Cor. 10:1-13). Therefore, we must stay under the cloud of His protection in order to be safe—this is a lesson most children can easily understand.

Concluding Comments:

Isaiah not only introduces "the Branch of Jehovah" but also confirms what Granddaddy stressed to me over and over as I was growing up—the majestic unity of the Bible even on such "minor" details as the pillar of cloud and fire in the wilderness as a picture of God's care and protection in Zion. The Bible cannot be the product of man. It is unique among the so-called sacred books of the world. This unity of story, prophecy and fulfillment, shadow and substance, type and antitype demonstrates beyond doubt that we have "not followed cunningly devised fables" (2 Pet. 1:16). Yes, fulfilled prophecy is the unsung message of the church and the strongest internal proof that the Bible is from God and not man.

God blesses and protects His people – Isaiah 4

God's protection and care of His people in the wilderness is a shadow of His protection and care of His Church today. The cloud by day and fire by night protected the Israelites from the heat of the sun and from the very cold nights. God helps us overcome temptation today (1Cor. 10:13).

©Sarah Fallis

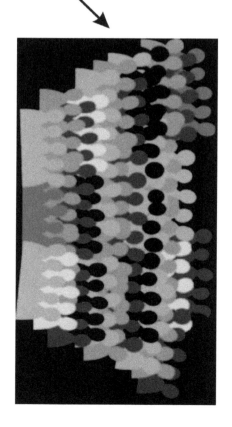

Isaiah 4:5

" ... then the LORD will create above every dwelling place of Mount Zion, and above her assemblies, a cloud and smoke by day and the shining of a flaming fire by night. For over all the glory there will be a covering."

The tabernacle was the place where God made His presence known among the people of Israel. God dwells in His people, the church, today (Eph. 2:19-22).

Figure 4.1

Old Testament

Isaiah 4:2-6

In that day the Branch of the LORD shall be beautiful and glorious;
And the fruit of the earth shall be excellent and appealing
For those of Israel who have escaped.

3 And it shall come to pass that he who is left in Zion and remains in Jerusalem will be called holy -- everyone who is recorded among the living in Jerusalem. 4 When the Lord has washed away the filth of the daughters of Zion, and purged the blood of Jerusalem from her midst, by the spirit of judgment and by the spirit of burning, 5 then the LORD will create above every dwelling place of Mount Zion, and above her assemblies, a cloud and smoke by day and the shining of a flaming fire by night. For over all the glory there will be a covering. 6 And there will be a tabernacle for shade in the daytime from the heat, for a place of refuge, and for a shelter from storm and rain.

New Testament

1 Peter 2:9

9 But you are a chosen generation, a royal priesthood, a holy nation, His own special people, that you may proclaim the praises of Him who called you out of darkness into His marvelous light.

1 Corinthians 10:13

No temptation has overtaken you except such as is common to man; but God is faithful, who will not allow you to be tempted beyond what you are able, but with the temptation will also make the way of escape, that you may be able to bear it.

2 Peter 1:2-3

2 Grace and peace be multiplied to you in the knowledge of God and of Jesus our Lord, 3 as His divine power has given to us all things that pertain to life and godliness, through the knowledge of Him who called us by glory and virtue,

Ephesians 1:3

Blessed be the God and Father of our Lord Jesus Christ, who has blessed us with every spiritual blessing in the heavenly places in Christ,

Revelation 2:10

Be faithful until death, and I will give you the crown of life.

You may want to read and discuss Romans 8:31-39 with older students.

Figure 4.2

Chapter 5
GOD IS ON THE THRONE!

*I*saiah's ministry spanned the reign of "Uzziah, Jotham, Ahaz, and Hezekiah, kings of Judah" (Isa. 1:1). King Uzziah died around 739 B.C., and this year is when Isaiah received the dramatic vision of God's glory. Uzziah became king when he was 16 and reigned 52 years (2 Chron. 26). In his early years, he sought to do God's will, and was a wealthy and powerful king because of God's blessings. [Although later, he became a leper. Because of his rebellious pride, he went into the temple to burn incense which was only the work of the priests (2 Chron. 26:16).] The nation of Judah had reached the zenith of wealth and renown similar to the days of Solomon. However, the kingdom was declining, and Uzziah's death marked the beginning of a downward spiral both economically and spiritually. Three other good kings would follow: Jotham, Hezekiah, and Josiah, but the nation was in gradual decline. Thus, Uzziah's death was a tragic time for God's prophet. He could see the spiritual depravity that was coming upon them, and he mourned the loss of the king and the coming loss of the nation. Jehovah knew Isaiah's grief and his concern for the future of Jerusalem and Judah. In Isaiah's lowest hour, Jehovah gives him a vision of His glory and a call to an even more difficult mission.

> In the year that King Uzziah died, I saw the Lord sitting on a throne, high and lifted up, and the train of His robe filled the temple. Above it stood seraphim; each one had six wings: with two he covered his face, with two he covered his feet, and with two he flew. And one cried to another and said: "Holy, holy, holy is the Lord of hosts; The whole earth is full of His glory!"

> And the posts of the door were shaken by the voice of him who cried out, and the house was filled with smoke.

> So I said: "Woe is me, for I am undone! Because I am a man of unclean lips, And I dwell in the midst of a people of unclean lips; For my eyes have seen the King, The Lord of hosts."

> Then one of the seraphim flew to me, having in his hand a live coal which he had taken with the tongs from the altar. And he touched my mouth with it, and said: "Behold, this has touched your lips; Your iniquity is taken away, And your sin purged."

Also I heard the voice of the Lord, saying: "Whom shall I send, And who will go for Us?" Then I said, "Here am I! Send me." And He said, "Go, and tell this people: 'Keep on hearing, but do not understand; Keep on seeing, but do not perceive.' "Make the heart of this people dull, And their ears heavy, And shut their eyes; Lest they see with their eyes, And hear with their ears, And understand with their heart, And return and be healed" (Isa. 6:1-10).

When you introduce this vision to children, you may want to relate back to Exodus 33:18-23 when Moses asked to see God's glory. God said He would "make all My goodness pass before you" (v.19); He placed Moses in the cleft of the rock and covered him so he could not see His face, since "no man shall see Me, and live" (v. 20). The apostle John reminds us of what God said to Moses: "No one has seen God at any time" (John 1:18). In John 12:27-41 John quotes from Isaiah 6 and adds that Isaiah said these things when he "saw His (*Jesus*) glory and spoke of Him" (v. 41). Thus, Isaiah saw Jesus, the eternal Word, in this vision. This is a good time to remind children that "Jesus has always been, but He has not always been a man." You may want to refer back to the shadow of Jesus in my first book. When Isaiah said in verse 5, "My eyes have seen the king, the LORD (*Jehovah*) of hosts," and John said in 12:41 that Isaiah "saw His (*Jesus*) glory and spoke of Him (*Jesus*)," we conclude that "Jehovah" of Isa. 6:5 is Jesus Christ. The writer of Hebrews confirms this truth in 1:3, as he says of Jesus that He is "the brightness of His (*God's*) glory and the express image of His (*God's*) person..." I don't want to get too technical and open a full discussion of the nature of the godhead. With children, the important thing is to help them see that Jesus has always existed, that He is eternal.

Isaiah describes the overwhelming majesty of this vision—Jehovah's royal robe flowed down from the throne that was "high and lifted up" (v.1), and filled the temple. The seraphim praise Him with "Holy, holy, holy is the LORD of Hosts; the whole earth is full of His glory!" Their praise is so magnificent and loud, that the doorposts of the temple shake. This scene is similar to the vision in Ezekiel 1 and in Revelation 4. In Ezekiel's vision, there are cherubim surrounding the throne, and in John's vision, there are four living creatures about the throne. The important concepts for children are what we learn about God and what our response to Him should be.

What do we learn about Jehovah from this vision? First, we see that He is above the creation; He is not a part of the universe. Second, God is not identical with the universe as in pantheism, but He is separate from it. Third, the creation is full of His power, work and glory. You may want to refer to Psalm 19, "The heavens declare the glory of God..." and to Romans 1:20, "For since the creation of the world His invisible attributes are clearly seen, being understood by the things that are made, even His eternal power and Godhead..." Fourth, we learn that God is worthy to be praised. He is holy—totally without sin and set apart from anything that is bad or evil.

How did Isaiah respond to this vision of Jehovah? Notice verse 5: "Woe is me, for I am undone! Because I am a man of unclean lips..." When Isaiah sees the pure, holy Jehovah on His throne, he sees his sinfulness in comparison to God's holiness. This is similar to Ezekiel's and John's response when they see the LORD of hosts on His throne. The more we know about God and the more we know God, the more concerned we will be about the sin in our lives. We will want to be pure and holy so we can be in God's presence, but like Isaiah, we are unclean. Yet, God does not leave Isaiah in this condition. Notice that a seraph took a coal from the altar and touched Isaiah's mouth with it and said, "Behold, this has touched your lips; your iniquity is taken away, and your sin purged" (v. 7). In the vision, Isaiah is given assurance that he is clean and pure before God. This is a good time to ask the children, "How do we become clean so we can be in God's presence?" When we realize we are sinful and need God's grace to save us, we will submit to His will in baptism (Rom. 6:1-4).

After Isaiah receives the assurance that he is clean and his sins are forgiven, he is ready for God to use. So the question comes from the Lord: "Whom shall I send, and who shall go for Us?" Immediately, Isaiah answers, "Here am I! Send me!" Isaiah volunteers because he knows God and is humble before the holy One of Israel. God cannot use people who will not submit to His will. He cannot use people who do not acknowledge their sins and desire to be forgiven. Isaiah is a good example of one who is humble and who desires to do whatever God instructs.

God commissions Isaiah in verses 9 and 10. Basically, He tells Isaiah to go and preach, but the people won't listen. They will hear his words, but they won't obey and they won't care. They will be so rebellious that they will be like talking to deaf and blind people. Would you want to preach to a group like that? It is interesting that God had referred to Judah as "my people" earlier, but in this commission, He tells Isaiah, "Go, and tell **this** people…" Their sin has increased so much that He can no longer call them His people. Isn't that sad? These people had a marvelous history with God. He had loved them and delivered them from Egypt and from other enemies as they journeyed to Canaan. He gave them food and water and brought them into a bountiful land. Now, they have left Him to serve the idols of the nations around them. How can anyone claim to belong to God and worship other gods that can do nothing for them? This was the depth to which they were sinking as Isaiah is called in this vision.

Isaiah asks only one question in verse 11: "Lord, how long?" If you were given a job like his, would you want to know how long you had to do it? I would! I think I could endure trying to teach people who were rebellious for a little while. I might be able to teach for a few years, but I wouldn't want to teach people who wouldn't listen and who didn't care about my message. God's answer is given in imagery, but He is basically telling Isaiah that he must do this work until the job is finished. One encouraging note is in verse 13 that a "tenth will be in it"—that is, a very small remnant will listen and be saved because of Isaiah's preaching.

Concluding Comments:

Some commentators have labeled this vision with the words, Look up, in, and out. That is, today, like Isaiah, we must look to God and see His glory and majesty. Then, we look in at ourselves and see our sin. In humility, we submit to the cleansing blood of Jesus in baptism. Lastly, we look out to others who need to hear the word of God. Jesus said in Matt. 28:18-20, "All authority has been given to Me in heaven and on earth. Go therefore and make disciples of all the nations, baptizing them in the name of the Father and of the Son and of the Holy Spirit, teaching them to observe all things that I have commanded you; and lo, I am with you always, even to the end of the age." Like Isaiah, will we say, "Here am I! Send me!"

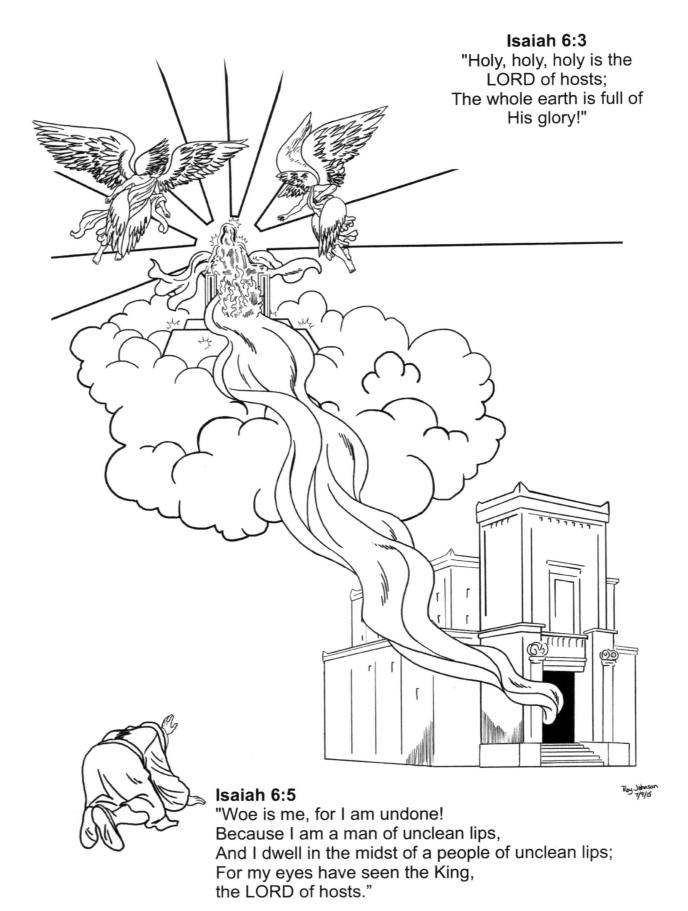

Isaiah 6:3
"Holy, holy, holy is the
LORD of hosts;
The whole earth is full of
His glory!"

Isaiah 6:5
"Woe is me, for I am undone!
Because I am a man of unclean lips,
And I dwell in the midst of a people of unclean lips;
For my eyes have seen the King,
the LORD of hosts."

Figure 5.1

6 Then one of the seraphim flew to me, having in his hand a live coal which he had taken with the tongs from the altar. 7 And he touched my mouth with it, and said:
"Behold, this has touched your lips;
Your iniquity is taken away,
And your sin purged." -- **Isaiah 6:6-7**

8 Also I heard the voice of the Lord, saying:
"Whom shall I send,
And who will go for Us?"
Then I said, "Here am I! Send me." **--Isaiah 6:8**

Figure 5.2

MANY WOULD NOT BELIEVE IN JESUS!

New Testament: John 12:37-41

But although He had done so _____ _____ before

them, they did _____ _____ in Him, that the word of

_____ might be _____, when he spoke:

"Lord, who has _____ *our report? And to whom has the arm of*

the Lord been _____ . " (This is from Isaiah 53:1, where Isaiah

tells about the death of Jesus. We will study it later this year.)

Therefore they could not _____, because Isaiah said again:

"He has _____ *their eyes and* _____ *their hearts,*

lest they should _____ *with their* _____, *lest they should*

_____ *with their* _____ *and* _____ *so*

that I should _____ *them."*   (Isaiah 6)

These things Isaiah said when he saw _____ _____ and spoke of Him.

Old Testament: Isaiah 6

"In the year that King Uzziah died, I saw the _____ sitting on a

_____ high and _____ up and the _____

of His _____ filled the _____. Above it stood seraphim;

each one had _____ wings: with two he covered his _____ , with

two he covered his _____ and with two he _____.   And one

cried to another and said: "_____, _____, _____ is the

_____ of hosts; the whole _____ is full of His _____."

Figure 5.3

1

After Isaiah saw this vision of God's glory, God asked in verse 8, "Who shall I send, and who will go for us?" Isaiah answered, "Here am I send me!" God then tells him how the people will respond to his preaching in verse 9:

"Keep on _____ but do not understand. Keep on _____ but do not perceive. Make the _____ of this people dull, and their _____ heavy, and shut their_____; lest they _____ with their eyes and _____ with their ears, and _____ with their heart, and return and be _____. "

This is what John quoted in the New Testament, and he said the people in Jesus' time responded to His message in the same way the people in the Old Testament responded to Isaiah's message. THEY WOULDN'T LISTEN, LEARN AND OBEY!!! This is sad! We want to be people who will listen and obey. Why should we obey Jesus? There are many reasons, but one is hidden in John 12 and Isaiah 6. Let's see if we can find that reason:

Isaiah said he saw the glory of the _____.
Whose glory did Isaiah see? _____ .
John said that Isaiah saw whose glory? _____.
And John said Isaiah was speaking about whom? _____.

From this, we can conclude that the main reason to obey Jesus is that

JESUS IS GOD!

Do you want to be like the people to whom Isaiah preached? _____
Do you want to be like the people to whom Jesus preached? _____

We want to listen with our _____ , see with our _____ and understand with our _____. If we do, that means we will _____ what Jesus says in His Word!

Figure 5.3

2

Chapter 6
THE SIGN - IMMANUEL

The prophecy of Isaiah 7:14 deals with the theme of God's faithfulness in fulfilling His promise and His discipline of the Northern Kingdom through Assyria. Isaiah 7 is delivered at the beginning of the prophecy concerning Assyria and Israel, and Isaiah 9 near the end; I will deal with Isaiah 9 in the next chapter. I am also referencing Micah's prophecy in 4:9 – 5:5 because it deals with that same theme. As I noted earlier, Isaiah and Micah are contemporaries. You may want to wait until you teach about the birth of Jesus to relate back to Isaiah 7:14 and Micah 5:2, or you may want to have one complete lesson on these prophecies, showing their fulfillment in Matt. 1:18-25, 2:1-6; Luke 1:26-38, 2:8-38; and John 1:1-18, using each of these New Testament passages in whatever detail you think your students are able to understand. Matthew and Luke are very straight forward, while John's account is probably best for more mature students, fifth grade and above.

The historical background of chapter 7 is important, but you don't have to belabor the details for children. If you are teaching on Wednesday night, and they are studying the Old Testament on Sunday morning, you may want to coordinate these lessons around the time frame of their Sunday lessons. However, these can be effectively taught by just a brief historical background and pointing to the timeline, showing where Isaiah stands in relation to Jesus. That is really the most important history to include in the lesson.

Briefly, King Ahaz of Judah is fearful of a plot by Rezin, king of Syria and Pekah, king of Israel, to overthrow his rule and place "the son of Tabel" as king in Judah (7:6). It might be interesting to show children how scared Ahaz and the leaders of the people were—Isaiah says their "hearts were moved as the trees... are moved by the wind" (7:2). They were shaking in their boots, to use an old Western term. The leaders of Judah are wringing their hands, wondering what to do, running here and there without making any certain decision.

God told Isaiah to take his son, whose name was prophetic, "a remnant shall return," and meet Ahaz by the aqueduct, probably a rather public place, and tell him, "It's not going to happen! The two kingdoms you fear will be destroyed shortly." He ends by challenging Ahaz and his companions: "If you will not believe, surely you shall not be established" (7:9b). Isaiah presses Ahaz to have faith instead of fear and ask for a sign from God, but Ahaz refuses. Then Isaiah announces God's sign, not to Ahaz, but to the whole house of David—"Behold, the virgin shall conceive and bear a Son, and shall call His name Immanuel" (7:14).

This is God's unique sign! Though the house of David is at this time represented by a weak and faithless king, God will still keep His greater promise. This sign, given to the house of David, would be fulfilled in the future by the house of David when Mary wrapped Immanuel in swaddling clothes and placed Him in a manger (Luke 2:7). There are some today who boldly say this prophecy does not refer to Mary and Jesus (Willis 2009, 537). However, the Holy Spirit instructed Matthew to write:

> Now the birth of Jesus Christ was as follows: After His mother Mary was betrothed to Joseph, before they came together, she was found with child of the Holy Spirit. Then Joseph her husband, being a just man, and not wanting to make her a public example, was minded to put her away secretly. But while he thought about these things, behold, an angel of the Lord appeared to him in a dream, saying, "Joseph, son of David, do not be afraid to take to you Mary your wife, for that which is conceived in her is of the Holy Spirit. And she will bring forth a Son, and you shall call His name JESUS, for He will save His people from their sins."

> So all this was done that it might be fulfilled which was spoken by the Lord through the prophet, saying: *"Behold, the virgin shall be with child, and bear a Son, and they shall call His name Immanuel,"* which is translated, "God with us" (Matt. 1:18-23).

The only person who could fulfill this prophecy is Jesus "who, being in the form of God... made Himself of no reputation, taking the form of a bondservant, and coming in the likeness of men..." (Phil. 26-7). How could the eternal Word become flesh (John 1:1, 14) without the intervention of God through the Holy Spirit in the womb of a virgin? Any other explanation of Jesus does not harmonize with other scripture regarding His nature and only reduces Him to an ordinary man. You will want to refer back to Isaiah 4 and "the Branch of Jehovah"—One is coming who will have the same nature as Jehovah. Hailey states it this way, which is hard to improve on: "What He was (God) He continued to be; what He was not (flesh) He became" (Hailey 1995, 100). I repeat, only the virgin birth can explain the nature of Jesus as recorded in the New Testament.

Children will be bombarded with the "god becoming man myth" from other religions and with the "absurdity" of this account from militant atheists. (I refer specifically to Richard Dawkins' The God Delusion, pages 117-123. He references Robert Gillooly who asserts that "all the essential features of the Jesus legend... are borrowed—every last one of them—from other religions already in existence in the Mediterranean and Near East region." Dawkins also compares the gospels to The Da Vinci Code, noting that both are fiction—the gospels are just ancient fiction.) When children enter college, they will meet biblical scholars and philosophy professors who have studied from such scholars like Dr. James Tabor who claims to be a biblical historian, only dealing with facts. He boldly asserts, "Women do not get pregnant without a male—ever. So Jesus had a human father... Dead bodies don't rise... So if the tomb was empty the historical conclusion is simple—Jesus' body was moved by someone and likely reburied in another location" (Tabor 2006, 233-234). You will not want to share all these scholarly objections with your children, but you need to be aware of what they will be challenged by even in our Christian schools and universities and perhaps even in Bible class if someone who has been influenced by these scholarly arguments is teaching them.

I met the scholarly objection to Isaiah 7:14 when I was in college. It was tempting to buy into it because of the Bible teacher I admired. However, Granddaddy's teaching on this subject kept nagging at me until I reasoned it out myself—basically and very simply, is the Holy Spirit lying in Matt. 1:23? I have also benefited from Dr. Furman Kearley's lesson notes on prophecy, especially as he points out that many prophecies had an immediate fulfillment during the time they were given, but a greater fulfillment in Christ. This is a very reasonable argument for Isaiah 7:14, especially relating to verses 15 – 17. Scholars will make all kinds of arguments that the Hebrew word "almah" in Isaiah just means "young woman" and not specifically "virgin." However, I must stand with the Holy Spirit, knowing that the Spirit of Christ was also in the prophets (1 Pet. 1: 11), inspiring them and guiding them in what they spoke and wrote, making the message of both the Old and New Testaments consistent in every detail. If you desire a fuller discussion of this concept, I recommend Homer Hailey's <u>A Commentary on Isaiah</u>, pages 84-88.

Micah 5:2 is quoted in Matthew's account of the birth of Jesus, and we usually just note that isolated verse as being fulfilled. However, when we review the whole context of Micah 4 through 5:5, we learn some tremendous truths about the Messiah. Recall from my Chapter 3 that Micah 4 is Messianic in that the prophet sees spiritual Zion exalted, God's Word going forth, all nations going into the Lord's house, and the peaceful character of the citizens of Zion. Micah continues in verse 6 with "In that day…" which is the same as "the latter days" of verse 1. In verses 6 – 8, he declares God's intention for the remnant of His people who would be faithful to Him— "So the Lord will reign over them in Mount Zion" (v. 7). In verses 9 – 12, he describes God's purpose and His relation to Israel in terms of the husband/wife relationship. (God had used this same analogy through Hosea as he preached to the Northern Kingdom during this same time, and there is an allusion to it in Isaiah 1:21.)

This may seem tedious or difficult to explain to younger children, and teachers should always use wisdom in knowing what their students can understand. In the prophets, God's relationship with His people is described in various ways—shepherd, king, father, husband are some that come to mind. In this passage, we see God sending Judah into Babylonian captivity—a painful experience for them. They will be in a foreign land for 70 years, but God has plans for them that they do not see at the time (Jer. 29:10-12). God affirms that same truth through Micah in 4:10-12 – "Be in pain and labor to bring forth, O daughter of Zion… And to Babylon you shall go, there you shall be delivered… Now also many nations have gathered against you, who say, 'Let her be defiled…' But they do not know the thoughts of the Lord, nor do they understand His counsel…" Micah sees the nation of Judah as a woman who is pregnant with the Messiah, and Jehovah as a caring, protective husband. Jehovah will send His wife into hiding as it were in Babylon until it is time for her to return to His land and give birth to the Messiah. (John uses similar imagery in Rev. 12; you may want to refer to that for children in fifth or sixth grade. I have actually referenced it for third and fourth grades when I've had students with a good Bible background in my class.)

With this as the background, Micah says, "'But you, Bethlehem Ephrathah, though you are little among the thousands of Judah, yet out of you shall come forth to Me the One to be Ruler in

Israel, whose goings forth are from of old, from everlasting.' Therefore He shall give them up, until the time that she who is in labor has given birth…" (5:2-3a). You recall that when wise men came seeking the one born "King of the Jews," Herod gathered the chief priests and scribes together to ask them; their reply was simply, "In Bethlehem of Judea, for thus it is written by the prophet…" and they quote Micah 5:2. This citation by Matthew as guided by the Holy Spirit, confirms that this prophecy was fulfilled in Jesus.

It is interesting to see all that was fulfilled in this prophecy. Micah is preaching in 730-700 B.C., but he looks down through over 100 years to 596 B.C. when God sends Judah to Babylon. Then, He draws back the curtain on God's eternal purpose, and shows the reason for the captivity, the birth of the One "whose goings forth are from old, from everlasting" in Bethlehem, and the glory of the spiritual Mount Zion.

Before I leave this passage, I want you to notice how the One born in Bethlehem is described—"whose goings forth are from of old, from everlasting" (v. 2). Do you see the magnitude of Micah's description? The eternally existing One, the I AM, Immanuel will be born in Bethlehem! This is another allusion to the virgin birth. The only way the One who is "before all things" (Col. 1:17) could take on the mantel of flesh is through the miraculous intervention of God in the womb of Mary.

Concluding Comments:

I said this in Chapter 1 relating to the reasons we need to teach the prophets to children, but I must say it again—children need to see the evidence of fulfilled prophecy in the scriptures so they will have a firm grasp of the fact that the Bible is from God. It is not a "sacred book" with man-made ideas; it is not even remotely similar to the Koran or Book of Mormon. One purpose of the Old Testament is for the examples, both good and bad, that we can use to help children understand that obedience to God's Word is important in their lives daily. However, a purpose we have neglected in teaching our children is stated by Paul in Rom. 15:4 – "For whatever things were written before were written for our learning, that we through the patience and comfort of the Scriptures might have hope." How do we have hope from those Old Testament Scriptures? As we read the prophets and see that God fulfilled all that He promised, we have hope that He is faithful and will fulfill the promises He has made to us. I can know that if I am faithful to Him, He will be faithful because I have the testimony of promise, picture and prophecy fulfilled in Christ and the church. Like Abraham of old, I can be "fully convinced that what He had promised He was also able to perform" (Rom. 4:21). In fact, if it is possible to be more than fully convinced, I can be more convinced than Abraham, because I have more evidence than he did. Do we want our children to be "fully convinced" of the truth of God's Word? Do we want them to be armed against the onslaught of militant atheists and world religions? Do we want them to be certain they have not followed myths? Then, we must teach the prophets!

Old Testament

New Testament

Isaiah 7:13-14

13 Then he said, "Hear now, O house of David! Is it a small thing for you to weary men, but will you weary my God also? 14 Therefore the Lord Himself will give you a sign: Behold, the virgin shall conceive and bear a Son, and shall call His name Immanuel.

Matthew 1:18-25

Now the birth of Jesus Christ was as follows: After His mother Mary was betrothed to Joseph, before they came together, she was found with child of the Holy Spirit. 19 Then Joseph her husband, being a just man, and not wanting to make her a public example, was minded to put her away secretly. 20 But while he thought about these things, behold, an angel of the Lord appeared to him in a dream, saying, "Joseph, son of David, do not be afraid to take to you Mary your wife, for that which is conceived in her is of the Holy Spirit. 21 And she will bring forth a Son, and you shall call His name JESUS, for He will save His people from their sins."

22 So all this was done that it might be fulfilled which was spoken by the Lord through the prophet, saying: 23 "Behold, the virgin shall be with child, and bear a Son, and they shall call His name Immanuel," which is translated, "God with us."

24 Then Joseph, being aroused from sleep, did as the angel of the Lord commanded him and took to him his wife, 25 and did not know her till she had brought forth her firstborn Son. And he called His name JESUS.

Figure 6.1

Chapter 7
THE CHILD BORN AND THE SON GIVEN

The prophecy of Isaiah 9:1-7 is related in time and theme to Isaiah 7:14 that I discussed in the previous chapter. In chapters 8 and 9, Isaiah describes the invasion of Israel and Judah by Assyria, but in chapter 10, he announces judgment on Assyria after God has used the Assyrians to accomplish his purpose. It is interesting to note that Assyria took the Northern Kingdom captive in 722 B.C. and invaded Judah. However, as you read the history recorded in 2 Kings 18 and 19, you see that Assyria did not take Jerusalem. This is what Isaiah prophesies of in chapter 10 which I will discuss in more detail in the next chapter. After describing the horror of Assyria's invasion, chapter 8 ends: "Then they will look to the earth, and see trouble and darkness, gloom of anguish; and they will be driven into darkness" (8:22). Chapter 9 begins with a message of hope and rejoicing:

> Nevertheless the gloom will not be upon her who is distressed, as when at first He lightly esteemed the land of Zebulun and the land of Naphtali, and afterward more heavily oppressed her, by the way of the sea, beyond the Jordan, in Galilee of the Gentiles. The people who walked in darkness have seen a great light; those who dwelt in the land of the shadow of death, upon them a light has shined.

> You have multiplied the nation and increased its joy; they rejoice before You according to the joy of harvest, as men rejoice when they divide the spoil. For You have broken the yoke of his burden And the staff of his shoulder, the rod of his oppressor, as in the day of Midian. For every warrior's sandal from the noisy battle, and garments rolled in blood, will be used for burning and fuel of fire.

> For unto us a Child is born, unto us a Son is given; and the government will be upon His shoulder. And His name will be called Wonderful, Counselor, Mighty God, Everlasting Father, Prince of Peace. Of the increase of His government and peace there will be no end, upon the throne of David and over His kingdom, to order it and establish it with judgment and justice from that time forward, even forever. The zeal of the Lord of hosts will perform this (Isa. 9:1-7).

Following the pattern of letting scripture interpret scripture, Matthew quotes verses 1 and 2 when he records the beginning of Jesus' ministry (Matt. 4:15-17). The land of Zebulun and Naphtali was northern most in Israel and suffered first from Assyria's invasion. In contrast, they would be the first to hear the glorious message of the Messiah and see the Light of the World shining into their lives. Jesus' birth was written beforehand, and so was the time and place for beginning His ministry.

Isaiah describes the great joy that comes to the land, noting that God (*You* of verses 3 and 4) is both the cause and the object of their rejoicing. Three important reasons are given for this rejoicing. In verse 4, God has delivered them from the oppressor. The historical allusion is to physical deliverance, but the Messianic context of this passage demands a spiritual deliverance. In verse 5, carnal warrior's armor and garments are burned. God's deliverance was not by physical warfare, but was a spiritual deliverance. This is reminiscent of Isaiah 2:4 and Micah 4:3-5. Then, in verses 6 and 7, Isaiah's reasons for rejoicing hit a crescendo: "For unto us a child is born, unto us a Son is given…" The child that is born is the one announced in 7:14 as a sign that God would not allow fearful leaders to thwart His purpose.

Some of the passages in the New Testament that demonstrate the fulfillment of this prophecy are:

John 1:9 – Jesus is the "true Light which gives light to every man coming into the world."

John 3:16 – "For God so loved the world that He gave His only begotten Son, that whosoever believes in Him should not perish but have everlasting life."

John 8:12 – "I am the light of the world. He who follows Me shall not walk in darkness, but have the light of life."

Luke 2:10-11 – At His birth, angels announced, "…for behold, I bring you good tidings of great joy which will be to all people. For there is born to you this day in the city of David a Savior, who is Christ the Lord."

Luke 24:52 – After Jesus' ascension into heaven, "And they worshiped Him, and returned to Jerusalem with great joy."

You may want to add other scriptures like Acts 8:39, the rejoicing of the eunuch from Ethiopia, or the numerous verses in Philippians as you build on this concept with older children. Joy in the new kingdom when the Messiah comes is a prominent theme in the prophets, and I will be referring to it as we see other pictures of the Messiah and His reign.

There are two other important concepts in this prophecy. The first is stated in the last part of verse 6—"the government shall be upon His shoulder." Also, verse 7 notes that there shall be no end to His government and that He shall rule on the throne of David. This is exactly what Gabriel promised to Mary of her Son in Luke 1:32-33 – "He will be great, and will be called the Son of the Highest; and the Lord God will give Him the throne of His father David. And He will reign over the house of Jacob forever, and of His kingdom there will be no end." Note, too, how this prophecy ties into Isaiah 2 relating to no end to peace.

Now, let's look at His names in verse 6:

Wonderful: This implies a sense of awe, amazement or great wonder. Jesus truly is the miracle of the ages, greater than our minds can fully grasp. Every time I consider the magnitude of the incarnation, I'm reminded of 1 Tim. 3:15 – "…and without controversy great is the mystery of godliness: God was manifested in the flesh, justified in the Spirit, seen by angels, preached among the Gentiles, believed on in the world, received up in glory." As I sit here at the computer, I'm thinking of the words to a children's song: "Wonderful, wonderful, Jesus is to me! Counselor, Prince of Peace, Mighty God is He. Saving me, keeping me from my sin and shame. Wonderful is my Redeemer! Praise His name!"

Counselor: "as God with us, He would give divine guidance and instruction compatible with God's nature and eternal purpose" (Hailey, p. 105). Jesus promised, "If anyone loves Me, he will keep My word; and My Father will love him, and We will come to him and make Our home with him" (John 14:23).

Mighty God: He is of the same essence as God, having the same power and might as God. Relate back to the discussion of the Branch of Jehovah in Chapter 4.

Everlasting Father: Just as His kingdom would have no end, so He has no end. In John 8:58, Jesus declared, "Before Abraham was, I AM." He thus indicated His eternal nature, His unity with the I AM of the burning bush in Exodus 3:14. The term "Father" can denote protector and provider (See Gen. 45:8; Job 29:16). In this way, the Son can be referred to as "Father."

Prince of Peace: Angels announced His birth with a message of peace on earth. Refer to the discussion of peace in Chapter 3 on Isaiah 2. You may want to add scriptures relating to peace in Christ that are special to you. I find that children respond more positively to our teaching when we make it personal.

I love how Isaiah ends this section: "The zeal of the Lord of hosts will perform this" (9:7b). Isaiah is telling the people who are burdened and feel there may be no hope that these blessings bear the seal of the Lord of hosts, the God of Israel. There can be no higher guarantee! As you trace out all the plan for man's redemption through promise, picture, and prophecy, you see God working. Our salvation is His work, His plan, His provision, His desire. Isaiah lets us know that the fulfillment of this magnificent prophecy does not rest on human power or wisdom, but rests squarely in God! This is what Paul meant when he said, "For by grace you have been saved through faith, and that not of yourselves; it is the gift of God, not of works, lest anyone should boast" (Eph. 2:8-9).

Concluding Comments:

I always try to focus the prophecy and fulfillment on the children by questions like those from the lesson in Isaiah 2—Are you in the picture? Fulfilled prophecy is the strongest proof that the Bible is from God, but if we don't make it personal for the students in our classrooms and for ourselves, it is just an academic theory. Asking students how we should respond to Jesus since He is "Wonderful, Counsellor, Mighty God, Everlasting Father, Prince of Peace" is a good activity for application. What implications would this have in our worship? In our daily lives?

I had an interesting surprise when I was teaching this prophecy to third and fourth graders. On the following Wednesday evening, several of the students brought a list of other names of Jesus from other Bible references! I had not suggested that to them, but this incident illustrates how bringing these fascinating lessons from the prophets into the lives of children can stimulate their interest in the Bible so they study and research on their own.

Old Testament

New Testament

Isaiah 9:1-2

Nevertheless the gloom will not be upon her who is distressed, as when at first He lightly esteemed the land of Zebulun and the land of Naphtali, and afterward more heavily oppressed her, by the way of the sea, beyond the Jordan, in Galilee of the Gentiles.
2 The people who walked in darkness have seen a great light; those who dwelt in the land of the shadow of death, upon them a light has shined.

Matthew 4:12-17

Now when Jesus heard that John had been put in prison, He departed to Galilee. 13 And leaving Nazareth, He came and dwelt in Capernaum, which is by the sea, in the regions of Zebulun and Naphtali, 14 that it might be fulfilled which was spoken by Isaiah the prophet, saying:

15 "The land of Zebulun and the land of Naphtali, by the way of the sea, beyond the Jordan, Galilee of the Gentiles:
16 The people who sat in darkness have seen a great light, and upon those who sat in the region and shadow of death light has dawned."

17 From that time Jesus began to preach and to say, "Repent, for the kingdom of heaven is at hand."

Isaiah 9:6-7

6 For unto us a Child is born,
Unto us a Son is given;
And the government will be upon His shoulder. And His name will be called Wonderful, Counselor, Mighty God, Everlasting Father, Prince of Peace.
7 Of the increase of His government and peace there will be no end, upon the throne of David and over His kingdom, To order it and establish it with judgment and justice from that time forward, even forever.
The zeal of the Lord of hosts will perform this.

Luke 1:30-33

30 Then the angel said to her, "Do not be afraid, Mary, for you have found favor with God. 31 And behold, you will conceive in your womb and bring forth a Son, and shall call His name JESUS. 32 He will be great, and will be called the Son of the Highest; and the Lord God will give Him the throne of His father David. 33 And He will reign over the house of Jacob forever, and of His kingdom there will be no end."

*Underline the words in Isaiah 9:6-7 that are names of Jesus.

Figure 7.1

Old Testament

Isaiah 9:1-2
Nevertheless the gloom will not be upon her who is distressed,
As when at first He lightly esteemed
The land of Zebulun and the land of Naphtali,
And afterward more heavily oppressed her,
By the way of the sea, beyond the Jordan,
In Galilee of the Gentiles.
2 The people who walked in darkness
Have seen a great light;
Those who dwelt in the land of the shadow of death,
Upon them a light has shined.

Isaiah 49:6
6 Indeed He says,
'It is too small a thing that You should be My Servant
To raise up the tribes of Jacob,
And to restore the preserved ones of Israel;
I will also give You as a light to the Gentiles,
That You should be My salvation to the ends of the earth.'"

New Testament

Luke 2:25-32
And behold, there was a man in Jerusalem whose name was Simeon, and this man was just and devout, waiting for the Consolation of Israel, and the Holy Spirit was upon him. 26 And it had been revealed to him by the Holy Spirit that he would not see death before he had seen the Lord's Christ. 27 So he came by the Spirit into the temple. And when the parents brought in the Child Jesus, to do for Him according to the custom of the law, 28 he took Him up in his arms and blessed God and said:
29 "Lord, now You are letting Your servant depart in peace,
According to Your word;
30 For my eyes have seen Your salvation
31 Which You have prepared before the face of all peoples,
32 A light to bring revelation to the Gentiles,
And the glory of Your people Israel."

Acts 13:44-48
44 On the next Sabbath almost the whole city came together to hear the word of God. 45 But when the Jews saw the multitudes, they were filled with envy; and contradicting and blaspheming, they opposed the things spoken by Paul. 46 Then Paul and Barnabas grew bold and said,"It was necessary that the word of God should be spoken to you first; but since you reject it, and judge yourselves unworthy of everlasting life, behold, we turn to the Gentiles. 47 For so the Lord has commanded us:
'I have set you as a light to the Gentiles,
That you should be for salvation to the ends of the earth.'"

Figure 7.2

Chapter 8
GOD'S AX, SAW, & ROD

*I*saiah chapters 10, 11, and 12 continue the theme of chapters 7 through 9—God's judgments on Israel and Judah through the instrumentality of Assyria, and the ultimate coming of Immanuel. I hope you will not let the length of this chapter and the material in Isaiah 10-12 overwhelm you as a teacher. You should plan several class periods for this prophecy, depending on the age and maturity of the children. I have taught this to third and fourth grades, and I usually spend three class periods on it. I think it is a very important lesson because of the popularity of the pictures of the "wolf and lamb" in religious circles. Also, this is the lesson where children begin to actually see what Old Testament prophecy is all about. They also see God as the Divine Woodcutter who is dealing with the nations according to His purpose to bring Christ into the world. Be prepared for an exciting and interesting journey through these pictures in Isaiah 10-12!

In chapter 10, we learn some interesting things about God and His using the pagan nations. I like to begin this section by asking the children if they know that God has an ax, a saw, and a rod. Figure 8.1 illustrates these tools like they may have appeared in the ancient world. We also discuss the purpose of each—an ax cuts down trees, a saw cuts the tree into pieces, a rod beats down enemies in battle. Sometime, either at the end or beginning of class, I ask the children if they know that God also has a wash pot. I don't tell them who it is, but I ask them to find out and bring the information to the next class. They always do. Now we have set the stage for the picture Isaiah paints in these chapters.

Before discussing the picture, it is helpful for teachers to know the context from 9:8 to 10:4. These verses tell us of the reason for God's discipline of His people. "For the people do not turn to Him… nor do they seek the LORD of hosts" (9:13). In verses 14-17, Isaiah lays the blame on the leaders, the elders, and the prophets who have caused the people to err. Though much of this is descriptive of both Israel and Judah, Isaiah's message is to Judah. In chapter 10, he pronounces woes on the tyrants who oppress the poor and helpless, and asks where they (the tyrants) will seek help when destruction comes (10:1-4).

I think it is helpful for children to see the sad state of Judah and Israel. They had every blessing from God; they had the assurance of His protection; they were His own special people—a holy nation. Yet, they had rejected His counsel and had desired to be like the nations around them. They pretended to worship God, but they were doing exactly what Moses warned about: "When the LORD your God cuts off from before you the nations… take heed to yourself that you are not ensnared to follow them… do not inquire after their gods saying, 'How did these nations serve their gods? I also will do likewise.' You shall not worship the LORD your God in that way…" (Deut. 12:29-31). I remember one of the girls in my third and fourth grade class commenting on God's judgement of His people: "When you think about it, they deserved it!" Lauren was right, and the prophets help us see that.

Assyria has been marching through all the neighboring nations and destroying them. They have taken the Northern Kingdom into captivity, and now they are thundering through Judah toward Jerusalem. God calls Isaiah to encourage the remnant—those who still are faithful to Him, but who are fearful as they see the approaching army. In the rest of chapter 10, God explains that He is using Assyria to refine His people, but He will not completely destroy them. And, here's the part the children love—when God is finished with Assyria, He will completely and utterly destroy them with a mighty devastation. Assyria will be gone from their land and eventually wiped out completely, and it will be obvious that God brought it about. With this as a summary, let's now turn to the picture of God, Assyria, and Judah.

The drawings by Jodie Boren and Roy Johnson help illustrate this section. You may want to use these in a power point or make transparencies or just copy the pictures for each student and have them follow along with the illustrations as you explain the scripture. Verse 5 lets us know that Assyria is God's rod; verse 6 says God is sending Assyria against Judah ("an ungodly nation"); and verse 7 tells us that Assyria doesn't intend to serve God. Assyria is only a vicious nation with a strong army. In fact, history demonstrates that Assyria was the most barbarous of the pagan nations. Kenny Barfield has pictures of reliefs at Nineveh graphically depicting the brutal torture of their victims—flaying them and tacking their skin to the walls, beheading and mutilating them in various ways. He also quotes from Ashurnarsipal II, king during the ninth century, where he takes great pride in the cruel treatment of his victims (Barfield 1995, 56-57). While teachers need to use wisdom in how much of these historical facts they share with their children, it is important to know that God was also acting in behalf of the good people in both the Jewish and Gentile world when He destroyed nations like Assyria. This is the nation, though, that God is using. Like Habakkuk, we may ask why or how God could and would do that, but the judge of all the earth will do right (Gen. 18:25), and His people can rest in that confidence (Hab. 2:4; 3:17-18).

The arrogance of Assyria is described in verses 8 through 14:

For he says:

"Are not my princes altogether kings?

Is not Calno like Carchemish?

Is not Hamath like Arpad?

Is not Samaria like Damascus?

As my hand has found the kingdoms of the idols,

Whose carved images excelled those of Jerusalem and Samaria,

As I have done to Samaria and her idols,

Shall I not do also to Jerusalem and her idols?"

Therefore it shall come to pass, when the Lord has performed all His work on Mount Zion and on Jerusalem, that He will say, "I will punish the fruit of the arrogant heart of the king of Assyria, and the glory of his haughty looks."

For he says:

"By the strength of my hand I have done it,

And by my wisdom, for I am prudent;

Also I have removed the boundaries of the people,

And have robbed their treasuries

So I have put down the inhabitants like a valiant man.

My hand has found like a nest the riches of the people,

And as one gathers eggs that are left,

I have gathered all the earth;

And there was no one who moved his wing,

Nor opened his mouth with even a peep."

In verses 8-11, the Assyrian boasts of his military superiority over all the nations he has conquered thus far. For younger children, just a general reference to these cities is enough, but for older students, you may want to locate them on a map of the ancient world. Homer Hailey has a good discussion of the cities and the date of this prophecy in <u>A Commentary of Isaiah</u>, pages 113, 114, but a good Bible dictionary will give you similar information. From the context, it is most probable this prophecy was spoken after the fall of Samaria in 722 B.C. and shortly before Sennacherib besieged Judah and Jerusalem in 702-701 B.C.

The Assyrian is guilty of blasphemy in verses 10 and 11, boasting that the elaborate and expensive idols of the nations he had conquered are more glorious than those of Jerusalem, and they had not protected their people from him. He reasons that Jehovah will not be able to stop him from taking Jerusalem. The imagery is interesting in verse 14, and children enjoy this picture of the Assyrian's bragging. Paraphrased, he says, "I've taken all the treasures of the nations as easy as gathering eggs, and no one 'opened his mouth with even a peep!'"

In verses 15-19, God answers in a loud roar, not a little peep! God first asks a series of rhetorical questions, each declaring that an ax, saw, rod or staff can do nothing unless someone uses them. Those tools must be wielded by a person, and have no power alone. In verse 5, God had identified the Assyrian as His rod, His instrument of destruction, so how could the Assyrian do any more or less than what God allowed? Isaiah pictures God as a Woodcutter, using his ax (Assyria) to cut down Israel and to humble Judah. Now, if God is accomplishing the work, how could the Assyrian brag about what he had done? You may want to bring a real or pretend set of these tools to class and ask the ax to cut down a tree, or the rod to beat up someone. Let the children see the folly of the boasting Assyrian. This can be extended to a lesson on the foolishness of boasting against God, or bragging about what we have done in His kingdom.

What will Jehovah do when He is finished with Assyria? He will "kindle a burning like the burning of a fire" that will consume the Assyrians in one day (Isa. 10:16-17). In all probability, this refers to the incident recorded in 2 Kings 19:22-36, 2 Chron. 32, and Isa. 37:36-38, when the Angel of the LORD came through the camp of the Assyrian army as it was threatening Jerusalem, and killed 185,000 in one day. Sennacherib returned home in disgrace and shame. He wasn't boasting about this military venture!

Isaiah continues to tell of the destruction of Assyria, using the imagery of a forest. God, acting as a divine Woodcutter, will now use another of His axes (Babylon) to cut down Assyria. In fact, this will be so devastating that there will be little to nothing left. "Then the rest of the trees of his forest will be so few in number that a child may write them" (v.19). Now, look at the Assyrian's glorious, conquering army! It will be like a "sick man wastes away" (v. 18). And, it is so small that even a young child can walk through it and count the soldiers! The complete destruction of Assyria would be several years later, but this defeat at Jerusalem set in motion the events that led to the rise of Babylon and destruction of Assyria. Previously, all nations were afraid of the Assyrian army, but seeing Sennacherib marching back to Nineveh, the conquered nations saw Assyria as vulnerable.

In verses 20-32, Isaiah pauses in his proclamation of Assyria's destruction to encourage the people. He does this through the recurring theme of the remnant—a remnant will escape, and of that remnant, a remnant will return to the land. The last part of verse 22 is interesting: "The destruction decreed shall overflow with righteousness." Again, we see the purpose of God's discipline. The destruction produces righteousness (Isa. 26:9). In verses 24 through 26, God tells the people not to fear the Assyrian, though he will strike them. This will not be for long, and then God will come as He did in Egypt and lift the burden of Assyria from them and take his yoke from them. These historical references let them know that deliverance from Assyria will not be from alliances or armies, but from His hand, alone. God enumerates Assyria's march through the countries and lets His people know that though he has been successful with others, he will only "shake his fist at the mount of the daughter of Zion, the hill of Jerusalem" (v. 32). This event is recorded in 2 Kings 19—the Assyrians will not even shoot an arrow into the city.

Isaiah returns to the imagery of a forest. He pictures Assyria's army outside Jerusalem like the immense forest of Lebanon—majestic and powerful. But now the divine Woodcutter has another ax, and "the Lord of hosts will lop off the bough with terror; those of high stature will be hewn down, and the haughty will be humbled. He will cut down the thickets of the forest with iron, and Lebanon will fall by the Mighty One" (vs. 33-34). Figure 8.3 is a graphic illustration of this picture combined with the one in verses 15-19.

Now, we enter the picture in Isaiah 11. Another felled forest stands in stark contrast to the totally devastated forest representing Assyria. Isaiah sees stumps in this new forest with the trace of life, and from the stump of Jesse (the father of David), a shoot or rod begins to grow. (Figure 8.4 helps the children see Isaiah's word picture.) God's promise has not been forgotten! He has disciplined His people and preserved the remnant to bring about our salvation! The house of David, though weakened by idolatrous and faithless kings, will bring forth the Messiah "as a root out of dry ground" (Isa. 53:2). This One will be distinctly different from the physical rulers of their past. Listen to Isaiah's description:

The Spirit of the LORD shall rest upon Him,

The Spirit of wisdom and understanding,

The Spirit of counsel and might,

The Spirit of knowledge and of the fear of the LORD.

His delight is in the fear of the LORD,

And He shall not judge by the sight of His eyes,

Nor decide by the hearing of His ears;

But with righteousness He shall judge the poor,

And decide with equity for the meek of the earth;

He shall strike the earth with the rod of His mouth,

And with the breath of His lips He shall slay the wicked.

Righteousness shall be the belt of His loins,

And faithfulness the belt of His waist (11:3-5).

In these verses, Isaiah personifies the "shoot" or "rod" or "Branch," and we are certain now that the picture is of a person, not a tree. Jesus Christ is the only person in history who fits Isaiah's description. "The Spirit of the Lord shall rest upon Him" (v. 2). At the baptism of Jesus, John the Baptist stated, "I saw the Spirit descending from heaven like a dove, and He remained upon Him. I did not know Him, but He who sent me to baptize with water said to me, 'Upon whom you see the Spirit descending, and remaining on Him, this is He who baptizes with the Holy Spirit'" (John 1:32-33). The scriptures supporting the nature of Jesus as revealed in this passage are too numerous to list. However, these in John's gospel are sufficient for my purpose:

John 3:34 . John the Baptist witnesses of Jesus, "For He whom God has sent speaks the words of God…"

John 4:34 . "Jesus said to them, 'My food is to do the will of Him who sent Me, and to finish His work.'"

John 5:30 . "As I hear, I judge, and My judgment is righteous, because I do not seek My own will but the will of the Father who sent Me."

John 6:38 . "For I have come down from heaven, not to do My own will, but the will of Him who sent Me."

John 7:16-18 . "Jesus answered them and said, 'My doctrine is not Mine, but His who sent Me. If anyone wills to do His will, he shall know concerning the doctrine, whether it is from God or whether I speak on My own authority. He who speaks from himself seeks his own glory; but He who seeks the glory of the One who sent Him is true, and no unrighteousness is in Him.'"

Next, Isaiah describes the character of those in the Messiah's kingdom:

The wolf also shall dwell with the lamb,

The leopard shall lie down with the young goat,

The calf and the young lion and the fatling together;

And a little child shall lead them.

The cow and the bear shall graze;

Their young ones shall lie down together;

And the lion shall eat straw like the ox.

The nursing child shall play by the cobra's hole,

And the weaned child shall put his hand in the viper's den.

They shall not hurt nor destroy in all My holy mountain,

For the earth shall be full of the knowledge of the LORD

As the waters cover the sea (Isa. 11:6-9).

Children can easily see this is figurative (or picture) language just as verses 1-5 were. The wolf usually lies down with the lamb inside him. The leopard will pounce on a young goat and have him for dinner. No parent would let a child be among these wild animals, and certainly not let a child play with a cobra or play near a viper's den. Children see quickly that this is a picture of unusual peace. Just like the shoot that grew out of the stump of a fallen tree is a picture of Jesus, so this is a picture of the peace that He brings into the lives of those who follow Him. And, notice where this takes place—not in the physical realm or earthly kingdoms of animals and people. Isaiah states clearly where this peace exists: "They shall not hurt nor destroy in all My holy mountain…" (v. 9). We have seen God's holy mountain previously in Isaiah 2 and Micah 4. In that picture, peace is described as people changing instruments of war into instruments of peace. We also saw that God's holy mountain is not a physical place on or in the earth, but it is the Mount Zion described in Hebrews 12: 22-24, which is His church. For a fuller discussion of the peace Jesus brings, refer back to Chapter 3 relating to Isaiah 2. You may also want to include John 14:27—"Peace I leave with you, My peace I give to you; not as the world gives do I give to you." Jesus states plainly that His peace is different; it is not "world peace."

Another way to illustrate this concept for children in about third grade and above is to remind them of Jesus' apostles—Matthew, a hated tax-collector and Simon the Zealot, who wanted to throw off Roman rule, and not pay taxes to Rome. Later as the gospel spread, we see Jews and Gentiles having harmony and peace with one another. "No iron curtain, color bar, class distinction or national frontier of today is more absolute than the cleavage between Jew and Gentile in antiquity" (Bruce 1961, 54). There are many good modern day examples of the unity and peace that Jesus brings into our society that no government, law, or other religion can bring. Hindus enforce the caste system. Buddhism tried to eliminate it, but created another type of exclusivism. Islam is a religion of division. Only Christ can break down barriers and unite those who otherwise might be enemies.

Why or how will this unusual peace come about? Isaiah answers that question, "For the earth shall be full of the knowledge of the Lord as the waters cover the sea" (v.9). Peace treaties between nations, the United Nations, the Peace Corps, and any other human organization or message cannot bring this peace. It comes only through the knowledge of God. And, notice, too, that this knowledge is for the whole earth. God's desire, even in the Old Testament, is for the salvation of all men. Isaiah's picture looked forward to Jesus' commission: "Go into all the world and preach the gospel to every creature" (Mark 16:15).

If there is any doubt that this is a picture of Jesus and His spiritual kingdom, verses 10 and 11 clearly remove that doubt. Note verse 10: "And in that day there shall be a Root of Jesse, who shall stand as a banner to the people; for the Gentiles shall seek Him, and His resting place shall be glorious." Paul quotes this verse in Romans 15:12 as he discusses the fact that Jesus is the fulfillment of the promise made "to the fathers, and that the Gentiles might Glorify God for His mercy." The phrase in verse 10, "in that day" refers to the "day" when the Gentiles will glorify God, having been saved by the blood of Jesus in the same way the Jews are saved.

How will children ever understand and remember all of this? First of all, it will take more than one 45 minute class period to teach the concepts of chapters 10-12. Second, on figure 8.5 on the Branch (tree), have the students write some of the words from verses 1-5 that describe Jesus. Third, I have used figure 8.5 to help them remember the picture and what it means, and I have included the additional pictures you will need in figures 8.5a and 8.5b. Give each child a copy of the figure of Jesus with the line noted for folding. Have him/her tape or glue that figure to the left side of figure 8.3 so that folded over, it will cover the Branch (tree). Then, give the students a copy of the sheet with the words "UNUSUAL PEACE" and various scriptures about peace on it. Have them tape or glue that sheet to the right side of 8.5 so that folded over, it will cover the picture of the wild and domesticated animals together.

After this activity, I usually come home and tell Gary, "I dare a Jehovah's Witness to knock on their door!" Sometime during the discussion of the picture in chapter 11, I show them pictures that are common in the physical interpretation of verses 6-9 and tell them that some of their friends may think this is right because so many pictures like this are distributed. I try to be kind in this, but to let them know that others have done with this passage what Peter says some do to other passages that are difficult to understand in 2 Peter 3:15-16 . "… which untaught and unstable people twist to their own destruction, as they do also the rest of the Scriptures." Then, I tell them that Isaiah 10 and 11 are really not difficult to understand, as they can see, but because many of us are not familiar with the prophets and the pictures they paint of the kingdom, we may be led astray or confused by false teachers. They always seem to "get it" at this point! When I have taught children these lessons from the prophets, this lesson is the one where the light seems to come on for them all. And, from this time on, they are anxious and ready to continue to look at the pictures of Jesus and His Kingdom.

There is still more to Isaiah's picture. I am going to include it here, but you may want to wait until a bit later to teach this part. Also, this is probably better for children in fifth grade and above. Isaiah is still speaking of "in that day" when the Branch rules, when there is unusual peace, and when the Root of Jesse stands as a banner for the people. He declares in verse 11, "It shall come to pass in that day that the Lord shall set His hand again the second time to recover the remnant of His people who are left, from Assyria and Egypt, from Pathros and Cush, from Elam and Shinar, from Hamath and the islands of the sea." The first time God recovered a remnant of His people was at the end of the 70 year Babylonian captivity under Ezra, Nehemiah, and Zerubbabel. This second gathering of the remnant was in the day of the Messiah, when He stands as a banner for the nations (v. 12). This second recovery of the remnant began in Acts 2 when devout Jews from all nations heard the message of the crucified and raised Messiah. As the gospel spread throughout the Roman Empire and beyond as recorded in Acts, the Messiah stood as a banner for all nations (refer again to Rom. 15:12). There are 7 nations mentioned in Isaiah 11:11, and Homer Hailey notes that seven is a number of completeness (Hailey 1985, 110). The gathering will include "the islands of the sea" (v.11) and those "from the four corners of the earth" (v.12). As you continue reading, former enemies will be at peace (like the picture in vs. 6-9), and many others will be obedient. This is compared to the time when God delivered His people from Egypt, making it evident that this is God's work, not man's.

Isaiah ends this picture with "There will be a highway for the remnant of His people who will be left from Assyria, as it was for Israel in the day that he came up from the land of Egypt" (v. 16). This highway is referred to again in Isaiah 35:8 as "the highway of holiness." We'll learn more about that highway later!

I wanted to include Isaiah 12 in this chapter because it is a fitting end of this picture of salvation in the day of the coming of the Branch, the banner for the nations. This is a picture of the praise and joy that comes to those who are in God's holy mountain. Twice, Isaiah says, "God is my salvation!" God had saved them from Assyria's threat, from Babylonian captivity, and now "in that day" they will acknowledge God's greater salvation again—"by grace you have been saved" (Eph. 2:8). God's past deliverance of His people is but a shadow of the marvelous deliverance we have from the one who kept us in bondage through the fear of death.

Look at the picture in verse 3: "Therefore with joy you will draw water from the wells of salvation." In His encounter with the Samaritan woman at Jacob's well, Jesus said, "Whoever drinks of this water will thirst again, but whoever drinks of the water that I shall give him will never thirst. But the water that I shall give him will become in him a fountain of water springing up into everlasting life" (John 4:13-14). She left her physical water pot to go with joy to the city and bring others to Him.

Notice the activity of those Isaiah describes in verses 4 and 5: They will "declare His deeds among the peoples…" Like Andrew who brought his brother to Jesus, Philip who found Nathaniel, and the woman of Samaria who brought a whole city to Him, people in His holy mountain will be evangelistic. You will want to refer back to Isaiah 2, when people come to the mountain of the Lord's house because others are saying, "Come let us go…" What is their message? "Cry out and shout, O inhabitant of Zion, for great is the Holy One of Israel in your midst!" (v.6). This is our message today. Let us never forget, "Great is the Holy One of Israel!"

Concluding Comments:

This chapter is rather long, but don't let that keep you from teaching this picture of the Messiah and His kingdom. In my experience, children like this prophecy better than most we study, and they understand more than you might think possible. Chapters 10 through 12 form a unit, and teachers need to know the background so they can be comfortable teaching this. You can make chapter 10 rather simple for children up through about 5th grade; the main concept is that God is using Assyria to cut down wicked nations like a woodcutter uses an ax. The ax begins to brag about his accomplishments and speak against God, but the great Woodcutter will also cut down Assyria. Then, tie into chapter 11—God has humbled Judah; a faithful remnant is left. From that faithful remnant, specifically the house of Jesse, the Messiah will come and set up His rule of peace and harmony among all people who will respond to His message. Chapter 12 highlights the joy that comes to those who are in this peaceful kingdom.

God's Ax, Rod, and Saw

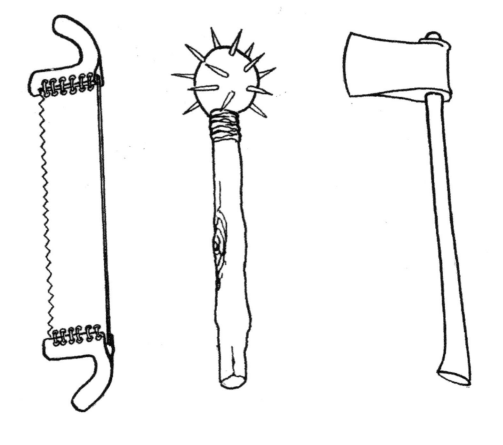

Isaiah 10:5-7

"Woe to Assyria, the rod of My anger
And the staff in whose hand is My indignation.

6 I will send him against an ungodly nation,
And against the people of My wrath
I will give him charge,
To seize the spoil, to take the prey,
And to tread them down like the mire of the streets.

7 Yet he does not mean so,
Nor does his heart think so;
But it is in his heart to destroy,
And cut off not a few nations.

Isaiah 10:15

15 Shall the ax boast itself against him who chops with it?
Or shall the saw exalt itself against him who saws with it?
As if a rod could wield itself against those who lift it up,
Or as if a staff could lift up, as if it were not wood!

Figure 8.1

God's Ax – Assyria

God used Assyria to cut down the sinful nation of Israel.

Assyria was God's tool.

Assyria did not mean to be serving God's purpose.

Assyria only wanted to destroy other nations.

Assyria was proud.

God would later use Babylon to cut down Assyria.

The Assyrian army doesn't know that God will use another ax (Babylon) to destroy them.

Art by Jodie Boren

Figure 8.2

God brought about the complete destruction of Assyria!

Babylon

Other tools God used*.

*See Barfield, pages 61-64.

Art by Roy Johnson

Figure 8.3

The Branch from the Root of Jesse

God used Assyria and Babylon to discipline His people, but He promised that "a remnant of them will return" (Isa. 10:22). Through that remnant of faithful people, God would bring Jesus into the world according to His promise made to Abraham, Isaac, Jacob, and David.

Write the names of the tribes of Israel on all the stumps that are left in this forest.

Draw a branch sprouting out of the stump of Jesse.

Read Matthew 1:1.
Did God fulfill His promise? _____

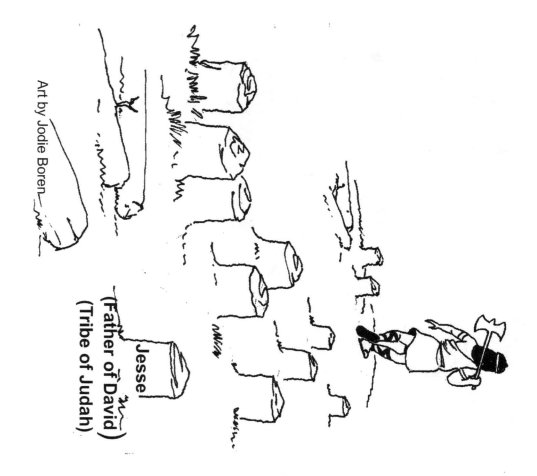

Art by Jodie Boren

Jesse
(Father of David)
(Tribe of Judah)

Figure 8.4

"They shall not hurt nor destroy in all My holy mountain." Isaiah 11:9

THE BRANCH

Art by Roy Johnson

Figure 8.5

Figure 8.5a

Fold along the line and glue or tape the blank side of this sheet to the back of figure 8.5 so that when folded, this covers the "Branch." You may need to trim the sheet or adjust the fold line.

Fold along this line.

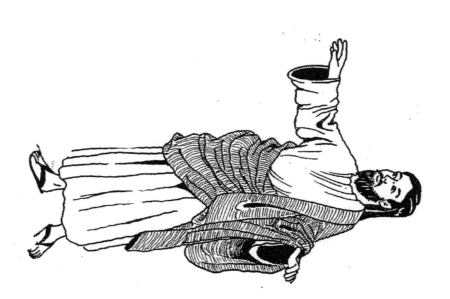

Isaiah 11:9

9 They shall not hurt nor destroy in all My holy mountain, for the earth shall be full of the knowledge of the LORD as the waters cover the sea.

PEACE
Unusual Peace

Luke 2:14

14 "Glory to God in the highest, and on earth peace, goodwill toward men!"

John 14:27-28

27 Peace I leave with you, My peace I give to you; not as the world gives do I give to you. Let not your heart be troubled, neither let it be afraid.

Ephesians 2:14-18

For He Himself is our peace, who has made both one, and has broken down the middle wall of separation, 15 having abolished in His flesh the enmity, that is, the law of commandments contained in ordinances, so as to create in Himself one new man from the two, thus making peace, 16 and that He might reconcile them both to God in one body through the cross, thereby putting to death the enmity. 17 And He came and preached peace to you who were afar off and to those who were near. 18 For through Him we both have access by one Spirit to the Father.

Fold along this line.

Fold along the line, then glue or tape the blank side to the back of figure 8.5 so that when folded over the picture, the scriptures cover the picture of the animals and children.

Figure 8.5b

Old Testament

Isaiah 11:1-5

There shall come forth a Rod from the stem of Jesse,
And a Branch shall grow out of his roots.
2 The Spirit of the LORD shall rest upon Him,
The Spirit of wisdom and understanding,
The Spirit of counsel and might,
The Spirit of knowledge and of the fear of the LORD.
3 His delight is in the fear of the LORD,
And He shall not judge by the sight of His eyes,
Nor decide by the hearing of His ears;
4 But with righteousness He shall judge the poor,
And decide with equity for the meek of the earth;
He shall strike the earth with the rod of His mouth,
And with the breath of His lips He shall slay the wicked.
5 Righteousness shall be the belt of His loins,
And faithfulness the belt of His waist.

New Testament

Matthew 1:1-6

The book of the genealogy of Jesus Christ, the Son of David, the Son of Abraham:
2 Abraham begot Isaac, Isaac begot Jacob, and Jacob begot Judah and his brothers. 3 Judah begot Perez and Zerah by Tamar, Perez begot Hezron, and Hezron begot Ram. 4 Ram begot Amminadab, Amminadab begot Nahshon, and Nahshon begot Salmon. 5 Salmon begot Boaz by Rahab, Boaz begot Obed by Ruth, Obed begot Jesse, 6 and Jesse begot David the king.

Luke 3:21-22

When all the people were baptized, it came to pass that Jesus also was baptized; and while He prayed, the heaven was opened. 22 And the Holy Spirit descended in bodily form like a dove upon Him, and a voice came from heaven which said, "You are My beloved Son; in You I am well pleased."

Matthew 7:28-29

28 And so it was, when Jesus had ended these sayings, that the people were astonished at His teaching, 29 for He taught them as one having authority, and not as the scribes.

Matthew 11:28-30
28 Come to Me, all you who labor and are heavy laden, and I will give you rest. 29 Take My yoke upon you and learn from Me, for I am gentle and lowly in heart, and you will find rest for your souls. 30 For My yoke is easy and My burden is light."

Figure 8.6

Old Testament

Isaiah 11:6-12

"The wolf also shall dwell with the lamb, the leopard shall lie down with the young goat, the calf and the young lion and the fatling together; and a little child shall lead them. 7 The cow and the bear shall graze; their young ones shall lie down together; and the lion shall eat straw like the ox. 8 The nursing child shall play by the cobra's hole, and the weaned child shall put his hand in the viper's den. 9 They shall not hurt nor destroy in all My holy mountain, for the earth shall be full of the knowledge of the LORD as the waters cover the sea. 10 "And in that day there shall be a Root of Jesse, Who shall stand as a banner to the people; for the Gentiles shall seek Him, and His resting place shall be glorious."
11 It shall come to pass in that day that the Lord shall set His hand again the second time To recover the remnant of His people who are left, from Assyria and Egypt, from Pathros and Cush, from Elam and Shinar, from Hamath and the islands of the sea.
12 He will set up a banner for the nations, and will assemble the outcasts of Israel, and gather together the dispersed of Judah from the four corners of the earth.

New Testament

John 14:27-28

27 Peace I leave with you, My peace I give to you; not as the world gives do I give to you. Let not your heart be troubled, neither let it be afraid.

Matthew 5:9

9 Blessed are the peacemakers,
For they shall be called sons of God.

Acts 2:5-12

And there were dwelling in Jerusalem Jews, devout men, from every nation under heaven. 6 And when this sound occurred, the multitude came together, and were confused, because everyone heard them speak in his own language. 7 Then they were all amazed and marveled, saying to one another, "Look, are not all these who speak Galileans? 8 And how is it that we hear, each in our own language in which we were born? 9 Parthians and Medes and Elamites, those dwelling in Mesopotamia, Judea and Cappadocia, Pontus and Asia, 10 Phrygia and Pamphylia, Egypt and the parts of Libya adjoining Cyrene, visitors from Rome, both Jews and proselytes, 11 Cretans and Arabs -- we hear them

Romans 15:9, 12

9 and that the Gentiles might glorify God for His mercy, as it is written:
" For this reason I will confess to You among the Gentiles,
And sing to Your name."

12 And again, Isaiah says:
"There shall be a root of Jesse;
And He who shall rise to reign over the Gentiles,
In Him the Gentiles shall hope."

Figure 8.7

"Therefore with joy you will draw water from the wells of salvation."

Isaiah 12:3

Jesus described the blessing of salvation that He brings to all people as "living water" (John 4:10).

Figure 8.8

Chapter 9
GOD'S BANQUET

What will it be like when Jesus comes? Isaiah paints a picture for us in chapter 25, and Jesus tells a parable that is parallel to this picture. Children enjoy this picture lesson, and Jodie Boren's illustrations are not only helpful, but appeal to the children's imaginations, especially figure 9.2. Let's look now at God's banquet:

And in this mountain

The LORD of hosts will make for all people

A feast of choice pieces,

A feast of wines on the lees,

Of fat things full of marrow,

Of well-refined wines on the lees.

And He will destroy on this mountain

The surface of the covering cast over all people,

And the veil that is spread over all nations.

He will swallow up death forever,

And the Lord GOD will wipe away tears from all faces;

The rebuke of His people

He will take away from all the earth;

For the LORD has spoken.

And it will be said in that day:

"Behold, this is our God;

We have waited for Him, and He will save us.

This is the LORD;

We have waited for Him;

We will be glad and rejoice in His salvation" (Isa. 25:6-9).

You may want to refer back to the discussion of "the mountain of the Lord's house" in Chapter 3 to remind the children that "in this mountain" is the same as the mountain in Isaiah 2, which is the same as Mount Zion in Heb. 12. A rich and interesting study of the Old Testament is to trace out Zion as it is used by David and the prophets. I will address that in more detail in a later chapter on Isaiah 60.

What will it be like when Jesus comes? Think about a gourmet banquet with all the finest foods prepared by the best chefs—that's what it will be like, only better! God is the chef for this banquet, and He prepares the very best from the finest ingredients. Notice that Isaiah is using the figure of a banquet to illustrate God's generosity and blessings. Sometimes I tell children Isaiah is telling us God's blessings are like Thanksgiving (or Christmas) dinner at Grandmother's house! All the family is there; they are laughing and enjoying being together; and all their favorite foods are on the table. (You may even ask the children what their favorite foods are and share yours. Just be careful that you don't focus more on the picture than on what it represents.)

A point I made in Chapter 7 is illustrated in this picture. It is God who prepares and provides. Those at the banquet didn't have to bring a dish as to a pot luck fellowship meal. They didn't have to work in the kitchen, serve the meal, or clean up afterward. Nor did they have to pay for the meal. God takes care of all of that. Does this remind you again of Eph. 2:8-9—"For by grace you have been saved through faith, and that not of yourselves; it is the gift of God, not of works, lest anyone should boast." However, those who are at the banquet did have to come to the table, as we will see in Jesus' parable.

Look for a moment at what's on God's banquet table. You will want to adjust this section depending on the age, biblical knowledge and maturity of your students. In the picture of the physical banquet, the best food is available. The physical banquet in God's mountain is a picture of the spiritual banquet in Mount Zion, so you will want to stress scriptures like Eph. 1:3—"Blessed be the God and Father of our Lord Jesus Christ, who has blessed us with every spiritual blessing in the heavenly places in Christ." For fifth grade and above, you might have them name some of the spiritual blessings. For younger children, you may need to list them. I'm smiling right now as I remember Tonya and what she would ask when she was little, "Mommy, are we rich?" I would always answer, "Yes, we're rich! We're rich in all the blessings God has given us!" Then, I would begin naming people and other things like a home, food, clothing, etc., and I would ask her to join me in naming those blessings. One day, when she was about eight, she was sitting in my lap and asked, "Mommy, are we rich? And, don't give me that 'rich in blessings' answer!" I lovingly told her those blessings were the only riches that were important, that we had enough money to take care of our basic needs, and that's all that mattered. All those who come to God's banquet are rich! Let's never forget that!

The imagery in verse 7 of a "covering cast over all people, and the veil that is spread over all nations..." refers to ignorance of His being and His Word. Sometimes children may think that the Jewish people were the only ones who could know God and reason that God is unfair, perhaps that He caused that veil and covering. But, Paul explains differently in Romans 1:20-21 – "For since the creation of the world His invisible attributes are clearly seen, being understood by the things that are made, even His eternal power and Godhead, so that they are without excuse, because, although they knew God, they did not glorify Him as God, nor were thankful, but became futile in their thoughts, and their foolish hearts were darkened." This is just an elaboration on what Paul preached at Lystra: "Nevertheless He did not leave Himself without witness, in that He did good, gave us rain from heaven and fruitful seasons, filling our hearts with food and gladness" (Acts 14:17). People could have known about God. The veil was over their hearts because they "did not like to retain God in their knowledge…" (Rom. 1:28a). God lifts the veil and covering through the knowledge of Jesus Christ. You may want to refer back to Chapter 6 in the discussion of Isaiah 9, that "the people who walked in darkness have seen a great Light…" and to Jesus' own statement as the Light of the World.

Verse 8—"He will swallow up death forever"—is quoted by Paul in 1 Cor. 15:54. If there was any doubt that this picture is Messianic, this quotation puts that doubt to rest. Death is swallowed up because Jesus conquered death. Again, it will depend on the age of the students you are teaching as to how much detail you include. With most students, you can summarize 1 Cor. 15, reading verses that they can relate to easily and show them that Paul says Jesus has been raised from the dead and because of that fact, we know we will be raised. I like to use also Heb. 2:14-18, that Jesus became flesh to release us from the fear of death by His resurrection and triumph over death. Also, Peter said of Him "whom God raised up, having loosed the pains of death, because it was not possible that He should be held by it" (Acts 2:24). "Death is swallowed up forever" for all those seated at God's banquet table in His holy mountain! Don't you want to be seated there? For children who are in later elementary or junior high who may be considering baptism, this is a good time to review how we can be seated at the banquet, having our sins washed away and enjoying all the spiritual blessings. For younger children, you can let them know they are seated beside their parents at the banquet, but there will come a time when they will want to make the decision to stay there and enjoy His bounty in their lives.

Verses 8 and 9 describe the joy as a result of the victory over death. God will "wipe away tears from all faces" (v. 8). This reminds me of Rev. 21:4—"And God will wipe away every tear from their eyes…" Tears and sadness give way to the blessed happiness of knowing that the one who had kept us in fear has been crushed. The promise of Gen. 3:15 has been realized! The redeemed are "glad and rejoice in His salvation" (v.9). Also, notice the same guarantee as in Isaiah 9—"For the Lord has spoken!" (v.8). What God has spoken carries with it all the authority and power of heaven and earth. "But the Lord is faithful, who will establish you and guard you from the evil one" (2 Thess. 3:3).

You can make a good application right here by telling the children that Satan doesn't want them to go to God's banquet and enjoy the blessings that are there. So, Satan has set up his banquet tables, too. One of his tables has just desserts and cotton candy—things that taste good, but can make us sick and don't nourish us if that is our complete diet. This would be like those who teach that we only have to say the sinner's prayer and that worship should be something we enjoy so they add rock bands and praise dancing to their worship. Satan has another table with food that has passed its "use by" date—things that were a part of the worship and service to God under the Old Testament, but have served their purpose and are not commanded in the new Testament. Another table Satan has is filled with spiritual "fast food"—books and ideas of men that make Jesus our casual friend and make Christianity into a voyage on a cruise ship instead of a spiritual battle. Then, there is Satan's table of junk food—pleasures of the world, trivial things that are really of no value, but can tempt us away from God's banquet table. I leave it to the teacher to use specific illustrations that the children can relate to in each category.

Now, let's consider the parallel parable Jesus told as recorded in Matt. 22:1-14 and Luke 14:15-24. Since most teachers are familiar with these accounts, I will just highlight the important points by way of summary. In Matthew's account, a king prepares a wedding feast for his son; in Luke's account, it is just a man who invited many to a "great supper." The king (man) sent his servants to invite people to the supper. Putting both accounts together, the response was negative, some made light of it, others made excuses, and still others mistreated the servants and killed them. This angered the king, so he declared that none of the first would be allowed to come to his banquet. Then he sent his servants to the "highways, byways, and hedges" and instructed them to invite all to come—the poor, the stranger, the good and the bad—"that my house may be filled" (Luke 14:23). When the banquet began, one guest wasn't dressed properly, and the king had him removed (Matt.22:11-13).

Jesus' parables have applications similar to Isaiah 25. Notice the feast in God's mountain was "for all nations," and in the parables various people from all walks of life are invited. The context in Matthew's account points to the historical rejection and rebellion of God's people in the way they treated God's messengers, even killing some of them (Matt. 23:31). I'm reminded of Paul's experience in Antioch as he said to the Jews, "It was necessary that the word of God should be spoken to you first; but since you reject it, and judge yourselves unworthy of everlasting life, behold, we turn to the Gentiles" (Acts 13:46). When I teach this to children, I stress also the accounts of the great commission and relate this prophecy back to Isaiah 2—all nations coming into the mountain of the Lord's house. The message of the prophets is an evangelistic message. I usually end repeating the concept that God wants His house to be full. I also ask that familiar question—are you in the picture? Related to that, what can you do to help God's house be full?

Concluding Comments:

Of course, there are many other lessons from the parables of the great supper, but children usually get these in their other classes. This is why I did not go into detail about the wedding garment and various excuses, etc. Those are side lessons as far as my overall purpose is concerned. I want children to see that Isaiah's picture is fulfilled in Christ and His church, that there are rich and marvelous blessings at God's banquet table, and that God is faithful—He will keep His word.

God's Bountiful Feast for All Nations

Isaiah 25:6

And in this mountain
The LORD of hosts will make for all people
A feast of choice pieces,
A feast of wines on the lees,
Of fat things full of marrow,
Of well-refined wines on the lees.

Art by Jodie Boren

Luke 14:16-24

16 Then He said to him, "A certain man gave a great supper and invited many, 17 and sent his servant at supper time to say to those who were invited, 'Come, for all things are now ready.' ... 23 Then the master said to the servant, 'Go out into the highways and hedges, and compel them to come in, that my house may be filled.'"

Figure 9.1

God Wants His House to be Full!

Art by Jodie Boren

John 3:16-17

16 For God so loved the world that He gave His only begotten Son, that whoever believes in Him should not perish but have everlasting life. 17 For God did not send His Son into the world to condemn the world, but that the world through Him might be saved.

Mark 16:15-17

15 And He said to them, "Go into all the world and preach the gospel to every creature. 16 He who believes and is baptized will be saved; but he who does not believe will be condemned.

2 Peter 3:9

9 The Lord is not slack concerning His promise, as some count slackness, but is longsuffering toward us, not willing that any should perish but that all should come to repentance.

Are you sitting at God's banquet table? How can you help others know about God and about the blessings that are in His banquet?

Figure 9.2

Old Testament

Isa 25:6-9

6 And in this mountain
The LORD of hosts will make for all people
A feast of choice pieces,
A feast of wines on the lees,
Of fat things full of marrow,
Of well-refined wines on the lees.
7 And He will destroy on this mountain
The surface of the covering cast over all people,
And the veil that is spread over all nations.
8 He will swallow up death forever,
And the Lord GOD will wipe away tears from all faces;
The rebuke of His people
He will take away from all the earth;
For the LORD has spoken.

9 And it will be said in that day:
"Behold, this is our God;
We have waited for Him, and He will save us.
This is the LORD;
We have waited for Him;
We will be glad and rejoice in His salvation."

New Testament

Luke 14:15-24

Now when one of those who sat at the table with Him heard these things, he said to Him,"Blessed is he who shall eat bread in the kingdom of God!"

16 Then He said to him, "A certain man gave a great supper and invited many, 17 and sent his servant at supper time to say to those who were invited, 'Come, for all things are now ready.' 18 But they all with one accord began to make excuses. The first said to him, 'I have bought a piece of ground, and I must go and see it. I ask you to have me excused.' 19 And another said, 'I have bought five yoke of oxen, and I am going to test them. I ask you to have me excused.' 20 Still another said, 'I have married a wife, and therefore I cannot come.' 21 So that servant came and reported these things to his master. Then the master of the house, being angry, said to his servant, 'Go out quickly into the streets and lanes of the city, and bring in here the poor and the maimed and the lame and the blind.' 22 And the servant said, 'Master, it is done as you commanded, and still there is room.' 23 Then the master said to the servant, 'Go out into the highways and hedges, and compel them to come in, that my house may be filled. 24 For I say to you that none of those men who were invited shall taste my supper.'"

Mark 16:15-17

15 And He said to them, "Go into all the world and preach the gospel to every creature. 16 He who believes and is baptized will be saved; but he who does not believe will be condemned.

Figure 9.3

GOD'S FEAST
ISAIAH 25: 6-9

1. Who will prepare a feast? (v. 6)_____

2. The feast will be for (v. 6) _____

3. The feast will be the best and most nutritious foods (v.6).

4. Verse 7 says God will destroy the "covering cast over all people and the veil that is spread over all nations. That is Isaiah's way of describing SIN. In Isaiah 9, he said, "The people who walked in _____ have seen a great _____." When a veil is over something, it is dark inside. When Jesus comes, God will destroy that _____ .

5. Verse 8: "He will swallow up _____ forever, and the Lord _____ will wipe away _____ from _____ faces..."

6. Verse 9: "Behold, this is our _____; we have waited for _____, and He will _____ us. This is the_____; we have waited for _____; we will be _____ and rejoice is His _____.

7. The picture of God's feast is Isaiah's way of telling us there will be joy, rejoicing and salvation when Jesus comes.

8. Ephesians 1:3 "...God has blessed us with _____ spiritual blessings in the _____ places in _____. This is how Paul said the same thing in the New Testament.

9. Jesus said, "Blessed are those who _____ and _____ for righteousness, for they shall be _____. " Matt. 5:6.

10. Isaiah's picture of God's feast is a "word-picture" describing God's blessings, His love and His care for all those who are in His family and who love Him. The best life is the one lived sitting at God's banquet table!

Figure 9.4

GOD'S GREAT FEAST
WHO WILL COME

In Isaiah 25:6-9, the prophet tells of a time when God would prepare a feast of good things for ALL PEOPLE. Isaiah said this feast would be in God's Holy Mountain. From our lesson in Isaiah 11, we have learned that "God's Holy Mountain" is a tem the prophets used for the CHURCH. When Jesus came, He preached about God's kingdom and said that the kingdom would come during the time when people who saw Him were still alive. (Read Mark 9:1.) Jesus told many parables about God's kingdom which is His Church. (Read Matthew 16:16-20.) One of the parables Jesus told is about a man who prepared a great supper and invited many to come. This is in Luke 14:16-24. Jesus' parable is like Isaiah's picture of the kingdom. Read Luke 14:16-24 and fill in the blanks in the summary below. Then write the circled letters at the bottom and use the number code to learn of God's desire for His feast in His house (church).

A certain man prepared a great ◯__ __ __ __ __ and invited many.

He sent his __ __ __ __ __ __◯ to tell the people who were invited, "Come

◯__ __ all __ __◯__ __ __ are now __ __ __ __◯" But they began to

make __ __ __◯__ __ __. So the man sent his servant to the

__ __ __◯__ __ __ and __ __◯__ __ __ of the city to bring in the __◯__ __,

the◯__ __ __ __ __ __, the◯__ __ __ __ and the◯__ __ __ __ __. There was

still room left for others, so he told the servant to go to the

◯__ __ __ __ __ __ __ and__ __◯__ __ __ and bring people to the supper.

Place the circled letters in order here:

__ __ __ __ __ __ __ __ __ __ __ __ __ __
1 2 3 4 5 6 7 8 9 10 11 12 13 14

WHAT IS GOD'S DESIRE FOR HIS CHURCH?

__ __ __ __ __ __ __ __ __ __ __ __ __ __ __ __ __ __ __ __ __ __ __
2 13 8 2   10 5   13 9 6 1 7   10 8 5   12 7   3 4 11 11 7 14

Read Matthew 28:18-20 and Mark 16:15-16 to see what our responsibility is as servants in God's house.

Figure 9.5

79

Chapter 10
THE PRECIOUS CORNERSTONE

*I*n chapter 28, Isaiah continues his warnings of coming destruction to Judah and Jerusalem. He uses both literal and figurative language to describe their condition. He calls the leaders drunkards who stagger and stumble in their judgment. Verse 8 is especially graphic, and it is interesting to see children's response to it: "For all tables are full of vomit and filth; no place is clean." Would you want to live in a place like that? In chapter 1, God had charged them, "Wash yourselves... put away the evil of your doings" (1:16). However, they continued in their sinful ways, so now God is going to cleanse them of their filth by preserving a faithful remnant in Babylonian captivity (1:9). Again, we see that their rebellion will not thwart God's purpose for the blessing He had promised to all nations through Abraham's Seed. As you read and study the prophets, it is interesting to see how often jewels of hope are sprinkled throughout their messages of woes, warnings and destruction. The whole story of the Bible can be written in these two verses: "God will provide for Himself the lamb..." (Gen. 22:8) and God is "...not willing that any should perish, but that all should come to repentance" (2 Pet. 3:9). This is what God has always desired—that we turn to Him and look to Him for the salvation He has so graciously provided.

I thoroughly enjoy teaching Isa. 28:16-22 to children! Jodie Boren's art makes this prophecy come alive. Also, as we see it fulfilled in the New Testament, there are many practical applications we can make, depending on the age of the children. Be prepared to spend at least two class periods on this prophecy. I begin by telling the children about the purpose of a cornerstone, ruler and plumb line. You may want to bring a ruler and plumb line to class to demonstrate these tools. Explain that when building a temple, the master builder would select the best stone to be the cornerstone. It had to be solid, and it had to be exact in the measurements, so that the walls and foundation could line up perpendicular to the stone and ensure a sound, secure, and beautiful temple. Then the builder would use his measuring line to make sure all additional stones were in line with the cornerstone horizontally, and he would use the plumb line to make certain the stones were exactly perpendicular to the cornerstone. The result would be the temple the builder intended, according to the plans laid out by the architect.

With this introduction about ancient building techniques, let's look at the prophecy:

Therefore thus says the Lord GOD:

"Behold, I lay in Zion a stone for a foundation,

A tried stone, a precious cornerstone, a sure foundation;

Whoever believes will not act hastily.

Also I will make justice the measuring line,

And righteousness the plummet;

The hail will sweep away the refuge of lies,

And the waters will overflow the hiding place.

Your covenant with death will be annulled,

And your agreement with Sheol will not stand;

When the overflowing scourge passes through,

Then you will be trampled down by it.

As often as it goes out it will take you;

For morning by morning it will pass over,

And by day and by night;

It will be a terror just to understand the report."

For the bed is too short to stretch out on,

And the covering so narrow that one cannot wrap himself in it (Isa. 28:16-20).

Isaiah is preaching to those who are trusting in an alliance with Assyria, as Hezekiah had done in the early years of his reign. He calls this their "covenant with death" and their "agreement with Sheol." God declares that those agreements will not stand. He will override them. How and why will He do so? He has laid a foundation stone in Zion! It is helpful to see the emphatic nature of Jehovah's statement in verse 16. "Literally, '*Behold Me* as Him who *has laid*'; namely, in My divine counsel; none save I could lay it" (Jamieson-Fausset-Brown Bible Commentary, Gospel Advocate software). Their plans would be annulled because God, in His eternal purpose and wisdom, had already laid the cornerstone in Zion. This figure can only refer to Jesus, and both Peter and Paul reference it, as we will see.

Isaiah is using the figure of a cornerstone in a building to tell us something about Jesus. Paul quotes Isaiah 28:16 in Romans 9:33 at the end of his discussion of the salvation of the Gentiles as well as the remnant of the Jews through the work of Jesus. He also uses this imagery in Eph. 2:20-22 when he says of Christians, "having been built on the foundation of the apostles and prophets, Jesus Christ, Himself, being the chief cornerstone." The characteristics of this stone are tried, precious, and sure. Notice that Jesus was tried—He was tempted by Satan in the wilderness, the Jewish leaders tried to catch Him in His words and asked Him what they considered unanswerable questions. He asked His accusers, "Which one of you convicts me of sin?" (John 8:46). Then, He was led through a mock trial and crucified on a Roman cross. This caused Paul to say, "For He made Him who knew no sin to be sin for us, that we might become the righteousness of God in Him" (2 Cor. 5:21). This cornerstone is also precious or costly. Peter reminds us that we are not redeemed with things of this world like silver and gold that the world considers valuable. He says our salvation is more costly—"the precious blood of Christ, as of a lamb without blemish and without spot" (1 Pet. 1:19). Lastly, because that cornerstone has been tested for solidarity and soundness, it is sure. That is, it can bear the weight of the superstructure of our redemption, like the cornerstone of ancient buildings could bear the weight of the building. Another part of the picture is the measuring line or ruler and the plummet (metal bob of a plumb line). Justice and righteousness will be the tools the divine Builder will use to line all the stones with the cornerstone.

Jesus used a similar cornerstone prophecy in Matt. 21:42 after the parable of the wicked vinedressers. When He ended the parable, He asked what the owner of the vineyard should do to those vinedressers, and the Jewish leaders answered correctly, "He will destroy those wicked men miserably, and lease his vineyard to other vinedressers who will render to him the fruits in their seasons" (Matt. 21:41). Then Jesus asked if they had read Psalm 118:22-24:

> The stone which the builders rejected
>
> Has become the chief cornerstone.
>
> This was the LORD's doing;
>
> It is marvelous in our eyes.
>
> This is the day the LORD has made;
>
> We will rejoice and be glad in it.

From this, we see clearly that the cornerstone of prophecy is definitely Jesus. The psalmist adds another dimension to the description of Jesus. Not only will He be tried, precious, and sure, but He will be rejected. Later, when Peter and John are arrested and appear before the rulers, elders, and scribes, Peter states plainly that Jesus is the "stone which was rejected by you builders, which has become the chief cornerstone" (Acts 4:11). He goes on to declare that Jesus' name is the only name in which there is salvation.

In 1 Peter 2, Peter combines both the prophecies in Isaiah 28 and Psalm 118 as he describes Christians as living stones in God's temple, similar to what Paul said in Eph. 2:19-22. Jesus is also a living stone, chosen by God, laid in Zion before the foundation of the world, but laid in time when the child born and son given (Isa. 9) conquered death, hell, and the grave. This picture of Christians as living stones has numerous applications for children and adults. Just like the stones in a physical building had to be in line with the cornerstone, so we who are living stones in God's temple must have our lives in harmony with Jesus and His word. You may want to tell children how the builders would have to cut the stones and make sure they were the right size and shape to fit into the building. Then, suggest things we need to cut out of our lives to be a living stone in God's temple. I leave the specifics of this application to the teacher, because it will depend on the age and maturity of your students as to what you select. Some to think about are saying bad words, telling lies, cheating, etc. I have turned this application to myself in the children's class. I've told them that some people think it would be fine for me (or other women teachers) to teach or preach to an audience of both men and women. However, I want to make sure I have my life in harmony with the cornerstone, so I refuse to do that. This lets children know, too, that it is a daily endeavor to keep our lives in line with the cornerstone. We must study His word, know His will for us. There is an extension of this application that Roy Johnson's drawing illustrates: How would the building look is some of the stones are out of place or not shaped correctly? I have left the "bad" stones blank for you to have the children write various applications you think are appropriate, like immodesty, gossip, etc.

Concluding Comments:

This prophecy definitely illustrates the folly of trying to build a successful life on anyone or anything other than Jesus. It's not smart to throw away the Cornerstone! Jesus is our sacrifice, example, high priest, king, and mediator. "I am the way, the truth, and the life. No one comes to the Father except through me" (John 14:6).

I can't leave this chapter without commenting on Psa. 118:24, "This is the day the LORD has made; we will rejoice and be glad in it." Have you heard that used to apply to a special day, like our Sunday worship, a Ladies' Day, special workshop, or just any day? While there is a sense in which every day is a day the Lord has made and a day for rejoicing, we lose the impact of this passage when we take it out of context and apply it like that. Notice that the Psalmist is not talking about any day. He is talking about the day the foundation stone is laid in Zion! That is the day in which we should rejoice and be glad. Jehovah has made salvation possible through the Cornerstone laid in Zion. Rejoice!

Foolish builders – throwing away the Cornerstone!

Isaiah 28:14-16
Psalm 118:22-24

Art by Jodie Boren

The cornerstone was the most important stone in ancient buildings. It was the stone that was perfect in all its measurements. Each stone was cut to be in line with the cornerstone so the building would be also perfect in all its measurements.
Jesus is the Cornerstone on which His temple (church) is built. The Jewish leaders (builders) rejected Jesus. They were like builders throwing away the perfect cornerstone.

1   Figure 10.1

Foolish Builders!

Isaiah 28:16

Therefore thus says the Lord GOD:

"Behold, I lay in Zion a stone for a foundation,
A tried stone, a precious cornerstone, a

Psalm 118:22-24

22 The stone which the builders rejected
Has become the chief cornerstone.
23 This was the LORD's doing;
It is marvelous in our eyes.
24 This is the day the LORD has made;
We will rejoice and be glad in it.

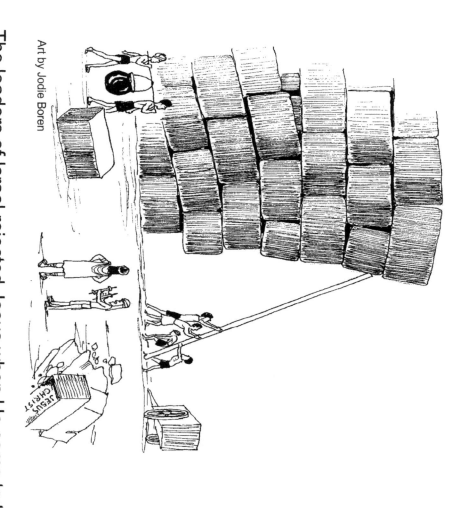

Art by Jodie Boren

The leaders of Israel rejected Jesus when He came to teach them about God. They had also rejected the message of God's prophets. That is like trying to build a building and throwing away the best stone that the master architect has chosen for the cornerstone. The building will not stand and be strong and secure. If we want our lives to be strong and secure, we will build our lives on Jesus and His word. Read Matthew 7:24-27 about the two builders--wise and foolish.

2

Figure 10.1

Christians are living stones in God's Temple!

Coming to Him as to a living stone, rejected indeed by men, but chosen by God and precious, 5 you also, as living stones, are being built up a spiritual house, a holy priesthood, to offer up spiritual sacrifices acceptable to God through Jesus Christ.--**1 Peter 2:4-5**

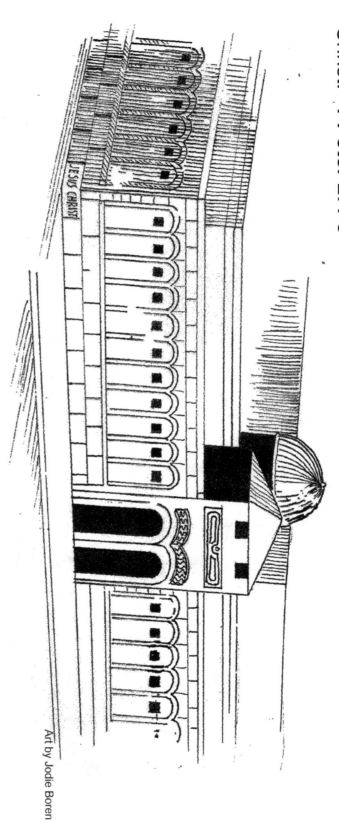

Art by Jodie Boren

Since you are living stones in God's Temple, you want to make sure your life is in line with the Cornerstone so the temple will be beautiful. Write your name on one of the stones. You may want to ask your friends in the class to write their names on a stone so you can all remember that you are living stones. You will want to help each other become more like Jesus who is the Cornerstone.

3

Figure 10.1

Living Stones in God's Temple

Foolish Builders – not lining up with the Cornerstone

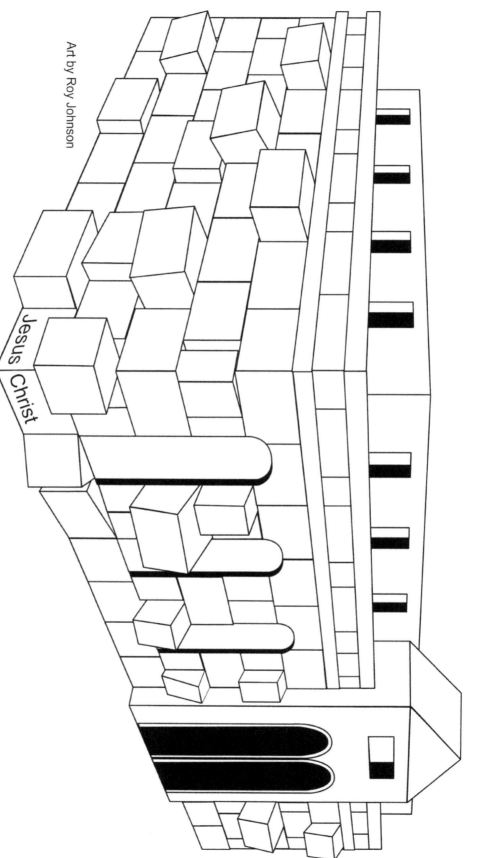

Art by Roy Johnson

Jesus Christ

Figure 10.1

Christians are "living stones" in God's temple. If His temple is strong and beautiful, every stone must be in line with the Cornerstone which is Jesus. This temple has some stones that are not in line with Jesus. It doesn't look like a very good temple, does it? Write some of the things that keep our lives from being like Jesus on the stones that are out of place. We want our lives to be like His. Write things that are like Jesus on the stones that are in place.

4

Your bed is too short and your cover is too small!

Isaiah 28:20
For the bed is too short to stretch out on,
And the covering so narrow that one cannot wrap
himself in it.

Art by Jodie Boren

This is Isaiah's picture of how foolish it is to reject God's Word.

Figure 10.1

Old Testament

Isaiah 28:16-17

Therefore thus says the Lord GOD:

"Behold, I lay in Zion a stone for a foundation,
A tried stone, a precious cornerstone, a sure foundation;
Whoever believes will not act hastily.
17 Also I will make justice the measuring line,
And righteousness the plummet;

Psalm 118:22-24

22 The stone which the builders rejected
Has become the chief cornerstone.
23 This was the LORD's doing;
It is marvelous in our eyes.
24 This is the day the LORD has made;
We will rejoice and be glad in it.

New Testament

Romans 9:33

33 As it is written: "Behold, I lay in Zion a stumbling stone and rock of offense, And whoever believes on Him will not be put to shame."

Ephesians 2:20-22

20 ...having been built on the foundation of the apostles and prophets, Jesus Christ Himself being the chief cornerstone, 21 in whom the whole building, being fitted together, grows into a holy temple in the Lord, 22 in whom you also are being built together for a dwelling place of God in the Spirit.

1 Peter 2:4-7

Coming to Him as to a living stone, rejected indeed by men, but chosen by God and precious, 5 you also, as living stones, are being built up a spiritual house, a holy priesthood, to offer up spiritual sacrifices acceptable to God through Jesus Christ. 6 Therefore it is also contained in the Scripture, "Behold, I lay in Zion a chief cornerstone, elect, precious, and he who believes on Him will by no means be put to shame." 7 Therefore, to you who believe, He is precious; but to those who are disobedient, "The stone which the builders rejected has become the chief cornerstone,"

Mark 12:10-11

10 Have you not even read this Scripture: The stone which the builders rejected has become the chief cornerstone. 11 This was the LORD's doing, and it is marvelous in our eyes'?"

Acts 4:10-12

11 This is the 'stone which was rejected by you builders, which has become the chief cornerstone.' 12 Nor is there salvation in any other, for there is no other name under heaven given among men by which we must be saved."

Figure 10.2

Read Isa. 28:16, 17, and find words that describe the cornerstone and fill in the blanks. Use the numbered letters for the message at the bottom of the page.

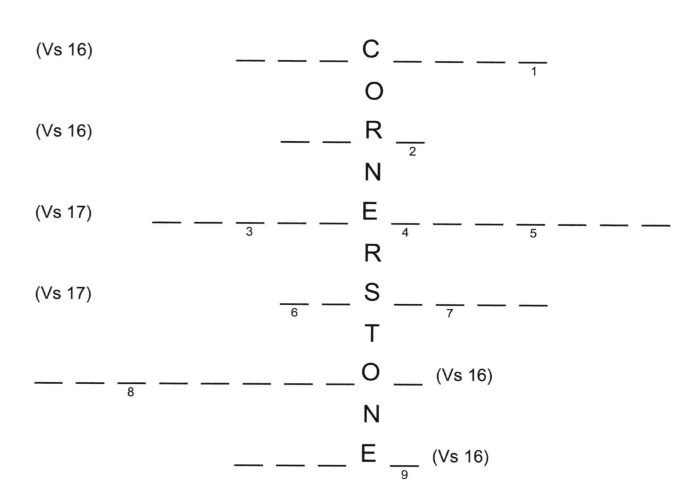

(Vs 16)   _ _ _ C _ _ _ _
                                    1

(Vs 16)   _ _ R _
                        2

(Vs 17)   _ _ _ _ _ E _ _ _ _ _ _ _ _
                  3   4   5

(Vs 17)   _ _ S _ _ _ _
                  6   7

_ _ _ _ _ _ _ _ O _ (Vs 16)
      8

_ _ _ E _ (Vs 16)
              9

_ _ _ _ _ _ _ _ _ _ , _
6 2 1 8 1   7 1   3 4 9 1

_ _ _
1 4 5

Figure 10.3

YOUR BED IS TOO SHORT AND YOUR COVER IS TOO SMALL

Isaiah and David both tell about a "chief corner stone" that God would lay in Zion (Isaiah 28:14-20 and Psalm 118:22-23). Jesus is that corner stone (Matthew 21:42). Isaiah 28:16 says the stone is a "p_____ corner stone" and David says in Psalm 118:22 it is the "stone which the b_____ r_____. "

Jesus is precious. He is God's Son. He lived a perfect life and always did what was right. He is our example of how to live. Jesus loved us enough to die for us -- to be the sacrifice for our sins. Many people loved Jesus, but the rulers of the Jews and the religious leaders did not. Jesus was not the kind of king they wanted. They wanted a king on earth who would make them the most powerful nation. That is what David means when he said the builders refused the corner stone. They were trying to build their lives without Jesus.

What are we like when we refuse Jesus? Isaiah 28:20 tells us: "For the _____ is too _____ to _____ out on, and the _____ so _____ that one cannot _____ himself in it."

Rejecting Jesus is foolish. It is like a person beginning to build a building and throwing away the cornerstone—the best-measured stone. It is also like a person trying to sleep on a bed that is much too short and trying to cover himself with a small baby-sized blanket. That just won't work! Many people today reject Jesus and try to live by their own rules. We don't want to reject Him. We want to hear His Word (the Bible) and do what He says in His Word. Happiness comes when we live like Jesus wants us to.

Figure 10.4

Matthew 7:24-27:

Therefore whoever _____ these _____ of Mine, and _____ them, I will liken him to a _____ man who built his house on the _____ : and the _____ descended, the _____ came, and the _____ blew and _____ on that house; and it did _____fall, for it was _____ on the _____.

But everyone who _____ these _____of Mine, and does _____ do them, will be like a _____ man who built his house on the _____: and the _____ descended, the _____ came, and the _____ blew and _____ on that and it _____. And _____ was its _____."

Isaiah, David and Jesus tell us how foolish it is to try to live without Jesus -- without doing His will. When we reject Jesus:

We build our house (life) on s_____. FOOLISH!

Our bed is too s_____. FOOLISH!

Our cover is too s_____. FOOLISH!

A life without Jesus is built on Satan's s_____. Such a life is too s_____ and too s_____. We want to be like the w_____ man and build our lives on J_____. When we do, our lives will be BIG in good works and our influence will be LONG because the good we do will last even after we die.

"...'Blessed are the dead who die in the Lord from now on...that they may rest from their labors, and their works follow them'" (Revelation 14:13).

2

Figure 10.4

Chapter 11
FLOWERS IN THE DESERT AND A HIGHWAY

*I*saiah 35 is another beautiful picture of what it will be like when Jesus comes. With his inspired paint brush, Isaiah paints first a wasteland and desert in chapter 34 to describe the plight of nations that reject God. He personifies the nations (v. 1) as Edom (vs. 5, 6). Such nations are pictured as a land soaked in blood, the streams have turned to dust, and it is the habitation of jackals and other wild beasts. The world without God is a dry, desolate place where men are covered with a "line of confusion and the stones of emptiness" (v.11). This is a picture of men's hearts when they reject God. For younger children, just a brief reference to this picture is sufficient. With older children, you may want to compare Paul's description of people who "refused to have God in their knowledge" in Romans 1:18-32, always using wisdom as to how to describe those sinful conditions. Another example is the world in Noah's time when "every intent of the thought of his (man's) heart was only evil continually" (Gen. 6:5).

What will it be like when Jesus comes? People's hearts and lives will be changed. On the canvas of the depressing picture of a barren wasteland, Isaiah dips his paint brush into vibrant colors and paints flowers blooming, water springing up, and a lush, green forest towering over the land. Now, we have a picture that is pleasant to see.

What does this picture show us about the Messiah and the effect of His coming into the world? Notice that this is a figure of men's hearts and lives. How do we know? Observe the personification in verses 1 and 2, the wasteland is glad, the desert rejoices, and the desert sings. Physical wastelands and deserts can't be glad, rejoice, or sing. This must be a picture of something else. Look at the situation for God's people when Jesus came: Religiously, their hearts and lives were like barren desert—unproductive and ugly. "There never was an age more dry and barren than that in which He was born" (Stalker 1949, 82). Jesus highlighted their situation in Matthew 23—they did their works to be seen; they loved special greetings and titles; they were "blind guides," twisting the Law to their advantage; they were like "whitewashed tombs;" and they made a pretense with long prayers in public areas. The Gentile world was also like a wasteland, having no hope, trusting in gods that were powerless.

When Jesus comes, the picture changes dramatically. His mission was to change the moral and spiritual wasteland into a lush garden, to transform Zion from a lowly remnant into a people ransomed by Jehovah (v. 10). The change was so great that Isaiah uses flowers and trees springing up suddenly as a figure of that change. In fulfillment of this prophecy, Jesus said, "I have come that they may have life, and have it more abundantly" (John 10:10). And, Paul tells us that Jesus brought "life and immortality to light through the gospel" (2 Tim. 1:10). You may want to relate back to Isaiah 9—the people in darkness have seen a great light. People now have hope! Their lives are productive! They rejoice in the knowledge of God.

There are two views on verses 5 and 6. I've studied the reasoning for both, and I present them simply so you can decide for yourself, or use the synthesis of the two. Some see verses 5 and 6 as relating to Jesus' physical miracles of healing the blind, deaf, and lame. It seems that verses 3 and 4 are a break in the figurative language—"Strengthen the weak hands… Be strong, do not fear! Behold your God will come… He will come and save you." This departure from figurative language would perhaps cause the reader to wonder when God would come to save. And, that answer is given in verse 6: "**Then** the eyes of the blind shall be opened, and the ears of the deaf shall be unstopped. **Then** the lame shall leap like a deer, and the tongue of the dumb sing." That is, when God comes to save, then these miracles will be a sign that He has actually come. If we compare this to the answer Jesus gave to the disciples of John the Baptist when John was in prison and questioning if Jesus were the Christ, we can see the strength of this reasoning: "Go and tell John the things you have seen and heard: that the blind see, the lame walk, the lepers are cleansed, the deaf hear, the dead are raised…" (Luke 7:22). Jesus used His miracles as proof to John that He was indeed the Messiah of prophecy.

Others see this as part of the figurative picture, especially since verses 5 and 6 are connected to verses 7 through 10 which depict flowers, water and forests growing up suddenly in the desert, and joyful people traveling on the Highway of Holiness. What causes this rejoicing? The spiritually blind can see, those who had not heard and understood the Word of the Lord could now hear and understand; and those who are lame spiritually can now leap and walk. For younger children, you might want to use this part of the picture to tell them Isaiah is comparing the spiritual joy people will have who obey Jesus to the joy those who were helped by His miracles had. For older children, use James Stalker's observation that His miracles were triumphs over the evil and sin in the world:

> But yet the misery of the world is the shadow of its sin. Material and moral evil, being thus intimately related, mutually illustrate each other. When He healed bodily blindness, it was a type of the healing of the inner eye; when He raised the dead, He meant to suggest that He was the Resurrection and the Life in the spiritual world as well; when He cleansed the leper, His triumph spoke of another over the leprosy of sin; when He multiplied the loaves, He followed the miracle with a discourse of the bread of life; when He stilled the storm, it was an assurance that He could speak peace to the troubled conscience (Stalker 1949, 63).

The relationship between Jesus' physical miracles and His spiritual mission is important to make, and it can be made with either viewpoint of verses 5 and 6. With children, I would not make a big deal of the difference between the two views, because I see Stalker's comment as a nice, biblical synthesis of the two.

Let's not lose the main message of Isaiah's picture. He repeats some elements of the picture after noting the miracles—"waters shall burst forth in the wilderness… the parched ground shall become a pool…" Jesus alone fulfills this part of the picture, for He provides the water that transforms: "…but whoever drinks of the water that I shall give him will never thirst. But the water that I shall give him will become in him a fountain of water springing up into everlasting life" (Jn. 4:14). "On the last day, that great day of the feast, Jesus stood and cried out, saying, 'If anyone thirsts, let him come to Me and drink. He who believes in Me, as the Scripture has said, out of his heart will flow rivers of living water.' But this He spoke concerning the Spirit, whom those believing in Him would receive; for the Holy Spirit was not yet given, because Jesus was not yet glorified" (John 7:37-38). With this repetition, Isaiah is emphasizing there is revived life and character of those who follow Jesus.

I have used the "Bible in Felt" to illustrate this picture. On the story board, I place the brown, earthy background. Then, I add the various flowers, green grass, reeds, trees and water. For an activity to illustrate this with the children, give them the picture of a wilderness (figure 11.1) and have them place stickers of various flowers and trees on the picture. You may want to use figure 11.1 twice: (1) Have the children color everything brown, gray and black, and have them write on it something like "People's hearts and lives without God." (2) Proceed with the above mentioned activity where they place pretty stickers on the picture, and have them write something like "People's hearts and lives when Jesus comes."

Isaiah 35, verses 8 through 10 continue with the picture and add another element to it:

A highway shall be there, and a road,

And it shall be called the Highway of Holiness.

The unclean shall not pass over it,

But it shall be for others.

Whoever walks the road, although a fool,

Shall not go astray.

No lion shall be there,

Nor shall any ravenous beast go up on it;

It shall not be found there.

But the redeemed shall walk there,

And the ransomed of the LORD shall return,

And come to Zion with singing,

With everlasting joy on their heads.

They shall obtain joy and gladness,

And sorrow and sighing shall flee away.

There are some things that are important about this Highway of Holiness, and I leave it to teachers to make age-appropriate applications of these concepts:

1. **Appointed by God**: The highway appears in the picture. It is not build by man, but given by God. Jesus said, "I am the way..." (John 14:6).

2. **Clean**: Its name is "Highway of Holiness"—only the clean can walk on it. Jesus spoke of the narrow and difficult way that only few would find in Matt. 7:13-14. This would be a good time to teach children how we become clean, having our sins washed away by the blood of Jesus in baptism (Acts 22:16; Rev. 1:5).

3. **Clearly marked**: This way is only for those who are wise and discerning. The NKJV translation of v. 8b is unfortunate—"...whoever walks on it, although a fool, shall not go astray." This makes it seem like the way is so simple a fool (uneducated, without knowledge) can easily walk on it. However, the word translated "fool" never means an uneducated person, but means one who despises wisdom and knowledge. The fool is also grouped with the unclean and the "ravenous beast" that shall not walk on it. Thus, the meaning is that the wayfarer (casual drifter), the fool, and anyone who would harm the people on the highway will not accidentally stumble upon it or walk on the highway (Hailey 1985, 297).

4. **Safe**: There will be no scary lions or beasts on the highway. For children, remind them that this is using a physical picture to teach a spiritual truth. Who would want to walk on a highway that had lions or bears on it? Just so, the Highway of Holiness has no enemies of God's people on it. Remember that Peter calls Satan a "roaring lion, walking about seeking whom he may devour" (1 Pet. 5:8). A very good application is that as long as we stay on that highway, we are safe, and Satan can't harm us.

5. **For the redeemed and ransomed**: This clearly lets us know it is not for the foolish who hate wisdom and knowledge (from point 3). The highway is for those who are holy, who are clean, who are redeemed, and who are ransomed by the working of God. As with Isaiah 2, you will want to make the point that younger children are walking on this highway holding to their parents' hands, but there will come a time when they must decide if they want to walk on this Highway of Holiness.

6. **Leads to Zion and everlasting joy**! As we noted several times, the writer of Hebrews lets us know that Zion of Old Testament prophecy is the "church of the Firstborn, who are registered in heaven..." (Heb. 12:23).

Concluding remarks:

What will it be like when Jesus comes? Let's back away a bit and see the whole picture Isaiah has painted for us. People who have lived without God, without hope, without purpose, whose lives are like a dry, barren desert will hear the gospel and obey it. When they do, their lives will have meaning and purpose, and they will be filled with joy; their lives will no longer be dry and desolate, but will be like a beautiful flower garden with towering trees and rivers of water flowing through it. The picture ends with sinners, both Jews and Gentiles, leaving their sinful ways and coming home to God through Christ with "songs of everlasting joy on their heads." Are you in the picture?

What will it be like when Jesus comes?

"The desert shall rejoice and blossom as a rose" (Isaiah 35)

Art by Roy Johnson

Figure 11.1

The Highway of Holiness

The joyful return of the remnant from Babylon on the highway to Jerusalem is a shadow of the joy people have when they come to the spiritual Mount Zion on the Highway of Holiness.

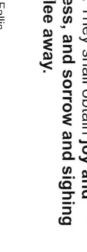

Isaiah 35:8-10

A highway shall be there, and a road, And it shall be called the Highway of Holiness....But the redeemed shall walk there, and the ransomed of the LORD shall return, and come to Zion with singing, with everlasting joy on their heads. They shall obtain **joy and gladness, and sorrow and sighing shall flee away.**

Acts 8:36-39

Now as they went down the road, they came to some water. And the eunuch said, "See, here is water. What hinders me from being baptized?" Then Philip said, "If you believe with all your heart, you may." And he answered and said, "I believe that Jesus Christ is the Son of God." And both Philip and the eunuch went down into the water, and he baptized him... and **he went on his way rejoicing.**

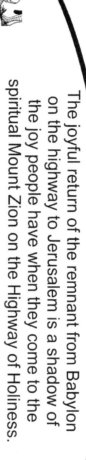

Figure 11.2

Old Testament

Isaiah 35:1-10

The wilderness and the wasteland shall be glad for them, and the desert shall rejoice and blossom as the rose; 2 It shall blossom abundantly and rejoice, even with joy and singing. The glory of Lebanon shall be given to it, The excellence of Carmel and Sharon. They shall see the glory of the LORD, the excellency of our God.
3 Strengthen the weak hands, and make firm the feeble knees. 4 Say to those who are fearful-hearted,"Be strong, do not fear! Behold, your God will come with vengeance, with the recompense of God; He will come and save you."
5 Then the eyes of the blind shall be opened, and the ears of the deaf shall be unstopped. 6 Then the lame shall leap like a deer, and the tongue of the dumb sing. For waters shall burst forth in the wilderness, and streams in the desert. 7 The parched ground shall become a pool, and the thirsty land springs of water; in the habitation of jackals, where each lay, there shall be grass with reeds and rushes.
8 A highway shall be there, and a road, and it shall be called the Highway of Holiness. The unclean shall not pass over it, but it shall be for others. Whoever walks the road, although a fool, shall not go astray. 9 No lion shall be there, nor shall any ravenous beast go up on it; it shall not be found there. But the redeemed shall walk there, 10 and the ransomed of the LORD shall return, and come to Zion with singing, with everlasting joy on their heads. They shall obtain joy and gladness, and sorrow and sighing shall flee away.

New Testament

Luke 2:8-12
Now there were in the same country shepherds living out in the fields, keeping watch over their flock by night. 9 And behold, an angel of the Lord stood before them, and the glory of the Lord shone around them, and they were greatly afraid. 10 Then the angel said to them,"Do not be afraid, for behold, I bring you good tidings of great joy which will be to all people. 11 For there is born to you this day in the city of David a Savior, who is Christ the Lord. 12 And this will be the sign to you: You will find a Babe wrapped in swaddling cloths, lying in a manger."

Mark 7:31-37

Again, departing from the region of Tyre and Sidon, He came through the midst of the region of Decapolis to the Sea of Galilee. 32 Then they brought to Him one who was deaf and had an impediment in his speech, and they begged Him to put His hand on him. 33 And He took him aside from the multitude, and put His fingers in his ears, and He spat and touched his tongue. 34 Then, looking up to heaven, He sighed, and said to him, "Ephphatha," that is, "Be opened."
35 Immediately his ears were opened, and the impediment of his tongue was loosed, and he spoke plainly. 36 Then He commanded them that they should tell no one; but the more He commanded them, the more widely they proclaimed it. 37 And they were astonished beyond measure, saying, "He has done all things well. He makes both the deaf to hear and the mute to speak."

Figure 11.3

The Spiritual Significance of the Miracles of Jesus

- Healed blind (John 9)→Spiritual blindness (John 9:39-41)

- Physical deafness (Mark 7:31-37)→Spiritual deafness (Mt. 13:15-16;Mk.8:18)

- Fed the 5,000 (John 6: 1-14)→"Bread of Life" (Jn. 6:35, 48)

- Raised Lazarus (John 11: 38-44)→"I am the resurrection and the life" (Jn. 11:25)

- Mute speak →spiritual power to praise Him & teach the gospel

- Lepers healed → leprosy of sin → forgiven

- Stilled the storm → bring peace to the troubled conscience

- Water to "best wine" → enrich quality of life

- Lame walk→spiritual strength → "go into all the world"

Figure 11.5

Background for Isaiah Chapters 40-66

Before introducing the next group of my favorite lessons from Isaiah, I think teachers need to be aware of the situation of Judah and the purpose of this latter half of the book. The tone of the book changes from admonition to assurance, or as Homer Hailey titles this section, "Hope for Troublous Times" (Hailey 1985, p. 325). Isaiah and Micah had preached to Judah during the Assyrian period when Israel was led captive and Sennacherib was threatening Jerusalem. Their work along with the influence of King Hezekiah turned enough people to Jehovah that they were spared the wrath of Assyria. However, Hezekiah showed all his treasures to the son of the king of Babylon, and the people also began again to turn away from God. Thus, Jehovah sent Isaiah to Hezekiah with this message, "'Behold, the days are coming when all that is in your house, and what your fathers have accumulated until this day, shall be carried to Babylon; nothing shall be left,' says the Lord" (Isa. 39:6).

Isaiah is now charged to comfort the people, to reassure them, to prepare them for the disaster that they have brought upon themselves so God will have a faithful remnant in captivity through whom He will work His purpose. The theme of this section is stated in 40:9 – "O Zion, you who bring good tidings, get up into the high mountain; O Jerusalem, you who bring good tidings, life up your voice with strength, lift it up, be not afraid; say to the cities of Judah, '**Behold your God**.'" They had left God to serve idols; this was their root sin from which all the immorality and injustice sprang. Though they would have to suffer the consequences for their sins, they needed to know that God was not detached from His people (40:31) and that He would forgive (43:25).

Isaiah extols God's greatness as Creator and Sustainer of the universe, especially in chapter 40. He is outside the universe, yet intimately involved with man. Since idolatry was the well spring of their sins, Isaiah shows the folly of idolatry beginning in chapter 40 and continuing throughout this section. As you read through these chapters, take special note of God's challenge to the idols. I am only going to analyze my favorite lessons for children from this section. However, I think you will see that these selections are representative of the main emphasis in these chapters.

Figure 12.0

Chapter 12
A VOICE IN THE WILDERNESS

*I*saiah chapter 40 can be considered an outline of the rest of the book because the prophet touches on every theme he will address in more detail later: comfort (vs. 1-2), revelation of the glory of the Lord through the Messiah (vs. 3-5), value of the Word of God (vs. 6-8), the mindlessness of idolatry (vs. 18-20), the majesty and power of God (vs. 9-26), and God's intimate relationship with those who trust Him (vs. 27-31). However, there are just two lessons for children I want to present from this chapter. The first deals with the "voice in the wilderness" and the second with "Behold your God."

Lesson 1: The Voice – Before discussing this further, it is good for teachers to remember that many historical events in the life of Israel and Judah foreshadowed the coming of Christ and His kingdom. From the vantage point of the Jews at that time, Isaiah was preparing them for the 70 year captivity and giving them assurance of their ultimate deliverance from Babylon. Remember, too, that he is speaking approximately 100 years before their captivity and almost 200 years before Cyrus will issue the decree for them to return. Both the Jews and "all flesh" will be amazed when Jehovah brings the captives home to rebuild their city and temple. However, Isaiah is also looking past the shadow to the time when all flesh will be in greater amazement as John the Baptizer preaches, "Prepare the way of the LORD; make His paths straight…" (Luke 3:4).

One way to introduce verses 3-5 to children is to ask them if they remember who prepared the way for Jesus to begin His preaching ministry. Or you might just say something like Granddaddy often said to me, "Did you know this is speaking about Jesus?" Then, you can go to the New Testament accounts and read where Matthew, Mark, Luke, and John quote this passage. It is interesting to note that Matthew and John only record verse 3, and Mark adds Malachi 3:1-2, whereas Luke records verses 3-5. The side-by-side scripture sheets and the illustrations for this prophecy will help you explain this prophecy and make the appropriate application for the children. Let's look at this prophecy:

> The voice of one crying in the wilderness: "Prepare the way of the Lord; Make straight in the desert a highway for our God. Every valley shall be exalted and every mountain and hill brought low; the crooked places shall be made straight and the rough places smooth; the glory of the Lord shall be revealed, and all flesh shall see it together; for the mouth of the Lord has spoken" (Isa. 40:3-5).

Again, Isaiah adds another dimension to the Messiah's coming—He will be the glory of the Lord (v. 5). This is exactly what John says of Him in 1:14: "And the Word became flesh and dwelt among us, and we beheld His glory, the glory as of the only begotten of the Father, full of grace and truth." Also, the Messiah will not come secretly. Someone special—The Voice—will announce His coming. Isaiah uses picture language of someone constructing a highway through rough and mountainous terrain. This special person (The Voice) will be like a highway builder. He will tear down hills and mountains and raise up valleys so there will be a smooth and level highway for the One who is the "glory of the Lord." You may ask the children if they have been in mountainous areas in our country and if they have been on highways through those areas. Perhaps you can bring pictures to show them roads that snake through such regions, twisting and turning, going up and down, around and through the mountains. This is not the kind of highway Isaiah is describing. The highway he sees is a straight, smooth, level highway through an area that had once been rugged and impassable.

When you put this prophecy together with its fulfillment in the New Testament, the meaning of the picture is clear. John the Baptizer announced that he was the fulfillment of this prophecy—that he was "The voice of one crying in the wilderness, 'Prepare the way of the LORD; make His paths straight…'" (Luke 3:4). This is also in fulfillment of what John's father, Zacharias, said at his birth, "…you will go before the face of the Lord to prepare His ways, to give knowledge of salvation to His people by the remission of their sins…" (Luke 1:76-77). John was not constructing a literal highway, but a spiritual highway. He was preparing men's hearts for Jesus' message of salvation and redemption.

Notice how Isaiah compares John's work to a highway builder. He will bring down mountains in people's hearts—mountains of anger, pride, selfishness, envy, anything that exalts men above God. Then, he will lift up valleys—valleys of discouragement, hopelessness, oppression. This is a good place in the lesson to use the picture sheet (figure 12.1) that has mountains and valleys, and have the children write *pride, anger, selfishness,* etc. on the mountains, and write words like "*no hope*" on the valleys. You may need to make two copies of this picture so the children will have one to write on for the mountains and one for the valleys. This helps them see the picture Isaiah is painting. Figure 12.2 shows the level and straight highway with an outline of a figure like Jesus to represent the glory of the Lord. I usually have the children put glue and glitter on the figure to illustrate that the glory of the Lord is special. John's message was one of repentance—that people must change their thinking and their lives to be ready for the kingdom of heaven. John also pointed people to Jesus as "the Lamb of God who takes away the sin of the world" (John 1:29). This is consistent with Isaiah's picture as well as with Malachi's prophecy in the time near the close of the Old Testament, about 250 years after Isaiah. "Behold, I send My messenger, and he will prepare the way before Me" (Mal. 3:1).

I think we should take every opportunity to point out the unity of the Bible's message, and this is an extremely good place to do so. Isaiah (740-700 B.C.) says that one known as "The Voice" will prepare the way for the LORD; about 250 years later, Malachi identifies "The Voice" as God's "messenger" who will prepare the way for Him. Then, about 400 years after Malachi, John begins preaching, preparing men's hearts for Jesus. In the process, he identifies himself as that voice and messenger. Isn't the Bible amazing? The chart (figure 12.4) helps you illustrate this to children. If you have a good timeline in your classroom, you can also illustrate the prophecy on it.

Lesson 2: Behold your God – The people of Israel had failed to obey God, not because they forgot His commandments, but because they forgot Him—they lost sight of Jehovah who had brought them into a bountiful land and had given them wealth and peace. This is a theme of both the prophets and the Psalms. In order to prepare the faithful remnant for their captivity and assure them of their deliverance, Isaiah had to remind them of who God is—I AM, creator, sustainer, shepherd, redeemer, and savior.

I have found it effective just to read verses 9-26 and comment on them as we read through them, asking the children to use their imaginations as they think about the way Isaiah describes God. I have also included a few illustrations you may want to use for this section—figures 12.5, 12.6. Pictures from the internet of the earth from space, pictures of oceans, sandy beaches, mountains, deserts, and huge forests will help you illustrate what Isaiah is saying. Following are some suggestions for teaching from this section:

V. 12 – God is one who can hold the waters of the sea in His hands, so He must be greater than the seas. How much water can you hold in your hands? He measures the heaven with a span. Do you know how much is a span? It is a unit of length based on the width of the expanded hand, approximately 9 inches. Now think about God being able to measure the sky with one span. God is greater than the sky! He can also weigh the mountains and hills in a balance scale. Imagine putting all the mountains and sands of the earth in a balance scale. You'd have to have a really huge scale, wouldn't you? Isaiah is telling us that God is greater than His creation. I have traveled in the world and in our nation, and each time I see majestic waterfalls, towering mountains, bountiful forests, starry nights, I think about the glory of God and His creative power. This is what Isaiah wants the remnant to focus on so they won't lose heart in Babylon.

Vs. 13-14 – Isaiah asks rhetorical questions like, "Who has taught God knowledge?" No one can teach God; He knows all things. He did not have to ask permission from anyone or seek help from any in His creation. For older children, this is a good place to refer to Job 38-40.

V. 15 – The nations are very little in God's sight—like a drop in a bucket full of water. This does not mean that God doesn't care for the people, but it is showing that God is greater than nations. I refer back to chapter 10 reminding the children how Assyria was God's ax, saw, and rod. Combining this with verse 17 that all nations are worthless before God, we see those who exalt themselves above Jehovah and do not desire to serve Him, but serve idols that are of no value, just like the idols they make (Psalm 135:15-18). We do become like the God (or gods) we worship.

V. 16 – There is not enough wood in the forests or enough animals in the earth to supply an adequate burnt offering to God. This reminds me of Psalm 50:7-15 – "…every beast of the field is Mine, and the cattle on a thousand hills… If I were hungry, I would not tell you; for the world is Mine and all its fullness." Jehovah does not need the sacrifices and burnt offerings. They were never to "feed" or "appease" Him, but to help the people see the seriousness of their sin and foreshadow the true sacrifice of the Lamb of God.

V. 22 – Jehovah "sits above the circle of the earth." What a powerful picture! Remind the children that Isaiah is using language we can understand to describe an eternal, all-powerful God that we cannot fully understand. This is a good place to use a picture of the earth from space to give the children an idea of the greatness of God that Isaiah paints for us. Jehovah also "…spreads them (the heavens) out like a tent to dwell in." These two portraits help us see God at once outside His creation, yet inhabiting it. It is helpful here to remind the children that when Isaiah wrote this about the earth, the popular idea in other cultures was that the earth was flat and/or that it was held up by Atlas or balanced on the back of a turtle. The Bible is not a book of science, but it is advanced and accurate in the scientific facts it reveals.

Vs. 27-31 – Jehovah never gets tired. He understands everything. I am not like that. I get tired; do you? There are many things I don't understand; what about you? Are there things you don't understand? God knows that we get tired and that we are weak (Psalm 103:13-14). But, He doesn't abandon us because of that. Instead, He gives us help and strength. "But those who wait on the LORD shall renew their strength; they shall mount up with wings like eagles, they shall run and not be weary, they shall walk and not faint" (40:31).

You can use the above basic narrative and alter it to suit the age of the children you are teaching. Our children today have seen many pictures from outer space like those from the Hubble Telescope or from our orbiting space craft, so they are aware of the grandeur of the universe. I sometimes share with the children that when I was a child, I would lie on a quilt on the lawn of my grandparent's house out in the country and look up at the starry sky. Of course, Granddaddy was quoting from Psalms, the prophets, or Job, reminding me of the wonder of God's creation. I tell them, also, about being in Africa only a few years ago. The nights are darker there because they do not have the amount of electricity we do. When I looked into the night sky, the stars were so bright and clear, I felt like I could reach up and grab one, but they were too far from me. Two songs always burst into my mind when I see something this marvelous in creation: "How Great Thou Art" and "Our God Is Alive." This portion of chapter 40 is a good lesson to use as a part of a review, because it reminds the children of the majesty of God.

Behold Your God!

Isaiah 40:12-14

12 Who has measured the waters in the hollow of His hand,
Measured heaven with a span
And calculated the dust of the earth in a measure?
Weighed the mountains in scales
And the hills in a balance?
13 Who has directed the Spirit of the LORD,
Or as His counselor has taught Him?
14 With whom did He take counsel, and who instructed Him,
And taught Him in the path of justice?
Who taught Him knowledge,
And showed Him the way of understanding?

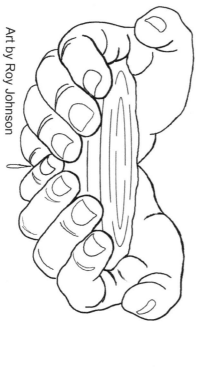

Art by Roy Johnson

Figure 12.01

Make Straight in the Desert a Highway for God
Isaiah 40:3-5

Art by Jodie Boren

Figure 12.1

John the Baptist – Preaching to prepare people for Jesus

Mark 1:1-8

The beginning of the gospel of Jesus Christ, the Son of God.
2 As it is written in the Prophets:

"Behold, I send My messenger before Your face,
Who will prepare Your way before You."
3 "The voice of one crying in the wilderness:
'Prepare the way of the LORD;
Make His paths straight.'"

4 John came baptizing in the wilderness and preaching a baptism of repentance for the remission of sins. 5 Then all the land of Judea, and those from Jerusalem, went out to him and were all baptized by him in the Jordan River, confessing their sins.

6 Now John was clothed with camel's hair and with a leather belt around his waist, and he ate locusts and wild honey. 7 And he preached, saying, "There comes One after me who is mightier than I, whose sandal strap I am not worthy to stoop down and loose. 8 I indeed baptized you with water, but He will baptize you with the Holy Spirit."

Roy Johnson
7/5/14

Figure 12.2

Art by Jodie Boren

Figure 12.3

ELIJAH, THE VOICE, THE MESSENGER

Jesus said to the apostles: " Elijah has come already, and they did not know him but did to him whatever they wished..."   Then the disciples understood that He spoke to them of John the Baptist.
Matthew 17:12-13

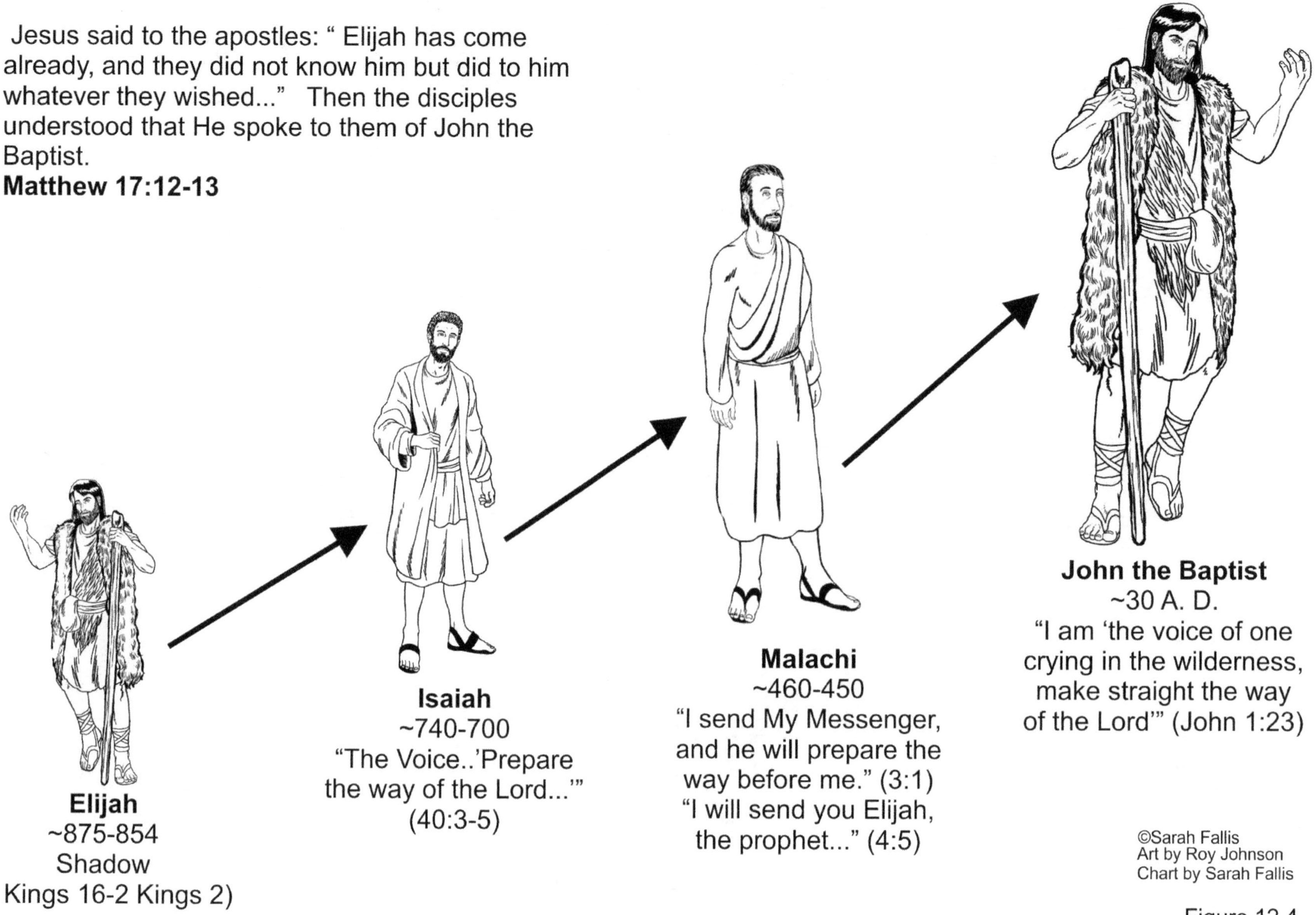

Elijah
~875-854
Shadow
(1 Kings 16-2 Kings 2)

Isaiah
~740-700
"The Voice.. 'Prepare the way of the Lord...' "
(40:3-5)

Malachi
~460-450
"I send My Messenger, and he will prepare the way before me." (3:1)
"I will send you Elijah, the prophet..." (4:5)

John the Baptist
~30 A. D.
"I am 'the voice of one crying in the wilderness, make straight the way of the Lord'" (John 1:23)

©Sarah Fallis
Art by Roy Johnson
Chart by Sarah Fallis

Figure 12.4

Old Testament

Isaiah 40:1-9

"Comfort, yes, comfort My people!"Says your God. 2 "Speak comfort to Jerusalem, and cry out to her, that her warfare is ended, that her iniquity is pardoned; for she has received from the LORD's hand double for all her sins."
3 The voice of one crying in the wilderness:"Prepare the way of the LORD; make straight in the desert a highway for our God. 4 Every valley shall be exalted and every mountain and hill brought low; the crooked places shall be made straight And the rough places smooth; 5 The glory of the LORD shall be revealed, and all flesh shall see it together; for the mouth of the LORD has spoken."
6 The voice said, "Cry out!"And he said, "What shall I cry?"
"All flesh is grass, and all its loveliness is like the flower of the field. 7 The grass withers, the flower fades, because the breath of the LORD blows upon it; surely the people are grass. 8 The grass withers, the flower fades, but the word of our God stands forever."
9 O Zion, you who bring good tidings, get up into the high mountain; O Jerusalem, you who bring good tidings, lift up your voice with strength, lift it up, be not afraid; say to the cities of Judah, **"Behold your God!"**

New Testament

Matthew 3:1-3
In those days John the Baptist came preaching in the wilderness of Judea, 2 and saying, "Repent, for the kingdom of heaven is at hand!" 3 For this is he who was spoken of by the prophet Isaiah, saying:

"The voice of one crying in the wilderness:
'Prepare the way of the LORD;
Make His paths straight.'"

Luke 3:1-6
Now in the fifteenth year of the reign of Tiberius Caesar, Pontius Pilate being governor of Judea, Herod being tetrarch of Galilee, his brother Philip tetrarch of Iturea and the region of Trachonitis, and Lysanias tetrarch of Abilene, 2 while Annas and Caiaphas were high priests, the word of God came to John the son of Zacharias in the wilderness. 3 And he went into all the region around the Jordan, preaching a baptism of repentance for the remission of sins, 4 as it is written in the book of the words of Isaiah the prophet, saying:

"The voice of one crying in the wilderness:
'Prepare the way of the LORD;
Make His paths straight.
5 Every valley shall be filled
And every mountain and hill brought low;
The crooked places shall be made straight
And the rough ways smooth;
6 And all flesh shall see the salvation of God.'"

Figure 12.5

Old Testament

Malachi 3:1

"Behold, I send My messenger,
And he will prepare the way before
Me.
And the Lord, whom you seek,
Will suddenly come to His temple,
Even the Messenger of the covenant,
In whom you delight.
Behold, He is coming,"
Says the LORD of hosts.

Malachi 4:5-6

5 Behold, I will send you Elijah the
prophet
Before the coming of the great and
dreadful day of the LORD.
6 And he will turn
The hearts of the fathers to the
children,
And the hearts of the children to their
fathers,
Lest I come and strike the earth with a
curse."

New Testament

Luke 1:13-17

13 But the angel said to him, "Do not
be afraid, Zacharias, for your prayer is
heard; and your wife Elizabeth will bear
you a son, and you shall call his name
John. 14 And you will have joy and
gladness, and many will rejoice at his
birth. 15 For he will be great in the sight
of the Lord, and shall drink neither wine
nor strong drink. He will also be filled
with the Holy Spirit, even from his
mother's womb. 16 And he will turn
many of the children of Israel to the
Lord their God. 17 He will also go
before Him in the spirit and power of
Elijah, 'to turn the hearts of the fathers
to the children,' and the disobedient to
the wisdom of the just, to make ready a
people prepared for the Lord."

Matthew 11:7-10, 13-15

7 As they departed, Jesus began to say
to the multitudes concerning John:
"What did you go out into the
wilderness to see? A reed shaken by
the wind? 8 But what did you go out to
see? A man clothed in soft garments?
Indeed, those who wear soft clothing
are in kings' houses. 9 But what did
you go out to see? A prophet? Yes, I
say to you, and more than a prophet.
10 For this is he of whom it is written:
"Behold, I send My messenger before
Your face, who will prepare Your way
before You.'

13 For all the prophets and the law
prophesied until John. 14 And if you
are willing to receive it, he is Elijah who
is to come. 15 He who has ears to
hear, let him hear!

Figure 12.6

JOHN THE BAPTIST

HIGHWAY BUILDER FOR GOD

Hundreds of years before he was born, God's prophets told about John the Baptist. Isaiah said he would be like a highway builder. Isaiah's word picture is a wilderness that has many mountains and valleys. Then, someone comes and lifts up the valleys, lowers the mountains, and makes all the crooked areas straight and the rough places smooth. That was a picture of what John the Baptist would do. He preached God's message, "Repent." Repent means to be sorry for the wrong things you have done and change your life from doing bad things to doing good.   In that way, John was preparing people to believe in Jesus when He came. So, John was building a "Highway for God." And, Isaiah said the glory of God would be on that highway. When Jesus came, He showed us God's glory.

"And the Word became flesh and dwelt among us, and we beheld His glory, the glory as of the only begotten of the Father, full of grace and truth." (John 1:14)

The prophet Malachi called John the Baptist God's messenger that would go before Him and prepare the people for His coming. Malachi also said that John would be similar to the prophet Elijah. You remember learning about Elijah. He was very brave. He challenged the false prophets of Baal to help God's people see that Baal was really no god at all. He also preached to King Ahab and Queen Jezebel and told them they were not doing what God wanted them to do.   John the Baptist was like Elijah because he was very brave in preaching God's Word. He preached to King Herod that what he was doing was wrong. You may remember that Herod had John killed because of that. John was a brave highway builder for God. Elijah is the "shadow" in the Old Testament, and John is the "substance" in the New Testament.

Figure 12.7

Chapter 13
THE FOLLY OF IDOLATRY

We usually don't like to use the word "stupid" when teaching children, but in relation to idolatry, that is the best description of those who would make and worship a wood, stone or metal image. Several times in Isaiah 41 through 48, the prophet presents the folly (or stupidity) of idolatry. As I noted earlier, when people forget Jehovah, they fall into idolatry. Some, like militant atheists, Muslims, Buddhists, and agnostics will not admit to worshiping idols. However, if you do some research about the place of science and intelligence, required pilgrimages and symbols, gold and emerald statues in ornate temples, and financial, political, or military power, you will definitely see that idols of some type play a part in these religions. Also, many who call themselves Christians venerate certain people as "saints" and have images they visit, kiss, or honor in some other way. Later, Ezekiel will explain that some who appear to be religious have "idols in their hearts" (Ez. 14:3). Our children are exposed to these religions on an almost daily basis, so Isaiah's message about the senseless and unthinking worship of an idol is very timely.

"I am the First, and I am the Last; besides Me there is no God…" (Isa. 44:6). Israel and Judah had forgotten the first of the Ten Commandments, and that was the primary reason for their captivity. Babylon was on the horizon, and Isaiah's task was to remind Judah of their special relationship with Jehovah and to give them additional evidence that He will fulfill the promise He made to their Fathers. It is interesting how people today, even religious people, speak of faith as "belief that something is true even without evidence." As we continue in this discussion, you will see that Jehovah never asks His people to believe without evidence. In fact, this is what He accuses the idolaters of doing—bowing to wood or stone without evidence that the wood or stone could do anything at all.

Throughout these chapters, God challenges the idols. He lays before them the contest—tell us the future, "declare to us things to come" so we can "know that you are gods" (41:22). He even makes the test a bit easier: "Yes, do good or do evil, that we may be dismayed…" (v.23). When Jehovah sets forth this challenge, He makes it plain that telling the past, present and future must be more than an educated guess. It must be specific events and people, and it must be fulfilled exactly. You may want to remind the children of Elijah and the prophets of Baal in 1 Kings 18. The prophets of Baal couldn't cause fire to come to a dry altar. God made His work even harder with the water that was poured around and on the altar, but His fire consumed the sacrifice on the soaked altar and all the water that was around it. God will meet and exceed this challenge as well.

However, let's first look at the folly of idolatry in chapter 44 and make some applications. Children enjoy this lesson, and Roy's art helps them see what Isaiah is describing. In verse 9, the prophet declares all images as useless. Then in verse 10, he asks, "Who would form a god or mold an image that profits him nothing?" The answer seems obvious—no one would want a worthless god. Although, that was exactly what the people were doing. Now, let's see the scenario he describes in verses 13-17:

> The craftsman stretches out his rule, he marks one out with chalk; he fashions it with a plane, he marks it out with the compass, and makes it like the figure of a man, according to the beauty of a man, that it may remain in the house. He cuts down cedars for himself, and takes the cypress and the oak; he secures it for himself among the trees of the forest. He plants a pine, and the rain nourishes it.

> Then it shall be for a man to burn, for he will take some of it and warm himself; yes, he kindles it and bakes bread; indeed he makes a god and worships it; he makes it a carved image, and falls down to it. He burns half of it in the fire; with this half he eats meat; he roasts a roast, and is satisfied. He even warms himself and says, "Ah! I am warm, I have seen the fire." And the rest of it he makes into a god, his carved image. He falls down before it and worships it, prays to it and says, "Deliver me, for you are my god!"

Look at the absurdity! A man cuts down a tree that he could not make grow on his own; the rain had to nourish it for it to grow. Next, he divides it into 3 parts; one part he uses to warm himself; one part he uses to cook his food; and one part he worships! How did he know which part of the tree was his god? Perhaps he cooked his food with his god. Maybe he burned his god so he could get warm. This is exactly what God says of such a person in verses 18-20. He says they do not even think about what they have done. They don't understand that, "I have burned half of it in the fire, yes, I have also baked bread on its coals; I have roasted meat and eaten it; and shall I make the rest of it an abomination? Shall I fall down before a block of wood?" You may also want to refer to other verses in this section that refer to idols—they must be fastened to a base so they won't fall (41:7); they must be carried either by the people or by their cattle (46:1, 7); they cannot answer when people call to them (46:7). In contrast, God hears and answers His people; He carries His people (46:4); and He will not fall.

This is the time for some good application, depending, again, on the age of the children. Ask what paper is made of. They know that paper comes from trees. Now, paper is used for good things—for books, even Bibles, and for paper to write on, and pretty cards and art. Paper is also used to make money. Now, do some people care more about money than they do about God? Do they trust in their investments more than in God's ability to save? You can also talk about other things that may be our idols—things that can become more important to us than God. What about the sports we like and the games we play? What about our friends? Can they become more important than God? Anything or anyone we allow to be more important to us than God, than worshiping and serving Him, is an idol. Here is a good place to remind them about Ezekiel's statement that the religious leaders had "idols in their hearts" (Ez. 14:3). We don't have to bow down to an image made of wood or stone. We can have hearts that are not in harmony with God's will. Do you want worship to be over soon so you can visit with your friends or watch your favorite TV program? Do you wish you didn't have to come on Wednesday evenings because you miss some favorite activity? Do you envy your friends who do not attend church because they have more time for fun things than you do? As a teacher, you can explore these ideas more and add to them. I only offer them to stimulate your thinking as to how to apply this lesson about idolatry.

The Test

As we noted earlier, Jehovah challenges the idols—"Tell us something so we can have evidence that you are gods!" Doesn't that make sense? If these idols are gods, they should know more than men, and they should be able to do more than men. A god who knows nothing and who can do nothing is nothing!

At this point, I usually ask children something like this, "If I told you I was the smartest and best mathematician in the whole world, would you want me to prove it?" They usually answer, "Yes!" I ask if a test question like, "What is 2 + 2?" would be hard enough for me to prove I'm the best mathematician. Of course not. Then, I ask them to think of a good, hard math question that might prove I'm the greatest mathematician. I always get interesting answers depending on the age of the children. One girl asked me to do long division; that was about the hardest math she could think of. A junior high girl asked, "What is the square root of pi?" While that is a harder question, none of those would give real proof to the world of mathematics. I would need to do something in mathematics that had never been done before. I would need to startle the world with my knowledge and be in the news. (As a teacher, you can think of your own scenario to use that would relate to your expertise or perhaps to someone the children know.)

Now, let's see the test that God gives. He asks the idols to tell the future (44:7). Remember, too, that God must pass the same test. He sets up a harder test for Himself; He tells what will happen to Judah in the future, how long they will be in Babylon, and who will let them return home. "Who says of Cyrus, 'He is My shepherd, and he shall perform all My pleasure, saying to Jerusalem, "You shall be built," and to the temple, "Your foundation shall be laid"'" (44:28). This must have sounded strange to the people. When Isaiah is speaking, the city of Jerusalem is standing firm and proud with bustling markets and teeming with people. The temple that Solomon built is in the midst of the city and it is filled with gold, silver and bronze. How absurd to have someone say, "You shall be built!" It is already built. There's no need. Notice, too, that Isaiah looks past the present into the distant future. In fact, he looks about 150 years ahead and names a king, Cyrus. This king had not even been born and his kingdom was not even "on the radar." Babylon was the rising star in the east, and God had already told them they would go to Babylon because of their sins. Who is this Cyrus? What is God talking about?

Jehovah mentions Cyrus again in chapter 45 and adds more information about him. "He shall build My city and let My exiles go free, not for price nor reward" (45:13). So Cyrus will not ask for money from the people when he lets them go back to Jerusalem. In fact, in verse 14, God says the wealth of nations like Egypt, Cush, and the Sabeans will be theirs when they go back home from Babylon. Not only that, but those nations will declare, "Surely God is in you, and there is no other; there is no other God."

Did God pass the test? All we have to do is turn to Ezra 1:1-4, 7-8:

> Now in the first year of Cyrus king of Persia, that the word of the LORD by the mouth of Jeremiah might be fulfilled, the LORD stirred up the spirit of Cyrus king of Persia, so that he made a proclamation throughout all his kingdom, and also put it in writing, saying,
>
> Thus says Cyrus king of Persia:
>
> All the kingdoms of the earth the LORD God of heaven has given me. And He has commanded me to build Him a house at Jerusalem which is in Judah. Who is among you of all His people? May his God be with him, and let him go up to Jerusalem which is in Judah, and build the house of the LORD God of Israel (He is God), which is in Jerusalem. And whoever is left in any place where he dwells, let the men of his place help him with silver and gold, with goods and livestock, besides the freewill offerings for the house of God which is in Jerusalem… King Cyrus also brought out the articles of the house of the LORD, which Nebuchadnezzar had taken from Jerusalem and put in the temple of his gods; and Cyrus king of Persia brought them out by the hand of Mithredath the treasurer, and counted them out to Sheshbazzar the prince of Judah.

Isaiah had told Hezekiah that Judah would go into Babylon as captives after his death, and Jeremiah had prophesied that their captivity would be 70 years. Isaiah had also told of God's proclamation about Cyrus 150 years before it happened. Notice that all the wealth the king of Babylon had taken, Cyrus gives back to the people. As you continue in the book of Ezra, Cyrus also gives them any financial assistance they need. Surely, God passed the test! The charts that I have to accompany this will help you, but you can also just point out these events on the timeline in the classroom, showing that God certainly did "declare the end from the beginning…" (46:10). I think it is important, also, when you teach about the return from Babylonian captivity, that you bring in these prophecies and "teach it backward" showing that these events were not accidental, but that God had foretold them 1-200 years previously.

It is interesting to notice from their history that the Jewish people were never entangled in idolatry after the Babylonian captivity. While that had been their downfall throughout their history, beginning at Mount Sinai with the golden calf, it would never again be a temptation. Why? In a word, Cyrus! They saw and they remembered. They had lost all their fortune, their homes, their temple and their city. Now, through God's servant, Cyrus, they regained it all. The evidence was clear. No idol would ever be in their land. This does not mean they were completely pleasing to God. In fact, the Jews had become so meticulous in obeying the Law, that they made it a burden as you see in the gospel accounts. Jesus would accuse them of many sins (Matt. 23), but idolatry was not one of them.

Concluding comments

I always think we should take every opportunity to show our children that the Bible is unique among all the sacred books and that faith in God is not an irrational, make-believe sort of thing. About a year ago, I was reading Jon Krakauer's book, Under the Banner of Heaven. This book is about a murder by some members of an extremist group in the Mormon Church. I know our young children are not reading this book, but some of our older teens may read it since it was a New York Times best seller and highly acclaimed by credible people in the literary world. The reason I'm referencing it is that as I was writing this chapter, I thought about some things I'd read that Krakauer says about faith. His views are not new, nor are they original. However, he does state them boldly, as if he has researched and knows this to be a fact like other things he supposedly researched for this work. Listen to this statement in the *Prologue*: "Faith is the very antithesis of reason, injudiciousness a crucial component of spiritual devotion" (Krakauer 2003, xxiii).

When he discusses the history of the Mormon church and the origin of the Book of Mormon, he is rather accurate about the Book of Mormon being a story that is not substantiated by history, archeology, or anthropology. He says this doesn't matter, because:

> All religious belief is a function of nonrational faith. And faith, by its very definition, tends to be impervious to intellectual argument or academic criticism. Polls routinely indicate, moreover, that nine out of ten Americans believe in God—most of us subscribe to one brand of religion or another. Those who would assail The Book of Mormon should bear in mind that its veracity is no more dubious than the veracity of the Bible, say, or the Qur'an, or the sacred texts of most other religions. The latter texts simply enjoy the considerable advantage of having made their public debut in the shadowy recesses of the ancient past, and are thus much harder to refute (Krakauer 2003, 70).

I repeat, this is not just his view, and because it is in a book our children may never read does not mean they will not be influenced by this kind of thinking. I've witnessed this in Dawkin's books, in several TED Talks online, and I've even heard some of my religious friends talk of faith in the same way. This is not biblical faith! This is faith like the people had in their idols—unreasonable, not based on any evidence at all. It is interesting that after pontificating so much on the nature of faith that Krakauer finally tells the reader in the appendix that he is an agnostic, that he does fear death, and that he hasn't been persuaded to make the "leap of faith" (Krakauer 2003, 341).

So, Krakauer says the Bible appeared in history so far back that it is harder to refute. I would ask him to research the evidence for the Bible in the same way and with the same exactness that he researched the court and police records for his book. How do we arm our children against such views of faith and of the veracity of the Bible? Peter tells us that one of the best ways is through fulfilled prophecy (2 Pet. 1:16-21). This is why I'm writing. God never asked us to shut our eyes, cross our fingers and make a "leap of faith." We can be assured that God will fulfill His promises to us because we have the historical record that He fulfilled all His unconditional promises to the Jews. Notice what He says to His people in Isaiah 46:9-10, "Remember the former things of old, for I am God, and there is no other; I am God, and there is none like Me, declaring the end from the beginning, and from ancient times things that are not yet done, saying, 'My counsel shall stand, and I will do all My pleasure.'"

At this point, it is good to stop and review some of the things we have learned. In Isaiah 2, God said His word and law would go forth from Jerusalem. Did He pass that test? Read Acts 2. Later in Isaiah 7, God said a virgin would bear Immanuel, and Micah said this would happen in Bethlehem. Did God pass that test? Read Matthew 1 and 2.

The Folly of Idolatry – Isaiah 44:6-20
Psalm 135:15-18 & Jeremiah 10:1-5

"He cuts down cedars for himself..."
Isa. 44:14

"Yes, he kindles it and bakes bread..."
Isa. 44:15

1

Ray Johnson
9/12/10

Figure 13.1

"Then it shall be for a man to burn,
for he will take some of it and warm himself..."

Isa. 44:15

"And the rest of it he makes into a god...
He falls down before it and worships it..."

Isa. 44:17

"And no one considers in his heart,...to say, 'I have burned half of it in the fire, yes, I have also baked bread on its coals...and shall I fall down before a block of wood?'"

Isa. 44:18-20.

Roy Johnson
6/22/15

This is the god Ganesh that Hindu people worship today.

Isaiah 46:5-7
5 "To whom will you liken Me, and make Me equal and compare Me, that we should be alike? 6 They lavish gold out of the bag, And weigh silver on the scales; They hire a goldsmith, and he makes it a god; They prostrate themselves, yes, they worship. 7 They bear it on the shoulder, they carry it and set it in its place, and it stands; From its place it shall not move. Though one cries out to it, yet it cannot answer nor save him out of his trouble.

Psalm 135:15-18
15 The idols of the nations are silver and gold,
The work of men's hands.
16 They have mouths, but they do not speak;
Eyes they have, but they do not see;
17 They have ears, but they do not hear;
Nor is there any breath in their mouths.
18 Those who make them are like them;
So is everyone who trusts in them.

The gods men make are worthless!

Idols Today

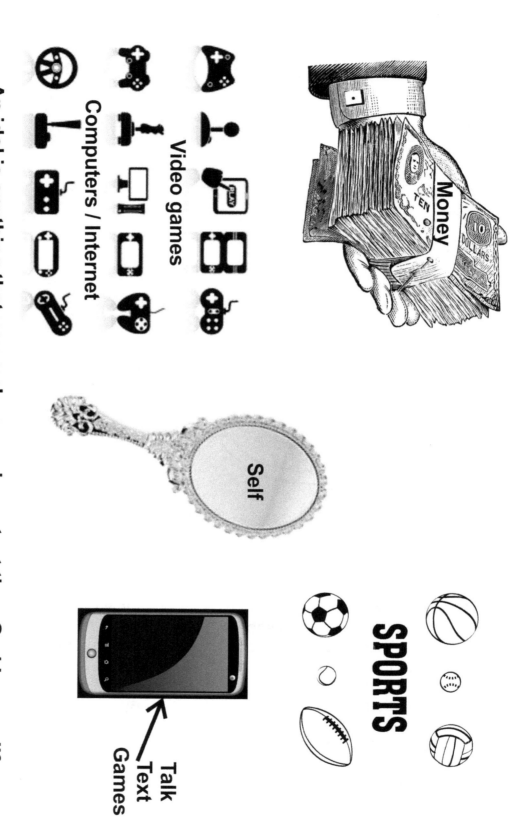

Money

Video games

Computers / Internet

Self

SPORTS

Talk
Text
Games

An idol is anything that you make more important than God in your life.
Can you think of other idols?

Figure 13.3

Isaiah 44:28 – God says of Cyrus, " '…he shall perform all My pleasure, saying to Jerusalem, " You shall be built," and to the temple, "Your foundation shall be laid." '"

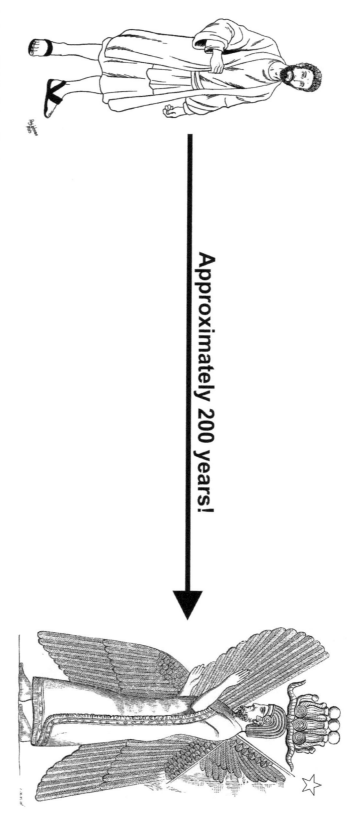

Approximately 200 years!

Isaiah – 745-695 B.C.

Cyrus of Persia ~ 536 B.C.

Read 2 Chronicles 36:22-23 and Ezra 1:1-4. Did God pass the test?

☆ This image of Cyrus is a copy of a bas-relief at Pasargadae. Cyrus is pictured as the guardian, wearing a crown of goat's horns and solar disks.

Figure 13.4

Chapter 14
THE SUFFERING SERVANT OF JEHOVAH

*I*saiah has painted several pictures of what it will be like when Jesus comes. In each of these, he has revealed something about Jesus that we did not know before. In this latter portion of the book, there are four outstanding passages that deal with the special Servant of Jehovah—the Messiah. These are Isaiah 42:1-9; 49:1-13; 50:4-11; and 52:13-53:12. Teachers of older children, teens, and adults may want to study and teach the first three of these selections called the "Servant Songs." I plan to discuss only the last song because of all Isaiah's prophetic pictures of the Messiah, this is the pinnacle.

Many scholars and commentators have tried to do justice to this passage, but some have robbed it of its Messianic message. For instance, Hailey, Jackson, Coffman, Kiser, Henry, and other conservative scholars agree that this prophecy finds its fulfillment in, and only in, Jesus Christ, the Messiah. Kiser quotes Polycarp the Lysian as saying this passage is the "golden *passional* of the Old Testament evangelist" (Kiser 1995, 178). In that same context, Kiser quotes Franz Delitzsch: "It looks as if it had been written beneath the cross upon Golgotha… and is the most central, the deepest, and the loftiest thing that the Old Testament prophecy, outstripping itself, has ever achieved." In contrast, the respected professor of Biblical Studies at Abilene Christian University, Dr. John Willis, agrees with the most liberal scholars and states that the suffering servant of this passage is the faithful remnant of Israel, suffering in behalf of the nations (Willis 2009, 566). I find it interesting that such men could hold that position when verse 9 clearly states of the servant, "… He had done no violence, nor was any deceit in His mouth." While the remnant of Israel had been faithful, they had not been without sin. I bring this to the teachers' attention because as children get older, they may be exposed to teaching similar to this from trusted professors or preachers who have studied under more liberal scholars. We need to be aware so we can give our children a firm foundation in the validity of Old Testament prophecy.

Another thing we as teachers need to be aware of is that some teachers will say that the Jewish rabbis did not understand Isaiah 53 to be Messianic. This is true. They had no concept of a suffering Messiah. Their idea of the Messiah was an earthly king like David who would restore their glory and power among the nations. While this might be interesting to observe, it has little to do with the true import of the passage. Remember that the rabbis and scribes did not recognize Jesus as their Messiah when He lived and taught among them, so why would we want to interpret the prophecies as they did? If they had understood their scriptures, they would have accepted their Messiah (John 5:39). F. F. Bruce makes the observation that between the times of Isaiah and the personal ministry of Christ, "No one identified the Suffering Servant of Isaiah with the Davidic Messiah, except Jesus" (Bruce 1954, 188). When it comes to understanding scripture, we should stand with Jesus rather than the Jewish scribes, rabbis, and modern liberal scholars.

In commenting on this for children, I approach it with reverence and awe. Each time I read it, I realize this truly is the summit of Isaiah's book and of all Old Testament Messianic prophecy. I usually just read the passage and comment on it in words the children can understand. I have included a page of word definitions from the New King James Version of this passage. You may use it or reword and improve it. You will also find the side-by-side scripture sheets helpful, and you may want to use them as you discuss the passage, having the students highlight the words quoted or alluded to.

A good way to introduce this to children is to refer back to the very first lesson about the prophets—Chapter 2 in this book. Peter tells us that the two main or great things which the Old Testament prophets indicated beforehand were the sufferings of Christ and the glory that should follow (1 Pet.1:11). You may also want to couple that verse with what Jesus said about the message of Moses, the Psalms, and all the prophets:

These are the words which I spoke to you while I was still with you, that all things must be fulfilled which were written in the Law of Moses and the Prophets and the Psalms concerning Me... Thus it is written, and thus it was necessary for the Christ to suffer and to rise from the dead the third day, and that repentance and remission of sins should be preached in His name to all nations, beginning at Jerusalem (Luke 24:44-47).

Stress to the children that Jesus said the Old Testament pointed to His suffering. You may want to use this time to review about the death for sin from the Garden of Eden to the Passover and to the Day of Atonement. All of these were spoken of by Moses, and if you have been teaching the Old Testament holistically, the children will be familiar with them. I have not dealt with the Psalms, but Psalm 22 is a companion song to this Servant Song in Isaiah 52/53. Since much of Psalm 22 is quoted or referred to at the crucifixion in the Gospels, it would be helpful to refer back to it when you are teaching about the death of Jesus.

Most scholars divide this servant song of Isaiah's into five sections of three verses each. I will follow that order in these brief comments:

1. The Servant's destiny, 52:13-15: Notice the introduction of this song, "Behold, My Servant..." Look, see, observe My Servant. The prophet signals our attention to his proclamation about the Servant of Jehovah. The destiny—exalted, extolled, and be very high. His exaltation comes after and because of His suffering—"so His visage was marred more than any man, and His form more than the sons of men" (v.14). You will need to consider the age of the children you are teaching when you describe how Jesus was treated (the scourging, mocking, crown of thorns, etc.) prior to His crucifixion. Explain that Jesus had not sinned even in what we would call a "little sin" and that He was being treated this way because of our sins. We sometimes don't realize how bad sin is, but when we see how Jesus was beaten, spit on, slapped, laughed at, and finally crucified, it helps us see how bad even those "little sins" are. For older children, you will want to relate this to Phil. 2:5-11, that God has "highly exalted" Jesus and given Him a "name that is above every name" because He was obedient even to death.

This stanza is really a summary of the whole song. It ends with the nations (the Gentiles) considering something that had not been told to them. The Jews had the benefit of the Law and prophets, but the Gentiles did not. However, Gentiles like Pilate, Felix and Caesar would be forced to consider Jesus and what He had accomplished. You may remember in the book of Acts that Gentiles were receptive to the gospel, often more than the Jews.

2. The Servant's rejection, 53:1-3: Jesus grew up as a "root out of dry ground." No one expects a plant to grow in very dry ground; it needs water and nutrients from the soil. This is a picture of how Jesus came into the Jewish world of the first century. We have mentioned this previously in Chapter 10, and you may want to review that with the children, referring again to what Jesus said about the scribes and Pharisees in Matt. 23. Also, the famed kingly house of David had fallen, and no king ruled on his throne in Jerusalem. How could Jesus flourish in such a dry and foreboding social and religious atmosphere? He grew under God's protection.

Jesus was rejected because He didn't fit their concepts of what the Messiah would be like. "He had no form or comeliness; and when we see Him, there is no beauty that we should desire Him" (53:2). Jesus did not come with the pomp of the worldly rulers, wearing a royal robe and riding in a chariot with servants and armies surrounding Him. Remind the students that He was born in a stable and laid in a manger, whereas earthly kings are born in palaces. He grew up in a poor, working-class family, so the people in general thought of Him as of no real value. They rejected Him, His works, and His message (Luke 4:22-30).

3. The Servant's Suffering, 53:4-6: This stanza begins with the Servant bearing our griefs and carrying our sorrows. Matthew, by inspiration, quotes that verse when he describes the general healing ministry of Jesus in Matt. 8:16-19. Numerous times, the gospel writers say that Jesus was "moved with compassion" or "had compassion" (Matt. 9:36; 14:14; 15:32; 18:27; 18:33; 20:34). Jesus—Immanuel, "God with us"—not only took upon Himself our fleshly nature, but He knew both physically and emotionally our hurts, our cares, our limitations, and our sorrows. He lived among us, not above us.

Verses 5 refers to the cruel treatment at His trial and crucifixion—wounded, crushed, pierced, bruised, chastised—all these Jesus endured for us. Then, verse 6 tells us why—all of us, "like sheep have gone astray"—so it was to bring us back to the Shepherd that He suffered. Then we learn that it was Jehovah (the LORD) who "laid on Him the iniquity of us all." Jehovah laid our sins on His Servant that we might be brought back to Him. In the original context, this may refer to the sins of the Jewish nation being laid on the Servant, but in the greater context of God's eternal purpose, it was the sins of the whole world. We cannot imagine the mental, emotional, and spiritual pain of feeling the crushing blow of the sins of the entire world, past, present and future, pressing upon the Sinless One.

4. The Servant's Submission, 53:7-9: His submission is described in agricultural terms that the people of that time could understand. I'm told by those who know about sheep and goats that goats when slaughtered respond with loud, wailing cries, but sheep when slaughtered are silent. Remind children of the facts of Jesus' trial—He made no defense and no accusations against His accusers, though they were the guilty ones. He was hurried through five illegal and arranged trials: before Annas, then the Sanhedrin, then Pilate, then to Herod, and finally to the judgment for His death. The Jewish trials were already arranged with false witnesses so the verdict was decided before the trials began. Pilate found "no fault in Him" (John 18:38; 19; 19:6) and tried to release Him. He silently and willingly submitted to these injustices.

His grave is with the wicked. He was crucified as a criminal between two thieves. He was mocked and ridiculed even while on the cross. Normally, the bodies of crucified criminals are tossed into a common grave, but Jesus' body was not. Notice even this minute detail of Isaiah's prophecy: "…but with the rich in His death" (v. 9):

> After this, Joseph of Arimathea, being a disciple of Jesus, but secretly, for fear of the Jews, asked Pilate that he might take away the body of Jesus; and Pilate gave him permission. So he came and took the body of Jesus. And Nicodemus, who at first came to Jesus by night, also came, bringing a mixture of myrrh and aloes, about a hundred pounds. Then they took the body of Jesus, and bound it in strips of linen with the spices, as the custom of the Jews is to bury. Now in the place where He was crucified there was a garden, and in the garden a new tomb in which no one had yet been laid. So there they laid Jesus, because of the Jews' Preparation Day, for the tomb was nearby (John 19:38-42).

5. The Servant's Victory and Reward, 53:10-12: This last stanza ties the song back to the first by showing the cause of His suffering, the outcome for us, and His ultimate exaltation. "It pleased the LORD to bruise Him" because it pleased Jehovah to save. The only way Jehovah could save us was through the sacrifice of "the Lamb of God who takes away the sin of the world" (John 1:29). Jesus' death for our sins was planned by God in eternity, not because He wanted to punish His Son, but because He wanted to save lost mankind. This was the only way.

Look, though, at the joyful outcome! I can think of no better passage to end this stanza with than Heb. 2:10-18:

> For it was fitting for Him, for whom are all things and by whom are all things, in bringing many sons to glory, to make the captain of their salvation perfect through sufferings. For both He who sanctifies and those who are being sanctified are all of one, for which reason He is not ashamed to call them brethren… Inasmuch then as the children have partaken of flesh and blood, He Himself likewise shared in the same, that through death He might destroy him who had the power of death, that is, the devil, and release those who through fear of death were all their lifetime subject

to bondage. For indeed He does not give aid to angels, but He does give aid to the seed of Abraham. Therefore, in all things He had to be made like His brethren, that He might be a merciful and faithful High Priest in things pertaining to God, to make propitiation for the sins of the people. For in that He Himself has suffered, being tempted, He is able to aid those who are tempted.

Concluding comments:

Like Isaiah, let us say, "Behold!" Let us look at the cross and see what God has accomplished in Jesus' suffering and death. This servant song is so majestic that I feel I have not done it justice in trying to explain to children. I think of it like the song "Jesus Loves Me"—we must keep singing it over and over until understanding comes. Also, let's not confine this to our teaching of the Old Testament or of the prophets. You can refer to the song of Isaiah 52/53 when you teach the life of Jesus, that He came to serve and "give His life a ransom for many" (Mark 10:45). When you teach about the feeding of the 5,000 and that the next day many of His disciples left Him, or when you tell students how the leaders of the Jews tried to catch Him in His words, you can refer to Isaiah's prophecy that He would be rejected by men. Of course, the classic use of Isaiah 53 is in Acts 8:26-40. This definitely proves that Isaiah was speaking of Jesus. Also, you can tie this into 1 Peter 1:12 that the prophets knew some of the things they said were not for them, but for us.

On a hot summer evening when I was thirteen, I went to a gospel meeting at the church of Christ in the northeast Texas community of Dodd City. Like any young girls, my cousins and friends and I were giggling and talking about our dresses—how many yards in our can-cans, etc. I remember sitting on the second row on the right side of the building that night. Usually these meetings were outside, but this was the first year the church had purchased a water cooler that provided some relief from the heat, so we were inside. Johnny Jackson, a preacher from Dallas, was preaching that meeting. This night his sermon was on the crucifixion of Jesus. He made Isaiah's prophecy come alive as he masterfully showed its fulfillment in the New Testament. As I sat there, I became oblivious to everything except the Word he preached. That night, the sacrifice of Jesus for my sins became more real to me than any time before. Yes, I knew the facts of the gospel, but that night I saw the gospel in its harmony, beauty, love and purity. Years later, as a young preacher's wife, Gary and I were going to the lectureship at Abilene Christian University. On the program for one of the keynote lessons was "Johnny Jackson – The Death of Jesus." I told Gary, "That one lesson will be worth the whole trip." It was. And, as I wrote this chapter, in my mind, I was sitting on the second row of that little church building in Dodd City.

WORDS WE NEED TO KNOW IN ISAIAH 53

1. Comeliness – handsome or beautiful. Someone who looks like royalty, or is good-looking.

2. Despised – hated, to look down on.

3. Acquainted – know about, aware of.

4. Esteem – to think well of, respect or honor.

5. Afflicted – caused pain or trouble, harass, torment persecute.

6. Transgressions – sins, breaking the law, crimes.

7. Chastisement – punishment, beaten.

8. Iniquity – sin, wickedness, wicked sin, relates to transgressions.

9. Deceit –lies or lying, cheat.

10. Spoil – things that have been gotten by a special effort. Usually in war, the winner takes all the valuable things from the looser. These things are called "spoils."

11. Intercession – helping another person; pleading for someone.

John 1:29

The next day John saw Jesus coming toward him, and said, "Behold! The Lamb of God who takes away the sin of the world!

Figure 14.1

THE CROSS – ISAIAH 52:13-53

His visage marred more than any man –
His appearance disfigured beyond any man

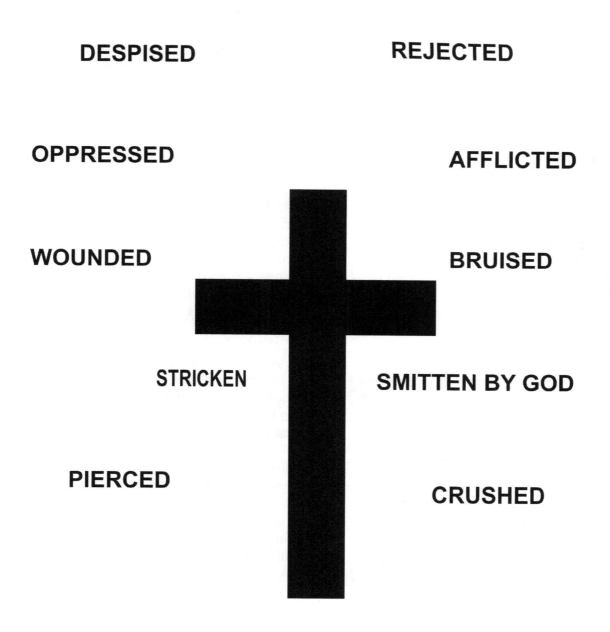

DESPISED

REJECTED

OPPRESSED

AFFLICTED

WOUNDED

BRUISED

STRICKEN

SMITTEN BY GOD

PIERCED

CRUSHED

The punishment that brought us peace was on Him

By His stripes (wounds) we are healed.

Figure 14.2

Isaiah 53:1-5

1 Who has believed our report? And to whom has the arm of the LORD been revealed?

1. Many of the Jews did not believe on Jesus, even though He did many miracles (John 12: 37-38).

2 For He shall grow up before Him as a tender plant, and as a root out of a dry ground. He has no form or comeliness; and when we see Him, there is no beauty that we should desire Him.

2. A plant does not grow easily in dry ground. Jesus was born in Bethlehem and grew up in Nazareth. He did not go to a major university, and He did not travel to the large cities. He also was not handsome or royal looking. People didn't follow Him because of His earthly power.

3 He is despised and rejected by men; a man of sorrows, and acquainted with grief. And we hid, as it were, our faces from Him; He was despised, and we did not esteem Him.

3&4. At first, people followed Jesus and they liked Him mainly because of the miracles of healing the sick. But many people did not like His teachings. Jesus was poor, and He knew about our troubles and sicknesses, too. He said once, "Foxes have holes, birds have nests, but the Son of Man hasn't a place to lay His head" (Matthew 8:20). When He healed the sick, the Bible says of Him, "He had compassion..." He really cared about people, but many of them did not care about Him. He was "a man of sorrows" because He was not popular with others and because He died for us.

4 Surely he has borne our griefs, and carried our sorrows; yet we esteemed Him stricken, smitten of God, and afflicted.

5 But He was wounded for our transgressions, He was bruised for our iniquities. The chastisement of our peace was upon Him; and with His stripes we are healed.

5. He died for us and because of our sins. Paul says in 2 Corinthians 5:21: "God made Him who had no sin to be sin for us, that we might become the righteousness of God in Him." That is, Jesus died that we might be saved! "With His stripes, we are healed."

1

Figure 14.3

Isaiah 53:6-10

6 All we like sheep have gone astray; we have turned every one to his own way; and the LORD has laid on Him the iniquity of us all.

6. We have all sinned (Romans 3:23). We have all tried to do things our way and live selfishly, but God put all our sins on Jesus. "God made Him who had no sin to be sin for us..." (2 Corinthians 5:23).

7 He was oppressed, and He was afflicted, yet He opened not His mouth. He was led as a lamb to the slaughter, and as a sheep before her shearers is silent, so He opened not His mouth.

7. Jesus did not scream and yell at His enemies when they took Him to the cross. In fact, He died willingly. He said, "No one takes my life. I have power to lay it down and I have power to take it up" (John 10:18). He could have called 12 legions of angels to save Him, but He didn't (Matthew 26:53).

8 He was taken from prison and from judgment. And who shall declare His generation? For He was cut off from the land of the living; for the transgression of my people He was stricken.

8. Jesus did not get a fair trial. The rulers brought in "false witnesses" to say things about Him (Mark 14:56). He died because of our sins!

9 And He made His grave with the wicked, and with the rich in His death; because He had done no violence, neither was any deceit in His mouth.

9. When He was crucified, two robbers were crucified at the same time (Matthew 27:38). Jesus' cross was between their crosses. But, after Jesus died, Joseph of Arimathea, a rich man who believed on Jesus, took His body and placed it in his new tomb.

10 Yet it pleased the LORD to bruise Him. He has put him to grief. When You make His soul an offering for sin, He shall see His seed, He shall prolong His days, and the pleasure of the LORD shall prosper in His hand

10. It was God's will that His Son die on the cross for our sins. This is the only way we can be saved. After 3 days, Jesus arose from the grave. He lived again on the earth for a while to show His disciples that He was God's Son, and then He went to heaven and lives now at God's right hand.

Figure 14.3

Isaiah 53:11-12

11 He shall see the labor of His soul and shall be satisfied. By His knowledge My righteous Servant shall justify many, for He shall bear their iniquities.

11. God was pleased or satisfied with what Jesus did when He died on the cross because that meant that God could save us.

12 Therefore I will divide Him a portion with the great, and He shall divide the spoil with the strong, because He poured out His soul unto death, and He was numbered with the transgressors, and He bore the sin of many, and made intercession for the transgressors.

12. Because Jesus died, God has given Him all power in heaven and on earth (Matthew 28:18). God has "highly exalted Jesus and has given Him a name that is above every name, that at the name of Jesus every knee should bow and every tongue confess that Jesus is Lord to the glory of God" (Philippians 2:9-11). Jesus is now "at the right hand of God, exalted" (Acts 2:36).

Jesus died for you and me!
This was in God's plan to save us from our sins.
Jesus is the "Lamb of God who takes away the sins of the world" (John 1:29).
God offered the sacrifice for sin in the Garden of Eden when He sacrificed
an animal (a lamb) to make tunics of skin to cover the shame of sin.
All the sacrifices for sin throughout the Old Testament were shadows
of that perfect sacrifice--the Lamb of God. Isaiah prophesied in detail
about the sacrifice of Jesus in chapter 53. This was about 700 years
before Jesus was born. Fulfilled prophecy is a proof that the Bible
is from God and not from man. The Bible is the only "sacred book"
that has one unifying theme and story--"For God so loved the world
that He gave His only begotten Son, that whoever believes in Him
should not perish but have everlasting life" (John 3:16).

Figure 14.3

Old Testament

Isaiah 53:1-6

1 Who has believed our report? And to whom has the arm of the LORD been revealed? 2 For He shall grow up before Him as a tender plant, and as a root out of dry ground. He has no form or comeliness; and when we see Him, there is no beauty that we should desire Him. 3 He is despised and rejected by men, a Man of sorrows and acquainted with grief. and we hid, as it were, our faces from Him; He was despised, and we did not esteem Him.

4 Surely He has borne our griefs and carried our sorrows; yet we esteemed Him stricken, smitten by God, and afflicted.

5 But He was wounded for our transgressions, He was bruised for our iniquities; the chastisement for our peace was upon Him, and by His stripes we are healed.

6 All we like sheep have gone astray; we have turned, every one, to his own way; and the LORD has laid on Him the iniquity of us all.

New Testament

John 12:37-38

But although He had done so many signs before them, they did not believe in Him, 38 that the word of Isaiah the prophet might be fulfilled, which he spoke:

"Lord, who has believed our report? And to whom has the arm of the LORD been revealed?"

Matthew 8:16-17

When evening had come, they brought to Him many who were demon-possessed. And He cast out the spirits with a word, and healed all who were sick, 17 that it might be fulfilled which was spoken by Isaiah the prophet, saying:

"He Himself took our infirmities And bore our sicknesses."

1 Peter 2:24-25

24... who Himself bore our sins in His own body on the tree, that we, having died to sins, might live for righteousness -- by whose stripes you were healed.

25 For you were like sheep going astray, but have now returned to the Shepherd and Overseer of your souls.

Figure 14.4

Old Testament

Isaiah 53:7-12

7 He was oppressed and He was afflicted, yet He opened not His mouth; He was led as a lamb to the slaughter, and as a sheep before its shearers is silent, so He opened not His mouth. 8 He was taken from prison and from judgment, and who will declare His generation? For He was cut off from the land of the living; for the transgressions of My people He was stricken.

9 And they made His grave with the wicked – but with the rich at His death, because He had done no violence, nor was any deceit in His mouth.
10 Yet it pleased the LORD to bruise Him; He has put Him to grief. when You make His soul an offering for sin, He shall see His seed, He shall prolong His days, and the pleasure of the LORD shall prosper in His hand. 11 He shall see the labor of His soul, and be satisfied. By His knowledge My righteous Servant shall justify many, for He shall bear their iniquities.

12 Therefore I will divide Him a portion with the great, and He shall divide the spoil with the strong, because He poured out His soul unto death, and He was numbered with the transgressors, and He bore the sin of many, and made intercession for the transgressors.

New Testament

Acts 8:30-36

30 So Philip ran to him, and heard him reading the prophet Isaiah, and said, "Do you understand what you are reading?" 31 And he said, "How can I, unless someone guides me?" And he asked Philip to come up and sit with him. 32 The place in the Scripture which he read was this:

"He was led as a sheep to the slaughter;
And as a lamb before its shearer is silent,
So He opened not His mouth.
33 In His humiliation His justice was taken away,
And who will declare His generation?
For His life is taken from the earth."

34 So the eunuch answered Philip and said, "I ask you, of whom does the prophet say this, of himself or of some other man?" 35 Then Philip opened his mouth, and beginning at this Scripture, preached Jesus to him.

1 Peter 2:21-22

21 For to this you were called, because Christ also suffered for us, leaving us an example, that you should follow His steps:
22 "Who committed no sin,
Nor was deceit found in His mouth";

Luke 22:37

37 For I say to you that this which is written must still be accomplished in Me: 'And He was numbered with the transgressors.' For the things concerning Me have an end."

Figure 14.4

Chapter 15
BEAUTIFUL ZION

*E*very time I think about the great biblical theme of "Zion," I'm reminded of Tchaikovsky's "1812 Overture." If you are familiar with that famous piece of music, you know that it begins very softly; the melody can hardly be heard. However, you dare not increase the volume, because as the piece continues, the sound intensifies until finally bells are ringing and cannons are firing as the orchestra reaches the magnificent crescendo.

The first mention of Zion in the Old Testament is in 2 Sam. 5:7: "Nevertheless David took the stronghold of Zion (that is, the City of David)." It is just a fortress that David conquered and later lived in. For that reason, it became known as the City of David. However, in God's eternal purpose, this physical stronghold has greater significance. "Zion" is mentioned 171 times in the Old Testament (NKJV); of those times, about 165 refer to the idealized Zion—the true stronghold for God's people, where God dwells, and where salvation is found. Several of these also refer to both the physical and spiritual Zion. I don't want to get too technical, but I need to mention, also, that sometimes Zion is compared and/or contrasted with Mount Sinai, and sometimes both figures are mixed as in Isaiah 2. Trace out many of those references for yourself, but I will mention just a few of my favorites here:

Ps. 2:6 – "I have set My King on My holy hill of Zion."

Ps. 14:7 – "Oh, that the salvation of Israel would come out of Zion!"

Ps. 50:2 – "Out of Zion, the perfection of beauty, God will shine forth."

Ps. 74:2 – "Remember Your congregation, which You have purchased of old, the tribe of Your inheritance, which You have redeemed—this Mount Zion where You have dwelt."

Ps. 132:13 – "For the LORD has chosen Zion; He has desired it for His dwelling place:"

Zech. 2:10-11 – "'Sing and rejoice, O daughter of Zion! For behold, I am coming and I will dwell in your midst,' says the LORD."

As you read some of the selections in the Old Testament about Zion, it is obvious that God is not speaking of a physical place on earth in which to dwell. Listen to the words of Solomon: "But will God indeed dwell with men on the earth? Behold, heaven and the heaven of heavens cannot contain You. How much less this temple which I have built!" (2 Chron. 6:18). When we turn to the New Testament, we hear the song about Zion reach the crescendo:

> **Heb. 12:22-24** – But you have come to Mount Zion and to the city of the living God, the heavenly Jerusalem, to an innumerable company of angels, to the general assembly and church of the firstborn who are registered in heaven, to God the Judge of all, to the spirits of just men made perfect, to Jesus the Mediator of the new covenant, and to the blood of sprinkling that speaks better things than that of Abel.

Of all the passages in the prophets about Zion, Isaiah 60 is the most detailed, beautiful, and interesting. Children are excited when they see the beauty of God's Holy City—what it will be like when the Redeemer comes to Zion (Isa. 59:20). There are also excellent applications as you will see in our discussion of this marvelous chapter. In this entire chapter, Jehovah is speaking to His people who, returning from Babylonian captivity, would see physical Zion and rejoice. However, that rejoicing cannot compare to the rejoicing when all nations see spiritual Zion. Also, the physical city of David and of Jerusalem never reached the height that is described in this chapter, so we know the prophet is speaking of a better city. This chapter and the two following are unique in that God has no rebuke of His people for their sins. Instead, He looks into the future when His true Zion, the work of His hand and the branch of His planting (60:21) will be a reality. Thus, as Hailey explains, "From the ashes of physical Zion, which fades into the background, arises the splendor of the new city under the Messiah. In highly poetic language the prophet extols the glory of Jehovah's holy city (v.14). As he does so, Isaiah weaves into the picture images from various realms of creation—light, man, animals, gold, incense, birds, the majestic trees of the forest" (Hailey 1985, 485-486).

I have taught this both to children and adults. When I teach adults, I usually read the entire chapter and then discuss it by grouping the verses in outline format: Zion is glorious because (1) Jehovah is present; (2) her children return; (3) the nations bring their wealth to her; (4) her people are righteous; and (5) Jehovah is her everlasting light. However, I've also taught this to adults by the same basic method I use with children. When I teach children, I usually read the chapter and explain it as we read through it. Sometimes, I ask the children to read it aloud. You can decide which works best for the children you are teaching. I have put my comments in braces after each verse (or group of verses) in case you want to use that with your students. To make this a little clearer, I have put the verses in italics and have the verse numbers on the left side instead of in paragraph form. You will want to choose what to say from each of these verses, considering the age and Bible knowledge of the children. I have the application lessons at the end.

Isaiah 60, Jehovah speaks:

1 *Arise, shine; for your light has come! And the glory of the LORD is risen upon you.* {In Isaiah 6, the seraphim shouted that "the whole earth is full of His glory." In a very special way, though, Jehovah is giving His glory to Zion.}

2 *For behold, the darkness shall cover the earth, and deep darkness the people; but the LORD will arise over you, and His glory will be seen upon you.*

3 *The Gentiles shall come to your light, and kings to the brightness of your rising.* {Remember what we learned in Isaiah 9—"the people who walked in darkness have seen a great light; those who dwelt in the land of the shadow of death, upon them a light has shined" (v. 2). Do you remember why those people had seen a great light? Verse 6 gives the answer. Also, from John 8:12, we learn that Jesus is the Light of the World. Teachers of older children will want to refer to John 1:4-9 as John discusses Jesus as the "true Light which gives light to every man."}

4 *Lift up your eyes all around, and see: They all gather together, they come to you; your sons shall come from afar, and your daughters shall be nursed at your side.* {These picture the returning remnant from Babylon, but also, those are returning to Zion with great joy because the Redeemer has come.}

5 *Then you shall see and become radiant, and your heart shall swell with joy; because the abundance of the sea shall be turned to you, the wealth of the Gentiles shall come to you.* {Zion will have great wealth! The next 2 verses describe the wealth in terms people of that time could understand. This is not to be taken literally, but is a picture of what it will be like when Jesus comes—what His people and His kingdom will be like. It will be magnificent and wealthy!}

6 *The multitude of camels shall cover your land, the dromedaries of Midian and Ephah; all those from Sheba shall come; they shall bring gold and incense, and they shall proclaim the praises of the LORD.*

7 *All the flocks of Kedar shall be gathered together to you, the rams of Nebaioth shall minister to you; they shall ascend with acceptance on My altar, and I will glorify the house of My glory.*

8 *Who are these who fly like a cloud, and like doves to their roosts?* {This question turns our attention from the wealth coming into the city to the people coming from afar—like doves coming home to roost.}

9 *Surely the coastlands shall wait for Me; and the ships of Tarshish will come first, to bring your sons from afar, their silver and their gold with them, to the name of the LORD your God, and to the Holy One of Israel, because He has glorified you.* {Those who had been scattered will return from distant lands, coming in ships, and they will bring their wealth, too. Notice that people are coming to Zion because they see she is glorified, that God is with her. Remember that Jesus said, "A city that is set on a hill cannot be hidden" (Matt. 5:14).}

10 *The sons of foreigners shall build up your walls, and their kings shall minister to you; for in My wrath I struck you, but in My favor I have had mercy on you.* {The sons of foreigners did not help build the walls of Jerusalem when the remnant returned. In fact, foreigners tried to keep them from building the wall (Neh. 4). Now, though, foreigners are involved in building up Zion. This reminds me of a prophecy made

by Amos about 40 years earlier: "On that day I will raise up the tabernacle of David which has fallen down, and repair its damages; I will raise up its ruins and rebuild it as in the days of old; that they may possess the remnant of Edom, and all the Gentiles who are called by My name" (Amos 9:11-12). In the New Testament, in Acts 15, when the leaders of the church met in Jerusalem to settle the question of whether the Gentiles can be saved by faith in Christ without circumcision and keeping the Law, James quotes these verses from Amos 9 and concludes with, "Known to God from eternity are all His works" (Acts 15:18). James is telling us that the salvation of the Gentiles was in God's eternal purpose and that Amos was predicting exactly that. When we look at Zion—the Church—today, we see people from every nation building in the kingdom. Is this what we saw in Isaiah 2? Did we see a similar picture in Isaiah 25—people from all nations seated at God's banquet table? This could not and did not happen until Jesus broke down "that middle wall of separation," created "in Himself one new man from the two," and reconciled "them both to God in one body through the cross" (Eph. 2:14-16).}

11 *Therefore your gates shall be open continually; they shall not be shut day or night, that men may bring to you the wealth of the Gentiles, and their kings in procession.* {No physical city in ancient times would leave the gates open continually, so this is another clue that this is not literal language. This suggests that only those who are supposed to come into Zion will come, and that no one is turned away. Children like this mention of wealth again, so don't overlook it!}

12 *For the nation and kingdom which will not serve you shall perish, and those nations shall be utterly ruined.* {It is true that some people will reject the gospel. Some will reject the wealth of God's blessings for the empty promises of Satan. Sadly, they will be destroyed.}

13 *The glory of Lebanon shall come to you, the cypress, the pine, and the box tree together, to beautify the place of My sanctuary; and I will make the place of My feet glorious.* {The trees of Lebanon adorned Solomon's temple, and you may want to ask the children if they remember that, or just remind them as you come to this verse. The finest woods will be in Zion in order that the place where God dwells will be glorious. As we noted at the first, God doesn't dwell in earthly, physical temples. This is another indication that the language is figurative.}

14 *Also the sons of those who afflicted you shall come bowing to you, and all those who despised you shall fall prostrate at the soles of your feet; and they shall call you The City of the LORD, Zion of the Holy One of Israel.* {Two important facts are alluded to here. First, former enemies will be coming to Zion and honoring the inhabitants of the great city. Refer back to the comments on verse 10. Second, the name of the city is important: "The City of the LORD, Zion of the Holy One of Israel." Zion is where God lives, and we'll see an application of that as we conclude.}

15 *Whereas you have been forsaken and hated, so that no one went through you, I will make you an eternal excellence, a joy of many generations.*

16 *You shall drink the milk of the Gentiles, and milk the breast of kings; you shall know that I, the LORD, am your Savior and your Redeemer, the Mighty One of Jacob.* {Israel's rebellion and sin could not thwart God's eternal purpose. God disciplined His people, preserved those who would be faithful, and worked His purpose through physical Zion to bring about the more glorious, wealthy, and prosperous spiritual Zion.}

17 *Instead of bronze I will bring gold, instead of iron I will bring silver, instead of wood, bronze, and instead of stones, iron. I will also make your officers peace, and your magistrates righteousness.* {Children like this verse! Everything is better in Zion! Notice the progression from good to better in verse 17. For older children, you may want to reference the theme of the book of Hebrews, that everything is better in Christ—a better sacrifice, a better altar, a better covenant, a better High Priest, a better tabernacle, a better city, and a better rest.}

18 *Violence shall no longer be heard in your land, neither wasting nor destruction within your borders; but you shall call your walls Salvation, and your gates Praise.* {There is safety in this city! We saw a similar picture on the highway of holiness in Isaiah 35:8-10; no lions or ravenous beasts were on it. Notice that the walls are "Salvation" and the gates are "Praise." Those who are in the city are saved, and they enter in humility and praise—joyful as they come into the city.}

19 *The sun shall no longer be your light by day, nor for brightness shall the moon give light to you; but the LORD will be to you an everlasting light, and your God your glory.*

20 *Your sun shall no longer go down, nor shall your moon withdraw itself; for the LORD will be your everlasting light, and the days of your mourning shall be ended.* {Jehovah is the everlasting light and glory of Zion! This verse also reminds me of the statement by Hailey that I quoted at the beginning: "From the ashes of physical Zion… arises the splendor of the new city under the Messiah." Their mourning has ended because they now see the glorious purpose for the salvation of all men that God was working through them.}

21 *Also your people shall all be righteous; they shall inherit the land forever, the branch of My planting, the work of My hands, that I may be glorified.* {I'm smiling as I begin this comment. I ask the children, "Who lives in Zion?" Then, I point them to verse 21, telling them or letting them discover that righteous people live there. However, they always correct me! They say, "No, not just righteous people, but rich and righteous people! Remember all the gold and silver and great treasure that people brought into Zion from all over the world?" And, I must agree. Rich and righteous people are citizens of Zion. Notice, too, that the Zion Isaiah is telling us about was not built by men, but by God. This is a strong indicator that Zion is a spiritual city, not a physical one built by men. We see also the reason for Zion's existence—"that

I may be glorified." I'm reminded of Ephesians 1:6, 12 where Paul tells us that God saved us that we might be "to the praise of the glory of His grace" (v. 6), and that His eternal purpose is "to the praise of His glory" (v.12).}

22 A little one shall become a thousand, and a small one a strong nation. I, the LORD, will hasten it in its time. {In the world's view, Israel was a small nation and the Jews were few in number. However, God had promised that Abraham's descendants would be in number like the sand on the seashore or the stars in the heavens. This was never true of the earthly nation, but it is true of the spiritual nation, for "...if you are Christ's, then you are Abraham's seed, and heirs according to the promise" (Gal. 3:26-29). What assurance do we have that all these blessings will be in Zion? Jehovah will bring it about at the right time. Does this remind you of Galatians 4:4? "But when the fullness of the time had come, God sent forth His son, born of a woman, born under the law, to redeem those who were under the law..."}

Hints on how to illustrate Isaiah 60:

I have used the "Bible in Felt" figures to illustrate all these verses. I had to construct a city from gold felt since one did not come with the set. Then, as I would read each verse, I would add figures to represent the things described. I had to be a bit creative, using figures of kings, queens, a treasure chest, a flock of sheep, etc. It wasn't as good as Roy Johnson's drawings that accompany this lesson, but it did get the message across. At verse 14, I placed a sign that said, "The City of the LORD, Zion of the Holy One of Israel." Then, at verse 18, I put the words "salvation" on the walls and "praise" on the gates of my felt city. For verses 19 and 20, I placed a bright figure of the sun that represented God as the light of the city. The felt is still a good way to illustrate Bible truths; children (and adults) respond to the colorful picture and remember the prophecy and its meaning.

Roy's pictures illustrate this prophecy well. He provided three panels, two showing the people and wealth coming into the city from each side (figures 15.1a and 15.1b) and the third with the two panels together (figure 15.2). You can use these in any way, depending on the age of the children. I've found that teens and adults respond well to these pictures. Figure 15.2 is good to give to each child and have him/her write the words on it from verses 14, 18, 19, and 20.

Some applications:

Figure 15.3 is another picture of Zion that Roy illustrated earlier. I added the plan of salvation so you could use it for the first major application: "How do we enter Zion, God's city?" I have included some scriptures that show us how we are saved, how we become the righteous people who can live in Zion. Another point you want to make with this application is that once we come into Zion, we need to stay there. Satan will try to get us to come out of the city and enter his "Fun and Games City." Also, as we are on our journey to Zion, Satan will try to lure us away to his city. You can use the example of "fool's gold" and of manmade diamonds or emeralds that can trick the person who doesn't know what the real jewels are like and who doesn't test them. Figure 15.5 shows Satan's city where we don't want to go.

I ask the children if Isaiah saw one city or several small cities inside the walls of Zion. They always answer correctly—Isaiah saw one city. Zion—where Jehovah dwells—is not made up of many separate cities with different ways to enter them. Figure 15.4 illustrates this application. You may want to use scriptures about the unity of the church like Matt. 16:15-16 and Eph. 4:4-6 with older children and teens.

Since world religions are right here in our neighborhoods and children are being inundated with the message that these are all equal, I have included figure 15.6 that will help you make the point that Zion is not equal with all those other cities. Zion is where Jehovah dwells. Zion is more valuable than all the riches in the entire world. Zion is eternal. Don't you want to live in Zion? I do!

Concluding comments:

We sing many songs about Zion, and children are usually familiar with most of them. One that I like to use at the end is "We're Marching to Zion." Children see immediately that we're actually living in Zion. However, I explain that there is also a sense in which we are marching to Zion, because we haven't entered the eternal rest in heaven. I share with them that when we sing this song in worship, I usually sing "we're living in Zion…" on the first verses and "we're marching to Zion…" on the last verse. Another song that I think tells the message of Isaiah better than any other is "Glorious Things of Thee are Spoken." I suggest you bring that to class and read it to your students or sing it with them. "Zion's Call" is another good song, and it can be used with Isaiah 2 as well.

This is one of my favorite prophecies to share with children. They quickly see the picture Jehovah paints through the words of Isaiah. Hopefully, this will help them value the church throughout their lives. If Zion is so valuable and beautiful, wouldn't we want all our friends and family to live there? "Zion's call is ringing, / Coming from the throne above, / While we hear it ringing, / Let us heed the call of love" (J. R. Baxter, Jr., 1944).

"The wealth of the Gentiles shall come to you."

Isaiah 60:5

The camels and dromedaries of Midian and Ephah and all those from Sheba shall come bringing gold and incense. They shall proclaim the praises of the LORD.

vs. 6-7

Figure 15.1a

"The Wealth of the Gentiles Shall Come to You."
Isaiah 60:5

"Surely the
coastlands shall
wait for Me;
And the ships of
Tarshish will come
first, to bring your
sons from afar,
their silver and their
gold with them,
to the name of the
LORD your God,
and to the Holy One
of Israel, because
He has glorified
you." (v.9)

Figure 15.1b

"The City of the LORD, Zion of the Holy One of Israel."
Isaiah 60:14

Art by Roy Johnson

"The sun shall no longer be your light by day, nor for brightness shall the moon give light to you; but the LORD will be to you an everlasting light, and your God your glory. Your sun shall no longer go down, nor shall your moon withdraw itself; for the LORD will be your everlasting light, and the days of your mourning shall be ended. Also **your people shall all be righteous**; they shall inherit the land forever, the branch of My planting, the work of My hands, **that I may be glorified**." – Isaiah 60:19-21

Don't you want to live in Zion where the rich and righteous people live?

Figure 15.2

THE CITY OF THE LORD, ZION OF THE HOLY ONE OF ISRAEL

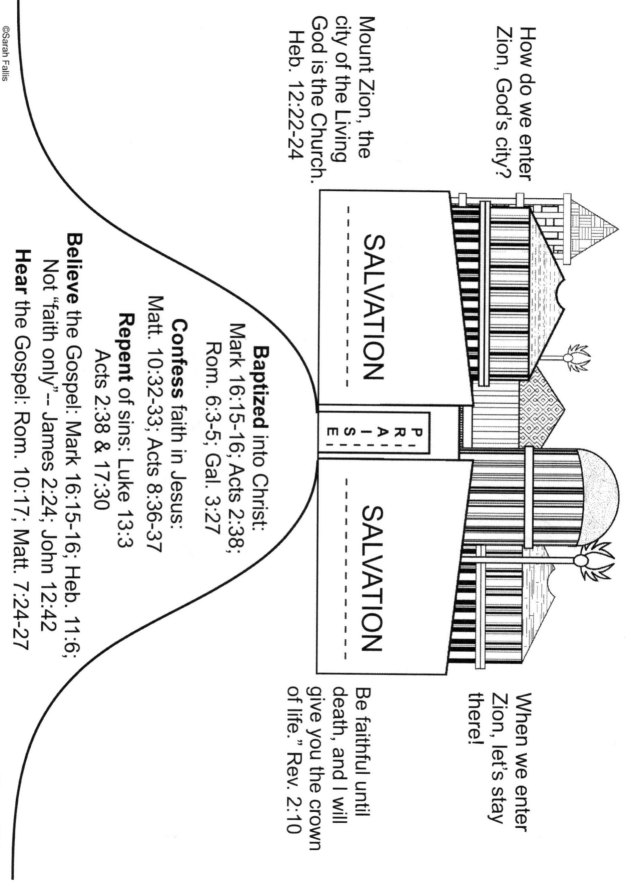

How do we enter Zion, God's city?

Mount Zion, the city of the Living God is the Church. Heb. 12:22-24

Baptized into Christ: Mark 16:15-16; Acts 2:38; Rom. 6:3-5; Gal. 3:27

Confess faith in Jesus: Matt. 10:32-33; Acts 8:36-37

Repent of sins: Luke 13:3 Acts 2:38 & 17:30

Believe the Gospel: Mark 16:15-16; Heb. 11:6; Not "faith only"-- James 2:24; John 12:42

Hear the Gospel: Rom. 10:17; Matt. 7:24-27

SALVATION

SALVATION

PRAISE

When we enter Zion, let's stay there!

Be faithful until death, and I will give you the crown of life." Rev. 2:10

Figure 15.3a

How do we enter Zion?
Read the verses and write the steps on the road.

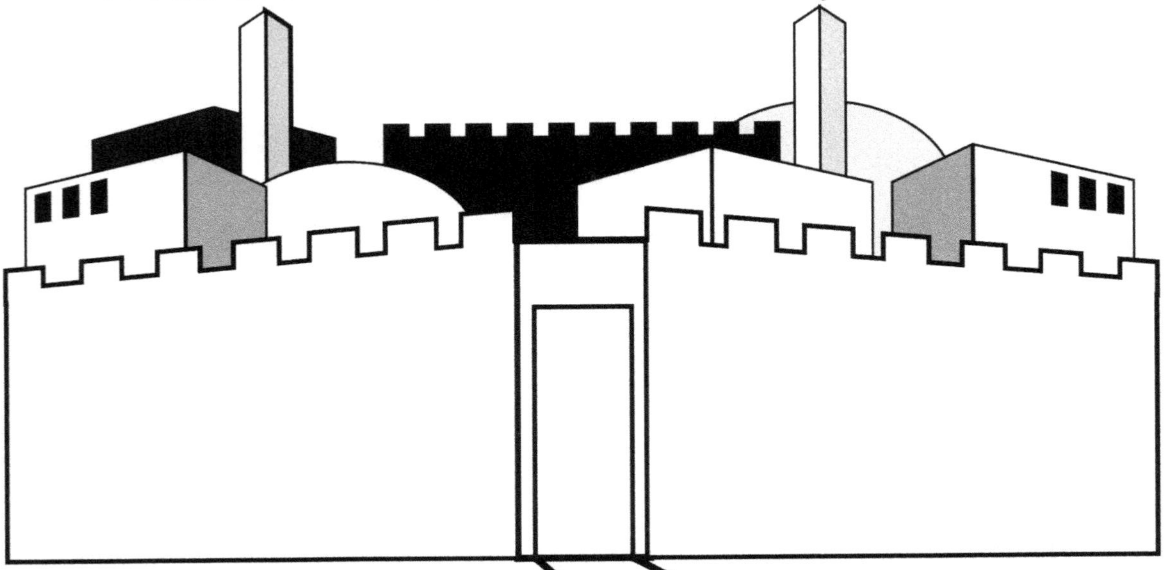

Write "salvation" on the walls.
Write "praise" on the gate.

Romans 10:17
Hebrews 11:6
Luke 13;3
Acts 8:36-37
Acts 2:38

Read Revelation 2:10
and write "stay in the city"
on one of the buildings.

Figure 15.3b

All who claim to be "Christians" are in God's City!

It doesn't matter what you believe as long as you are sincere.

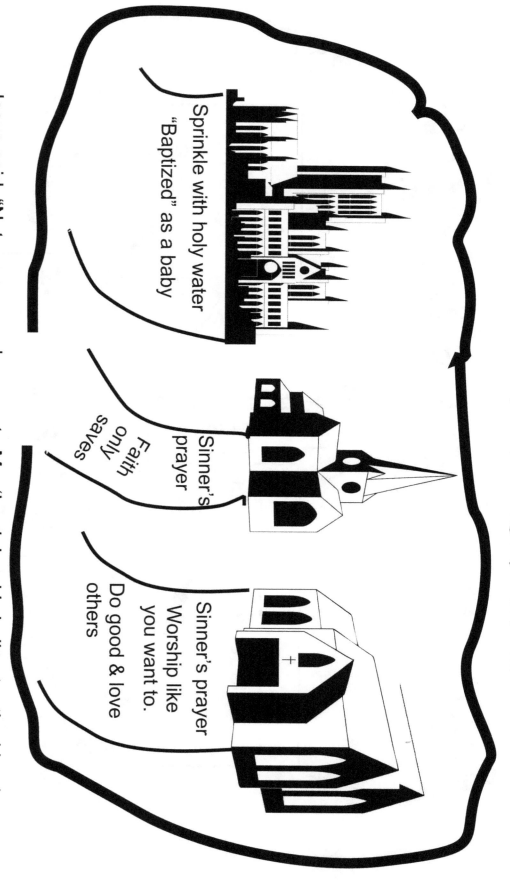

Sprinkle with holy water

"Baptized" as a baby

Sinner's prayer

Faith only saves

Sinner's prayer

Worship like you want to.

Do good & love others

Jesus said, "Not everyone who says to Me, 'Lord, Lord,' shall enter the kingdom of heaven, but he who does the will of My Father in heaven." – Matt. 7:21

Figure 15.4

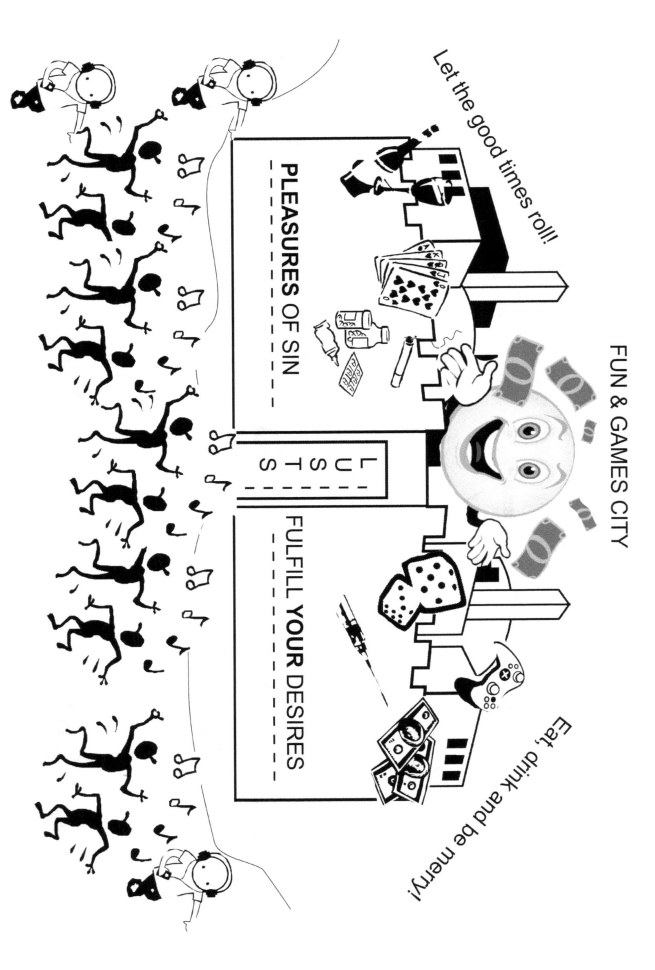

Let the good times roll!

FUN & GAMES CITY

Eat, drink and be merry!

PLEASURES OF SIN

LUST

FULFILL YOUR DESIRES

©Sarah Fallis

They don't know: "**The wages of sin is death.**"-- Rom. 6:23

Figure 15.5

ANY CITY IS GREAT!

Choose the path you want to walk.

Every path leads to deity.

Choose the god you like best.

They don't know: Jesus said, "I am the way, the truth, and the life. **No one comes to the Father except through me.**" --John 14:6

©Sarah Fallis

Figure 15.6

Chapter 16
NEW CLOTHES AND A NEW NAME

*I*saiah chapters 61 and 62 continue the theme of Zion's future glory, but from different perspectives and with different figures. However, after studying chapter 60, it is natural and easy to key back into the beautiful picture Jehovah creates as He pours forth His glory on His people. The speaker in verses 1-3 comes on the scene suddenly and without introduction, but there are at least two clues to His identity. First, "The Spirit of the Lord God is upon Me…" (v. 1) is a phrase we have heard before. Children will remember that in Isa. 11:2, the Spirit was on the Branch of Jehovah. Second, Jesus quotes this passage in Luke 4, saying it is fulfilled in Him. Teachers, note that Jesus said, "**Today** this Scripture is **fulfilled** in your hearing" (v.21). He did not say that sometime in the past the Scripture was fulfilled in the remnant of Israel, which is a popular liberal interpretation. He did not say that sometime in the future the Scripture would be fulfilled on earth when He comes again. Also, Jesus did not say, "I'm applying this Scripture to me so you will believe I am the Messiah." This is a popular teaching that is more subtly stated similar to: "Luke applied this to Christ to convince the Jews." Our children will hear such things from teachers they admire as they become adults, and we need to arm them with the Scripture.

I usually introduce chapter 61 to my students in the same way Granddaddy did to me. I read verses 1 and 2 and then ask, "Do you know that's speaking of Jesus?" Children in first through third grades may need you to go to Luke 4 and read that passage, but children a little older or who have good Bible knowledge will probably be able to answer the question without your help. They may not know exactly where it is located, but they will remember this dramatic event in Nazareth. You can use the scripture sheet at this point, having them highlight similar statements in the Old and New Testament in the same color. I also read or have them read 61:3 and ask if that sounds familiar. "To give them beauty for ashes, the oil of joy for mourning, the garment of praise for the spirit of heaviness" reminds us of 60:17, that everything in Zion is better. And, "…that they may be called trees of righteousness, the planting of the LORD, that He may be glorified" relates back to 60:21. Thus, the One who is speaking is the Messiah, the Redeemer who will come to Zion (59:20), Jehovah's righteous Servant (53:11), and the Branch of Jehovah (4:2).

Verses 4 and 5 relate back to chapter 60:10, and verse 7 relates to 60:17, so I usually just refer to those briefly. Notice verse 6: "But you shall be named the priests of the LORD, they shall call you the servants of our God." In the New Testament, Peter refers to Christians as "a holy priesthood" (1 Pet. 2:5) and John says that Jesus has made us "kings and priests to God" (Rev. 1:6). This is a point I usually make with older students. Also, the "everlasting covenant" in verse 8 is a concept that I tell students we will put on "hold" until we get to Jeremiah.

Now, we come to the last two verses of chapter 61, and children (especially the girls) enjoy this picture:

> I will greatly rejoice in the LORD,
>
> My soul shall be joyful in my God;
>
> For He has clothed me with the garments of salvation,
>
> He has covered me with the robe of righteousness,
>
> As a bridegroom decks himself with ornaments,
>
> And as a bride adorns herself with her jewels.
>
> For as the earth brings forth its bud,
>
> As the garden causes the things that are sown in it to spring forth,
>
> So the Lord GOD will cause righteousness and praise to spring forth before all the nations.

Questions and comments like this peak their interest: I like new, pretty clothes, don't you? Did you know God is giving His people new clothes? Have you been to a wedding? People always want to know what the bride's dress was like. If you read about weddings, there is always a detailed description of the brides' dress. Even though we don't get as excited about what the groom wears as we do about the bride, the groom usually wears a formal tuxedo, not tacky jeans. And, when we go to a wedding, we usually wear our nice clothes, don't we?

This is the picture Isaiah is painting for us to tell us how special we are to God. God gives us salvation and righteousness to wear. We don't earn this clothing; God gives it to us by His grace. The scripture sheets for this lesson will help you illustrate the meaning of this passage. I always refer to Isaiah 64:6, that "…all our righteousnesses are like filthy rags." This is how we are dressed without Christ, in dirty, ragged clothing. That's not a pretty picture. And, if you have on dirty clothes, you have to take them off before you can put on clean and beautiful clothes. You may even want to remind the children that the fig leaves Adam and the woman made to cover their nakedness were not a good covering. God shed the blood of an animal to provide proper clothing for them, and this was a shadow of how He would provide "garments of salvation" and "robes of righteousness" for us through the shedding of Jesus' blood—"the Lamb of God who takes away the sin of the world" (John 1:29).

Chapter 62 continues this theme of God's love for His people. I have two main lessons for children from this chapter in the first 3 verses:

> For Zion's sake I will not hold My peace,
>
> And for Jerusalem's sake I will not rest,
>
> Until her righteousness goes forth as brightness,

And her salvation as a lamp that burns.

2 The Gentiles shall see your righteousness,

And all kings your glory.

You shall be called by a new name,

Which the mouth of the LORD will name.

3 You shall also be a crown of glory

In the hand of the LORD,

And a royal diadem

In the hand of your God.

Lesson 1: A good way to introduce this lesson to children is to ask: Do you know people who think they are really special and that act like they are better than anyone else? Many of the Jews acted that way, because they had misunderstood the purpose for which God had chosen them. Before they were taken into Babylonian captivity, they thought they were especially important because the temple was in Jerusalem. They didn't think anyone could harm them since they had the temple. Even years after they returned to their homeland, many of them still had that idea.

God's glorious city, "the Zion of the Holy One of Israel," would be open to all people. Gentiles would come, bringing their wealth into His city, and foreigners would build the walls. This was a new idea to the Jewish people. Jehovah would bring about a totally new event in the earth when He sacrificed His Son, raised Him from the dead, and built His church. A new event, a new concept of God's city, demands a new name. And, Jehovah would be the one to give that name.

When would He give that new name? In verse 2, we see that Gentiles and kings had to see the righteousness and glory of Zion before the new name would be given. Now, let's review the book of Acts. Only Jews, Samaritans, and proselytes had become Christians in the first nine chapters. In chapter 10, God instructs Peter to go to Cornelius, who is a Gentile. Peter obeys and preaches to Cornelius and his household. They are baptized, and Peter stays there a few days. This is something new! God has accepted Gentiles into His kingdom in the same way He accepted the Jews. In Acts 11, Peter had to explain his actions to the Jewish Christians in Jerusalem. "When they heard these things they became silent; and they glorified God, saying, 'Then God has also granted to the Gentiles repentance to life'" (v. 18).

As we continue in Acts 11, several who had been scattered beyond Jerusalem because of the persecution after Stephen's death (8:4) began preaching to the Greeks, "and a great number believed and turned to the Lord" (11:21). The church in Jerusalem sent Barnabas to Antioch, which was becoming a center for the large Gentile church. After encouraging the disciples, he went to Tarsus to find Saul (11:22-25). Why was it important to bring Saul to Antioch? Remember what Jesus had told Ananias about Saul in Acts 9:15: "…he is a chosen vessel of Mine to bear My name before Gentiles, kings, and the children of Israel…" Now the stage is set for the new name. "And the disciples were first called Christians in Antioch" (11:26). The new name that Jehovah would give His new creation would come when Gentiles and kings see the glory and righteous of Zion. That happened in Antioch, so it is fitting that the new name be given there. Notice, too, that Saul was to "bear My name before Gentiles..." The new name wasn't given until Saul—the name-bearer—arrived in Antioch.

Note to teachers: I realize there is some disagreement among good people about this "new name." Hailey says the identity is not clear and suggests it could be the names "Hephzibah" and "Beulah" mentioned in 62:4, or perhaps just a name that is known only to Jehovah and the inhabitants of Zion, citing Rev. 2:17; 3:12; 19:12 (Hailey 1985, 497). Keil and Delitzsch don't mention the name in their comments on Isaiah 62. There is a good argument for the name being "Christian" from the Greek word translated "were called" in Acts 11:26—that one of the meanings of that word is "by divine proclamation or intimation" (Strong's Definitions, PC Study Bible). As I studied this, I found Coffman's explanation to be the best. He mentions Saul (Paul) as the name-bearer and brings all the facts in Acts together with the conditions of the prophecy in Isaiah. You can read that free on www.StudyLight.org.

Lesson 2: God's love for Zion is pictured in verse 3; Zion is a "crown of glory" and "royal diadem" in Jehovah's hand. I tell children about visiting Scotland many years ago. We went into the castle at Edinburgh and saw the crown jewels of Scotland. On display were crowns worn by special kings and queens in their history and many other jewels like necklaces and scepters. These were in a very secure area and guards were stationed at the entry and exit. If you haven't had such an experience, you may want to bring pictures of the crown jewels of England or France, for instance. We are God's crown jewels! He wants us to always shine forth His beauty to others. Another mention of God's people as His jewels in Mal. 3:17, "'They shall be Mine,' says the LORD of hosts, 'On the day that I make them My jewels.'" Christians are God's special treasure!

There is an excellent application that flows from this short verse. Three times in Psalms, the declaration is made that the world and everything in it belongs to Jehovah (Ps. 24:1; 50:12; 89:11). How special is the world to Him? Peter tells us that the earth and everything in it will eventually be burned up (2 Pet. 3:10). So, the world is not the most special thing God owns, since He will destroy it someday. What is special to God? His treasures! His crown jewels! Now, there is a thief in this world, and he knows what is valuable to Jehovah. Satan is the thief, and he wants to steal you from God. Just like a thief has a tool kit, Satan does, too. He'll try to trick you, to deceive you, to make you quit listening to the truth, to discourage you, to make you think you're not important. He will use your friends or some of your family; he may use popularity or the sports or hobbies you enjoy. He may even try to make you think you're so smart you don't need God. You and I must be on guard so he can't steal us away from God (2 Cor. 2:11; 1 Pet. 5:8).

Concluding Comments:

This is the last of my favorite lessons for children from Isaiah. However, as I was studying Isaiah afresh for this book, I found some other lessons I want to teach. Those will have to be for another day. I hope these lessons have stirred your interest not only in Isaiah, but in all the prophets. Now, I'm looking forward to sharing some of my favorite lessons from the other prophets.

Old Testament

Isaiah 61:1-3

"The Spirit of the Lord GOD is upon Me,
Because the LORD has anointed Me
To preach good tidings to the poor;
He has sent Me to heal the brokenhearted,
To proclaim liberty to the captives,
And the opening of the prison to those who
are bound;
2 To proclaim the acceptable year of the
LORD,
And the day of vengeance of our God;
To comfort all who mourn,
3 To console those who mourn in Zion,
To give them beauty for ashes,
The oil of joy for mourning,
The garment of praise for the spirit of
heaviness;
That they may be called trees of
righteousness,
The planting of the LORD, that He may be
glorified."

Isaiah 53:2-3
He has no form or comeliness;
And when we see Him,
There is no beauty that we
should desire Him.
3 He is despised and rejected
by men,

New Testament

Luke 4:16-22

So He came to Nazareth, where He had
been brought up. And as His custom
was, He went into the synagogue on the
Sabbath day, and stood up to read. 17
And He was handed the book of the
prophet Isaiah. And when He had
opened the book, He found the place
where it was written:

18 "The Spirit of the LORD is upon Me,
Because He has anointed Me
To preach the gospel to the poor;
He has sent Me to heal the
brokenhearted,To proclaim liberty to the
captives
And recovery of sight to the blind,
To set at liberty those who are
oppressed;
19 To proclaim the acceptable year of the
LORD."

20 Then He closed the book, and gave it
back to the attendant and sat down. And
the eyes of all who were in the
synagogue were fixed on Him. 21 And
He began to say to them, "Today this
Scripture is fulfilled in your hearing." 22
So all bore witness to Him, and marveled
at the gracious words which proceeded
out of His mouth. And they said,"Is this
not Joseph's son?"

Luke 4:28-30

28 So all those in the synagogue, when
they heard these things, were filled with
wrath, 29 and rose up and thrust Him out
of the city; and they led Him to the brow
of the hill on which their city was built,
that they might throw Him down over the
cliff. 30 Then passing through the midst
of them, He went His way.

Figure 16.1

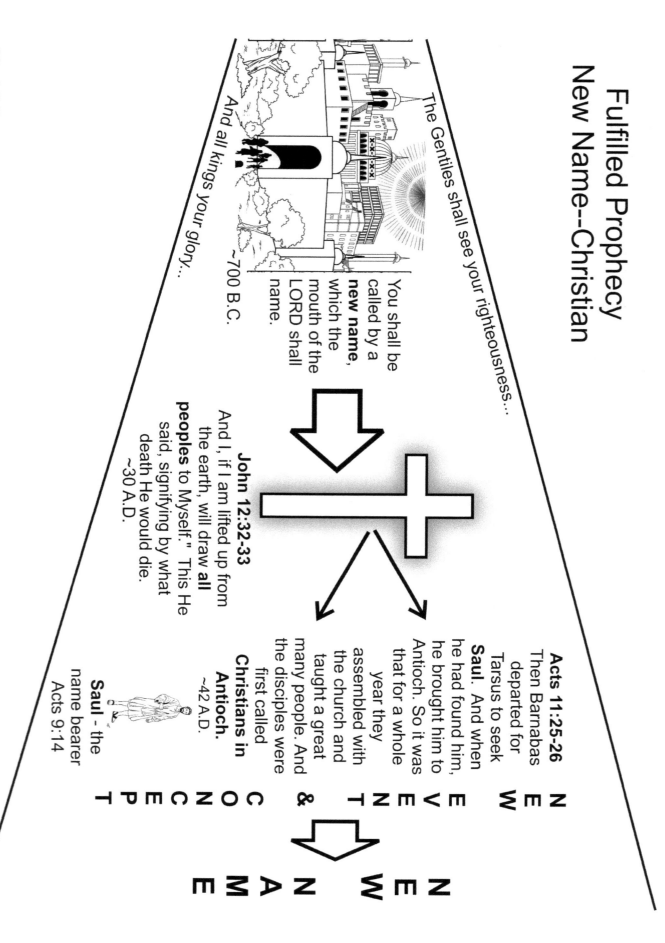

Fulfilled Prophecy
New Name--Christian

The Gentiles shall see your righteousness...

You shall be called by a **new name**, which the mouth of the LORD shall name.

And all kings your glory...

~700 B.C.

John 12:32-33
And I, if I am lifted up from the earth, will draw **all peoples** to Myself." This He said, signifying by what death He would die.
~30 A.D.

Acts 11:25-26
Then Barnabas departed for Tarsus to seek **Saul**. And when he had found him, he brought him to Antioch. So it was that for a whole year they assembled with the church and taught a great many people. And the disciples were first called **Christians in Antioch.**
~42 A.D.

Saul - the name bearer
Acts 9:14

N E W

N E V E N T

&

C O N C U

T P E T

N E W

N A M E

Figure 16.2

Background for Jeremiah, Ezekiel, and Daniel

Near the end of King Hezekiah's reign, Isaiah had told him that all his treasures, all the wealth of the people, and all of his descendants would be taken to Babylon after he died (Isa. 39:4-8; 2 Kings 20:15-19). This was approximately 100 years before Nebuchadnezzar came to Jerusalem and began the first of three deportations of Jews to Babylon. Though Josiah, Hezekiah's great-grandson, was zealous in destroying the idols and restoring true worship, his reforms could not make a permanent change in the hearts of the people. Judgement from God through Nebuchadnezzar had to come.

Jeremiah was the oldest of the three and began preaching when Ezekiel was about 5 years old. He warned of the destruction and pleaded with the people to surrender to Babylon so they would not be completely destroyed. They preferred the message of the false prophets, even after Nebuchadnezzar had taken two groups to Babylon. The end finally came when King Zedekiah rebelled. Jeremiah chose to stay with the few remaining Jews in the land. They rebelled and went to Egypt, taking Jeremiah with them. He died in Egypt with people who hated his message, but feared he was actually speaking for God.

Daniel was taken to Babylon in the first group of captives in 606, when Nebuchadnezzar took the brightest and best to serve in his palace. Daniel was God's prophet in the courts of the various kings of both Babylon and Persia. Through Daniel, God demonstrated numerous times that He truly is the God of all nations, not just the national god of the Jews.

Ezekiel was in the second group of 10,000 captives that included King Jehoiachin and the best of the people—artisans, soldiers, and princes. They were settled outside the city of Babylon in concentration camp type facilities. God called Ezekiel to demonstrate God's justice in His judgment, to extend His mercy toward those who would repent, and to prepare them for the destruction of Jerusalem and a long captivity. This was a most difficult task and required an unusual man. Ezekiel was that man.

Figure 17.0

Chapter 17
FOUR OBJECT LESSONS FROM JEREMIAH

Jeremiah had a very difficult task, and his ministry was plagued with constant persecution. When God called him, he first protested that he was too young to do the work, but God thought otherwise and assured Jeremiah, "Do not be afraid… I will be with you to deliver you" (1:8). Then He commissioned Jeremiah, "See, I have this day set you over the nations and over the kingdoms, to root out and to pull down, to destroy and to throw down, to build and to plant" (1:10). Would you like that job? There are two figures of speech used here: an agricultural picture and a construction picture.

Let's look at the agricultural picture first. The situation in Judah and Jerusalem could be described like a vineyard that has been overgrown with weeds, thorns, bushes, shrubs, and all kinds of vegetation that is worthless. It is about to choke out the good plants that are struggling to survive. Isaiah used a similar figure in Isa. 5:1-7. If any of the good plants can be saved and if new ones can be planted, this vineyard needs some major work—root out and destroy all the worthless vegetation. I grew up on a farm, and clearing land for planting is definitely harder than planting a new crop. Jeremiah is charged with both duties.

Now let's look at the construction picture. All of us have probably seen the demolition of old, useless buildings. Today, we do that with specially placed explosives, and the building comes down quickly. However, there is still the clearing out of all the debris before a new building can be constructed. What if you had to tear down those old buildings with the tools available in Jeremiah's time? And, what if you were the only one doing it? That would be a really tough job! After the old building is destroyed and the debris is cleared, a new building can be built.

Both of these pictures describe the condition of the people. Their hearts were filled with greed, idolatry, hatred, covetousness, and all kinds of evil. Their lives demonstrated the condition of their hearts. They bribed officials; they oppressed the poor; they offered sacrifices to idols, sometimes even burning their children to Molech. Their thinking was so perverted that they thought no one could destroy them because God's temple was in Jerusalem. In fact, they had done what no other nation had done—they had changed gods. "Has a nation changed its gods, which are not gods? But My people have changed their Glory for what does not profit" (2:11). This reminds me of Psalm 106:19-20 – "They made a calf in Horeb, / And worshiped the molded image. / Thus they changed their glory / Into the image of an ox that eats grass." Thus, God is the glory of His people. What a challenging and interesting thought! In the verses following, God uses another figure of speech. He says the people have left Him, "the fountain of living waters, and hewn themselves cisterns—broken cisterns that can hold no water" (v. 13).

Jeremiah was preaching the message of God's judgment with love for his people and sorrow in his heart. You would think that the other prophets and priests would appreciate his message and encourage him in his work, but that's where he met his greatest opposition. The prophets were saying Babylon would not destroy the city or the temple. And, when Nebuchadnezzar took two groups to Babylon in 606 and 597 B.C., the other prophets were saying their captivity would be only two years and there was nothing more to fear. Jeremiah's warnings fell on willfully deaf ears and into purposefully hardened hearts. Wickedness had overtaken God's people so there was no remedy. His message was destroyed by the king; he was imprisoned and put in stocks; he was laughed at, ridiculed, and scorned publicly. Many times he was discouraged and sometimes he wanted to give up, but in the prophet's own words, "His word was in my heart like a burning fire shut up in my bones; I was weary of holding it back, and I could not" (20:9). Jeremiah had to speak God's word!

The earlier generations had not listened to Isaiah's eloquent sermons and passionate pleadings. His masterful pictures of the Messiah and Zion seemed like "fairy tales" to them. Now, God would use Jeremiah and employ other methods along with the preaching to get His message across to the people. Jeremiah used several parables and illustrations like the broken cisterns and God's word as fire in his heart. He also used visual aids or object lessons. These are interesting to children and help them see that God wanted the people to understand His message and repent. In this chapter, I will deal with four of these object lessons, and you will find Roy's illustrations helpful as you teach these to children.

Object Lesson 1 – The Linen Sash:

Thus the LORD said to me: "Go and get yourself a linen sash, and put it around your waist, but do not put it in water." So I got a sash according to the word of the LORD, and put it around my waist.

And the word of the LORD came to me the second time, saying, "Take the sash that you acquired, which is around your waist, and arise, go to the Euphrates, and hide it there in a hole in the rock." So I went and hid it by the Euphrates, as the LORD commanded me.

Now it came to pass after many days that the LORD said to me, "Arise, go to the Euphrates, and take from there the sash which I commanded you to hide there." Then I went to the Euphrates and dug, and I took the sash from the place where I had hidden it; and there was the sash, ruined. It was profitable for nothing.

Then the word of the LORD came to me, saying, "Thus says the LORD: 'In this manner I will ruin the pride of Judah and the great pride of Jerusalem. This evil people, who refuse to hear My words, who follow the dictates of their hearts, and walk after other gods to serve them and worship them, shall be just like this sash which is profitable for nothing. For as the sash clings to the waist of a man, so I have caused the whole house of Israel and the whole house of Judah to cling to Me,' says the LORD, 'that they may become My people, for renown, for praise, and for glory; but they would not hear" (Jer. 13:1-11).

God explains the lesson to Jeremiah, and the picture is easy for children to see. You remember that God had promised Abraham that He would make a great nation of his descendants and bless all nations through One special person (Gen. 12:1-3; Gen 22:16). This promise was renewed to Isaac and to Jacob, showing them that they had a unique relationship with Him. In his farewell address to the newly formed nation, Moses reminded the people,

"For you are a holy people to the LORD your God; the LORD your God has chosen you to be a people for Himself, a special treasure above all the peoples on the face of the earth" (Deut. 7:6). As long as the people remained close to God and kept His Law, like the sash tied about Jeremiah's waist, they were safe and valuable. However, notice how Jehovah ends this explanation of the object lesson—"but they would not hear." How sad! They had become like that sash that Jeremiah hid in the rocky area. They were ragged, useless, and worthless. What do we do with clothing that is ragged and useless? We throw it away. This is what Jehovah was going to have to do with His people, those who were His special treasure. Figure 17.1 illustrates this object lesson.

Now, let's think about us and what we can learn from this object lesson. As long as we stay close to Jehovah, as long as we study His word, do His will, and live for Him even when it isn't the popular thing to do, we are valuable—God's special treasure. But, if we determine to go our own way, if we decide we know what is best for us, if we listen to Satan and follow friends, family, or teachers that would lead us away from God, we become worthless like a holey, shredded piece of cloth. I just thought of a play on words from this object lesson: Do you want to be holy or holey?

Object Lesson 2 – The Broken Flask:

Thus says the LORD: "Go and get a potter's earthen flask, and take some of the elders of the people and some of the elders of the priests. And go out to the Valley of the Son of Hinnom, which is by the entry of the Potsherd Gate; and proclaim there the words that I will tell you, and say, 'Hear the word of the LORD, O kings of Judah and inhabitants of Jerusalem. Thus says the LORD of hosts, the God of Israel: "Behold, I will bring such a catastrophe on this place, that whoever hears of it, his ears will tingle.

"Because they have forsaken Me and made this an alien place, because they have burned incense in it to other gods whom neither they, their fathers, nor the kings of Judah have known, and have filled this place with the blood of the innocents (they have also built the high places of Baal, to burn their sons with fire for burnt offerings to Baal, which I did not command or speak, nor did it come into My mind), therefore behold, the days are coming," says the LORD, "that this place shall no more be called Tophet or the Valley of the Son of Hinnom, but the Valley of Slaughter. And I will make void the counsel of Judah and Jerusalem in this place, and I will cause them to fall by the sword before their enemies and by the hands of those who seek their lives; their corpses I will give as meat for the birds of the heaven and for the beasts of the earth. I will make this city desolate and a hissing; everyone who passes by it will be astonished and hiss because of all its plagues. And I will cause them to eat the flesh of their sons and the flesh of their daughters, and everyone shall eat the flesh of his friend in the siege and in the desperation with which their enemies and those who seek their lives shall drive them to despair.'"

"Then you shall break the flask in the sight of the men who go with you, and say to them, 'Thus says the LORD of hosts: "Even so I will break this people and this city, as one breaks a potter's vessel, which cannot be made whole again; and they shall bury them in Tophet till there is no place to bury. Thus I will do to this place," says the LORD, "and to its inhabitants, and make this city like Tophet. And the houses of Jerusalem and the houses of the kings of Judah shall be defiled like the place of Tophet, because of all the houses on whose roofs they have burned incense to all the host of heaven, and poured out drink offerings to other gods"'" (Jer. 19:1-13).

This object lesson is probably best for children in fifth grade or above because there is some very graphic description of the unusual and extreme catastrophe that is coming on Judah. When you teach this, I think it is important to do some research into the worship of Baal, Ashtoreth, and Molech. Sometimes we give our students the idea that worship of idols just involved bowing down to wood, stone, or other engraved and ornate images. This worship involved all kinds of sexual immorality. Many of the symbols were also sexual in nature. The "sacred pillars" that are mentioned throughout the Old Testament were probably phallic symbols. Some may have been representations of gods or goddess, but whatever their exact meaning, they had something to do with pagan worship. There's an interesting comment about Asa, king of Judah, in 1 Kings 15:13 – "Also he removed Maachah his grandmother from being queen mother, because she had made an obscene image of Asherah. And Asa cut down her obscene image and burned it by the Brook Kidron." We have already noted that worship of Molech involved child sacrifice, and this passage in Jeremiah states that was true of Baal worship as well. Of course, teachers should use wisdom in explaining this to children. I remember a kindergarten teacher telling me that she just explained to her children that when people worshiped these other gods, it caused them to do many horrible things like mothers and fathers not loving each other and not really caring for their children.

Homer Hailey, in commenting on Israel's failure to become what God had desired, lists two contributing factors—wealth in the form of a rich and fertile land, and worship of the Canaanite gods. Why would God's people be tempted to worship Baal and these other gods? I find it hard to improve on Hailey's explanation, and I offer it here to help you decide how to best present this concept to the children in your classes:

Canaanitish gods were totally immoral. I mean by that, the worshipers were expected to engage in every sensual and immoral practice their minds could invent as acts of worship to their gods. The Canaanitish women practiced prostitution as a part of the worship of their fertility deity; their festivals and pagan rites were of the most sensual and lascivious sort, and sexual orgies were a normal and accepted part of their religious practice. All of this, of course, would have a strong appeal to the men of Israel, and tend to draw them away from the strict moral code which God had laid down to govern them. God's laws were strict and unyielding; they demanded that the desires and lusts of the flesh be held fully in check. Now, adding all of these things together—an unusual and strange prosperity, a sensual worship, in strong contrast to the strong moral and uncompromising conduct called for by the law of Moses—it is not too great a surprise to find the men of Israel slipping again and again into apostasy (Hailey 1985, 40-41).

The coming destruction is also described in very disturbing and graphic images. Notice especially verse 9: "And I will cause them to eat the flesh of their sons and the flesh of their daughters, and everyone shall eat the flesh of his friend in the siege and in the desperation with which their enemies and those who seek their lives shall drive them to despair." This is not a pretty picture. Jehovah had warned them prior to entering the Promised Land that if they departed from His way, such a disaster would come upon them (Deut. 28:49-57). This same thing happened earlier in the siege of Samaria, recorded in 2 Kings 6:28-29. Jeremiah agonizes about what had happened in Lam. 4:10: "The hands of compassionate women boiled their own children; they became food for them because of the destruction of the daughter of my people." Josephus records that similar events occurred during the destruction of Jerusalem in A.D. 70 (Keesee 2011, 413).

The broken flask could not be mended. Such was the condition of the nation after Babylon razed the city and burned the temple. As we look down through Judah's history from captivity onward, the remnant did return and rebuild the city and the temple as God had promised. However, the nation never attained the prominence and glory that it had under the reigns of David and Solomon. It was still like a shattered flask. The people looked for the Messiah, but not for the Messiah God would send. Like many today, they wanted an earthly king on the throne of David in Jerusalem, but Jeremiah dispels that hope in 22:30, speaking of Coniah – "Thus says the LORD: / 'Write this man down as childless, / A man who shall not prosper in his days; / For none of his descendants shall prosper, / Sitting on the throne of David, / And ruling anymore in Judah.'" Jehoiachin (Coniah) had seven sons, but he would never have a descendent ruling on David's throne in Jerusalem. His grandson, Zerubbabel, was a leader of the people and returned with Ezra; he served in several capacities, but never as king. Jesus is a descendant of Coniah (Matt. 1:11-13), so His rule is not earthly and David's throne of prophecy is not in physical Jerusalem, but in the "Jerusalem above… which is the mother of us all" (Gal. 4:26). This discussion may seem a little too technical for children, but I remember wondering how we could know that Jesus was really on David's throne and that David's throne was a heavenly throne, not an earthly one. This may be like singing "Jesus Loves Me" to a baby, trusting that full understanding will come. Children may not see the complete significance of this concept, but let's sow the seed so they will not be swept away by the popular false doctrine of the "rapture" and Jesus' future thousand year reign in Jerusalem. Figure 17.2 illustrates the flask.

Object Lesson 3 – The Yoke:

In the beginning of the reign of Jehoiakim the son of Josiah, king of Judah, this word came to Jeremiah from the LORD, saying, 2 "Thus says the LORD to me: 'Make for yourselves bonds and yokes, and put them on your neck, 3 and send them to the king of Edom, the king of Moab, the king of the Ammonites, the king of Tyre, and the king of Sidon, by the hand of the messengers who come to Jerusalem to Zedekiah king of Judah. 4 And command them to say to their masters, "Thus says the LORD of hosts, the God of Israel -- thus you shall say to your masters: 5'I have made the earth, the man and the beast that are on the ground, by My great power and by My outstretched arm, and have given it to whom it seemed proper to Me. 6 And now I have given all these lands into the hand of Nebuchadnezzar the king of Babylon, My servant; and the beasts of the field I have also given him to serve him. 7 So all nations shall serve him and his son and his son's son, until the time of his land comes; and then many nations and great kings shall make him serve them. 8 And it shall be, that the nation and kingdom which will not serve Nebuchadnezzar the king of Babylon, and which will not put its neck under the yoke of the king of Babylon, that nation I will punish,' says the LORD, 'with the sword, the famine, and the pestilence, until I have consumed them by his hand. 9 Therefore do not listen to your prophets, your diviners, your dreamers, your soothsayers, or your sorcerers, who speak to you, saying, "You shall not serve the king of Babylon." 10 For they prophesy a lie to you, to remove you far from your land; and I will drive you out, and you will perish. 11 But the nations that bring their necks under the yoke of the king of Babylon and serve him, I will let them remain in their own land,' says the LORD, 'and they shall till it and dwell in it'"'" (Jer. 27:1-11).

This object lesson demonstrates God's concern for and rule over nations other than just Judah. He promised that those who would serve Babylon would dwell in their land. God's willingness to allow even pagan nations to listen and continue for a time suggests His desire that they, too, have an opportunity to repent and turn to Him. Imagine seeing Jeremiah wearing that yoke! The people did not want to be in bondage to any nation, and false prophets were feeding their imaginations. Jeremiah tells both Judah and the pagan nations not to listen to diviners, prophets, and soothsayers who say differently.

Judah preferred the message of Hananiah who said, 'Within two full years I will bring back to this place all the vessels of the LORD's house, that Nebuchadnezzar king of Babylon took away from this place and carried to Babylon. And I will bring back to this place Jeconiah the son of Jehoiakim, king of Judah, with all the captives of Judah who went to Babylon,' says the LORD, 'for I will break the yoke of the king of Babylon'" (Jer. 28:3-4). That sounded much more hopeful than Jeremiah's message of doom. Hananiah also decided to be very dramatic. He took the yoke from Jeremiah's neck and broke it in front of the people, telling them that God had broken Nebuchadnezzar's yoke. That was even more impressive. Surely it was true. God sent Jeremiah back with the message: "You have broken the yokes of wood, but you have made in their place yokes of iron" (28:13). God's message to Hananiah also carried some bad news—he would die that year because he had made the people believe in lies. This should have been a warning to the people, because he did die before the year's end, but they continued to trust in his words and those of other false prophets.

An important lesson for us is that we need to be able to distinguish between false teaching and truth. Jesus said some would come to us as "wolves in sheep's clothing" (Matt. 7:15), and Paul warned the elders in Ephesus that false teachers would arise from their own group (Acts 20:29). How can we know the difference? Paul told the Ephesians to be watchful and remember what he had taught them. Jesus said a similar thing and added that we would know them by their fruit, by the kind of lives they live. Use figure 17.3 for this object lesson.

Object Lesson 4 – Buy a Field:

6 And Jeremiah said, "The word of the LORD came to me, saying, 7 'Behold, Hanamel the son of Shallum your uncle will come to you, saying, "Buy my field which is in Anathoth, for the right of redemption is yours to buy it."'" 8 Then Hanamel my uncle's son came to me in the court of the prison according to the word of the LORD, and said to me, 'Please buy my field that is in Anathoth, which is in the country of Benjamin; for the right of inheritance is yours, and the redemption yours; buy it for yourself.' Then I knew that this was the word of the LORD. 9 So I bought the field from Hanamel, the son of my uncle who was in Anathoth, and weighed out to him the money -- seventeen shekels of silver. 10 And I signed the deed and sealed it, took witnesses, and weighed the money on the scales. 11 So I took the purchase deed, both that which was sealed according to the law and custom, and that which was open; 12 and I gave the purchase deed to Baruch the son of Neriah, son of Mahseiah, in the presence of Hanamel my uncle's son, and in the presence of the witnesses who signed the purchase deed, before all the Jews who sat in the court of the prison.

13 Then I charged Baruch before them, saying, 14 "Thus says the LORD of hosts, the God of Israel: 'Take these deeds, both this purchase deed which is sealed and this deed which is open, and put them in an earthen vessel, that they may last many days.' 15 For thus says the LORD of hosts, the God of Israel: 'Houses and fields and vineyards shall be possessed again in this land'" (Jer. 32:6-15).

It is significant that this event occurred while Nebuchadnezzar was besieging Jerusalem. Why would Jehovah want Jeremiah to purchase some land, seal the purchase in front of the people, and preserve the papers in an earthen vessel? The answer is given in verse 15, but Jeremiah still has difficulty understanding the meaning, so in the next several verses, he goes to God in prayer, asking what this means since all the people are going to Babylon and the city will soon be destroyed. God answers that this was another object lesson to impress on the people that a remnant will return, family lands will be returned to the lawful owners, and the people will again dwell in the land. This lesson demonstrates to us that God keeps His promises, and we can trust Him. Figure 17.4 will help the children remember this lesson.

Concluding Comments:

As I was writing this chapter, reliving the agony of Jeremiah as he preached to the people, I was reminded of God's overwhelming love for His people even when they had gone so far into sin there was little hope. He sent His prophets all throughout their history with the same message: "Repent, turn to Me, and I will forgive." Though they were going headlong into idolatry and must be given into the hands of Babylon, God would not give them up without a struggle. I saw that struggle more poignantly through the eyes of Jeremiah. His tears are God's tears. His agony is God's agony. His love is God's love. Let us never forget God's undying love for us, and let us take the warnings of Jeremiah and remain close to God; He will protect us and provide for us. For those of us who are teachers, let us remember to deliver God's message with God's heart so others will see and be saved.

"Get yourself a linen sash, and put it around your waist..." (13:1).

"Take the sash... go to the Euphrates, and hide it there in a hole in the rock" (13:4).

"Go... and take the sash..." (13:6).

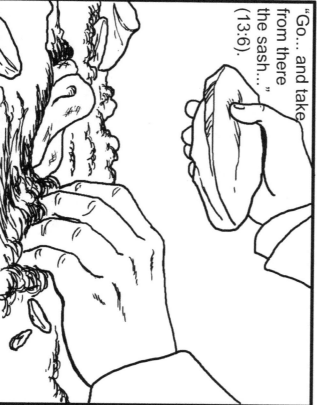

"...and there was the sash, ruined. It was profitable for nothing" (13:7).

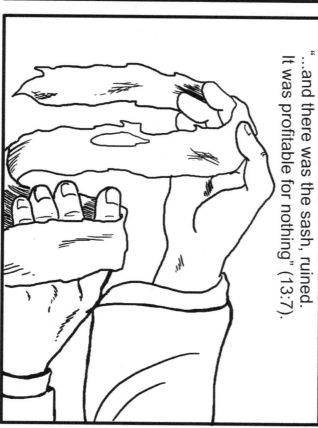

Figure 17.1

Roy Johnson 8/19/14

Object Lesson 2 – The Broken Flask - Jeremiah 19

Figure 17.2

Object Lesson 3 – The Yokes - Jeremiah 27 - 28

"Make bonds and yokes and put them on your neck, and send them..." (27:2-3).

"Hananiah took the yoke of Jeremiah's neck and broke it" (28:10).

Figure 17.3

Object Lesson 4 – Buying a Field - Jeremiah32

"And I signed the deed and sealed it, took witnesses, and weighed the money on the scales. 11 So I took the purchase deed, both that which was sealed according to the law and custom, and that which was open; 12 and I gave the purchase deed to Baruch the son of Neriah, son of Mahseiah, in the presence of Hanamel my uncle's son, and in the presence of the witnesses who signed the purchase deed, before all the Jews who sat in the court of the prison" (32:10-12).

"For thus says the LORD:'Just as I have brought all this great calamity on this people, so I will bring on them all the good that I have promised them... Men will buy fields for money, sign deeds and seal them, and take witnesses... for I will cause their captives to return,' says the LORD"(32:42-44).

Figure 17.4

Chapter 18
THE BRANCH AND THE COVENANT

When Jesus asked His disciples, "Who do men say that I, the Son of Man, am?" (Matt. 16:13), their answer included Jeremiah. We sometimes compare Jeremiah and Jesus on the basis of Jesus having wept over the city of Jerusalem like Jeremiah did, thus both of them would be known as "weeping prophets." However, Jesus' question comes before that event, so the people saw more than that as a means of comparison. As I thought about Jeremiah and Jesus, they both taught with parables, illustrations, and object lessons. They taught passionately with love for God and for the people. And, they were hated, maligned, and persecuted for their message. While they had much in common, Jesus is greater than Jeremiah, and Jeremiah spoke of Him. Jeremiah and the Messianic hope is the main focus of this chapter, although I do plan to include one of my favorite lessons at the end.

Lesson 1—The Branch: Though Jeremiah's message is of destruction and judgement, his acute suffering is counterbalanced with glimmers of hope for a brighter future for his people when Jehovah causes to grow "to David a Branch of righteousness" (Jer. 23:5; 33:15). These two selections say almost exactly the same thing, and I want to deal with them in a side-by-side manner to more easily make a comparison without repetition. You may want to give a copy of figure 18.1 to each of the children so they can see the references on one page. Also, I will analyze the verses with an adaptation of Dayton Keesee's analysis on page 464 of his *Truth for Today Commentary* on Jeremiah 1-25. I have used his basic outline, but I have added scriptures we have referred to in previous lessons and those I think children can more easily understand. This lesson may be best for children 6th grade and above.

I will raise up—The messianic branch (shoot) would be raised up by the direct action of God. We have already seen that concept in Isaiah 11:1-5 and 53:2. You can read similar statements of the fulfillment in Acts 13:22-23, "From this man's (*David's*) seed, according to the promise, God raised up for Israel a Savior – Jesus."

For David—The promised Messiah would be the descendent of David and rule on David's throne (God's throne) forever. Nathan, the prophet, announced this to David in 2 Sam. 7:12-16, "…And your house and your kingdom shall be established forever before you. Your throne shall be established forever." Isaiah alludes to it in chapter 9:6, "…the government shall be upon His shoulders..." And, in verse 7, he states plainly that the Son of verse 6 will rule "upon the throne of David and over His kingdom." The angel Gabriel also promised this to Mary of her Son, "And behold, you will conceive in your womb and bring forth a Son, and shall call His name JESUS. He will be great, and will be called the Son of the Highest; and the Lord God will give Him the throne of His father David. And He will reign over the house of Jacob forever, and of His kingdom there will be no end" (Luke 1:31-33).

A branch of righteousness—The Messiah was called "the Branch of Jehovah" in Isaiah 4, and we discussed that in Chapter 4, specifically that He has the same nature of Jehovah. Here, though, He is spoken of as a "Branch for (or to) David" which would indicate His human parentage and nature. Zachariah will also describe the Messiah as "the Branch." Those who know the Hebrew language point out that in Isaiah 11:1 a different Hebrew word is used for the English word "branch." That is true, but as we saw in our discussion of that prophecy, the meaning is clear—"the branch" of Isaiah 11 is the Messiah who will rule in a kingdom of unusual peace. Don't let this distract you from teaching with certainty from the context of that passage.

Righteous—The Messiah would be a righteous branch. While other descendants of David needed forgiveness, the Messiah would be sinless. Remember Isaiah 53:9 – "... because He had done no violence, nor was any deceit in His mouth." Paul affirms of Jesus, "For He made Him who knew no sin to be sin for us, that we might become the righteousness of God in Him" (2 Cor. 5:21).

Reign as king—The Messiah would reign as King over His kingdom. On the first Pentecost after Jesus' death and resurrection, Peter declared when His reign began: "Therefore, being exalted to the right hand of God..." (Acts 2:33). John the Baptizer, Jesus and His apostles all preached, "The kingdom of heaven is at hand..." (Matt. 3:2; 4:17; 10:7). However, after the death, resurrection, and ascension of Jesus, every mention of the kingdom is in the present time (Col. 1:13-20; Rev. 3:21).

Act wisely—The Messiah would rule in wisdom. In the picture of the Branch in Isaiah 11, the prophet says, "The Spirit of the LORD shall rest upon Him, the Spirit of wisdom and understanding" (v. 2). Jesus' critics asked, "Where did this Man get this wisdom and these mighty works?" (Matt. 13:54).

Do justice and righteousness in the land—This is the same promise Isaiah made of the Messiah, "...upon the throne of David and over His kingdom, to order it and establish it with judgment and justice..." (9:7). And, he makes that promise again in chapter 11, "with righteousness He shall judge the poor... Righteousness shall be the belt of His loins..." (vs. 4, 5).

Judah will be saved, and Israel will dwell securely—Israel and Judah would be reunited under the rule of the Messiah. When we have lessons from Ezekiel who was preaching during this time to the captives, we will see an interesting picture that he shows us of this promise (Ezek. 37:19). Jeremiah is telling the people they will be blessed, be saved from all their enemies, and be secure. He is using figures of speech that they could understand and relate to. All the blessings of the Messiah's rule, as we have seen, are spiritual in nature, not physical. And, the rule of the Messiah is over a kingdom that is "not of this world" (John 18:36).

The LORD our righteousness—This title clearly refers to Jesus. I found it interesting that Zedekiah's name means "The LORD is my righteousness." He certainly didn't live up to his name! In contrast to Zedekiah, a fearful, unrighteous king, the Messiah would be a righteous king. And, in contrast to the selfish shepherds (leaders) of Judah, He would be the ideal shepherd (Ezek. 34:23-31; John 10:1-18). Go back to the side-by-side sheet for Jer. 23 and 33, and compare 23:6 with 33:16. I underlined the phrases for emphasis. In chapter 23, the name "The LORD our righteousness" refers to the Branch; in chapter 33, the name refers to the city of Jerusalem. Is there a contradiction? First, note that these passages are highlighting the characteristics of the Messiah's rule, so the Jerusalem mentioned in 33:16 is not the physical city, for Paul says of it, "...Jerusalem which now is, and is in bondage with her children — but the Jerusalem above is free, which is the mother of us all" (Gal. 4:25-26). The Messiah rules over the free Jerusalem—Zion of Old Testament prophecy and fulfilled in the New Testament in Heb. 12:22ff. Remember from Isaiah 60 that the citizens of Zion are all righteous (v. 21), and from Isaiah 61 that God has clothed us with the robe of righteousness (v. 10). The Messiah is righteous, and those in His kingdom share in His righteousness. Don't you want to be a part of that Jerusalem which is above and is free? That's where the righteous people live, ruled by the righteous King!

Jeremiah concludes this section by declaring the significance of the return from Babylonian captivity:

"Therefore, behold, the days are coming," says the LORD, "that they shall no longer say, 'As the LORD lives who brought up the children of Israel from the land of Egypt,' but, 'As the LORD lives who brought up and led the descendants of the house of Israel from the north country and from all the countries where I had driven them' And they shall dwell in their own land" (23:7-8).

Until this time, the most significant event in their history had been their deliverance from Egyptian bondage when a new nation was formed and the Law was given at Mount Sinai. Now, Jehovah was working a new and greater deliverance with a brighter future. When He brought them out of Babylon and settled them in their land, the stage was set for the coming of the Messiah—the most significant event in their history.

Chapter 33 ends with the announcement that David would never lack a man on his throne and the Levitical priesthood would, likewise, never lack a man to serve as High Priest. The priesthood of Levi and sacrifices were restored when Israel returned to their land, but the throne of David was not restored. After Jerusalem was destroyed in 70 A.D., the priesthood and sacrifices were completely discontinued and have never been restored in Jerusalem. Did God not fulfill His promise? Let's remember that Jesus is a "priest after the order of Melchizedek" (Ps. 110:4; Heb. 6:20) who was both priest and king (Gen. 14:18). If you have been teaching holistically, children will be familiar with this promise. However, you may want to refer back to Chapter 7, "Priest and King," in my first book to review this concept with them. Jesus is both king and priest, and He forever serves in those offices in the Jerusalem that is free, the spiritual Jerusalem, Zion of Old Testament prophecy.

I think it is interesting to see the parallels that Jeremiah may be alluding to in both these chapters. Deliverance from Egypt resulted in freedom from slavery, the birth of the nation of Israel, the giving of the Law at Mount Sinai, and the ordination of the priesthood. Later, God would choose David as the ideal shepherd-king. Deliverance from Babylonian captivity would result in God's greater blessings that He foreshadowed through these events in Israel's history—the coming of the Messiah. From His work, we are delivered from the slavery of sin, a new spiritual kingdom is born, a new law is proclaimed from Mount Zion, and a new perpetual priesthood is ordained.

Lesson 2—The New Covenant: What are some of the things we have seen that God had promised when the Messiah comes? This is a good time to review some of the prophecies. The children will supply many good answers, but I offer these to stimulate your thinking: The LORD'S house is established and exalted above all earthly kingdoms; God's Law is proclaimed from Zion; all nations are invited to enjoy the blessings in this kingdom; a Shepherd and King rules out of Zion; and people come rejoicing to Zion, walking on a Highway of Holiness. None of this could happen under the Law of Moses. That Law was only given to the Jewish people at Mount Sinai (Mal. 4:4). Also, the Law contained specific restrictions regarding Gentiles; they were welcome "at a distance" in the court of the Gentiles in the temple. They could convert to Judaism, but that involved being circumcised and keeping the Law.

In the New Testament, Paul describes the Law as a "middle wall of separation," and declares that Jesus "abolished in His flesh the enmity, that is, the law of commandments contained in ordinances, so as to create in Himself one new man from the two, thus making peace, and that He might reconcile them both to God in one body through the cross" (Eph. 2:14-16). If Jesus abolished the Law, then there is something new in its place. This discussion brings to our next major lesson from Jeremiah—the new covenant from chapter 31.

The Old Covenant (Law) was given by God and was perfect for the purpose it served. It was never meant to be a permanent law for God's people. You may want to refer back to the veil over Moses' face when he came to the people after being in Jehovah's presence. Paul tells us in 2 Cor. 3:13 that Moses put that veil over his face "so that the children of Israel could not look steadily at the end of what was passing away." The Law, from its very inception, was designed to pass away and be replaced. This is why the writer of Hebrews will say, "For if that first covenant had been faultless, then no place would have been sought for a second" (8:7).

The writer of Hebrews tells us in chapter 7 that the Levitical priesthood under that Law was also imperfect or faulty. This connects back to the discussion of Jer. 33:18. An imperfect priesthood occupied by imperfect men must be replaced with the perfect priesthood of Christ, which is an "unchangeable priesthood" (Heb. 7:24). That is the only way the promise of verse 18 could be fulfilled: "nor shall the priests, the Levites, lack a man to offer burnt offerings before Me to kindle grain offerings, and to sacrifice continually." I don't want to go into a commentary on Hebrews, but I do think it is important for teachers to read Hebrews 7-10 prior to teaching this part of Jeremiah.

You will find the side-by-side scripture sheets for Jer.31:31-34 and Heb. 8:8-12 (figure 18.2) to be helpful. I have also included a chart, "Distinctions between the Two Covenants" (figure 18.3) copied from Dayton Keesee's commentary of Jeremiah, pages105-106. I suggest you select from that the concepts and scriptures that are appropriate for the students you are teaching and make a chart similar to this for your class.

Lesson 3—Racing Horses: This is probably my favorite lesson from Jeremiah, and I thought I would just put it in this chapter for your consideration. It is especially good for teachers and for leaders who sometimes get discouraged. However, children face similar situations when they think God has been unfair: Why are all the kids who don't go to church getting all the awards, and I don't? Why do others make fun of me when I'm just trying to obey God? They call me "teacher's pet" and other names just because I try to be good. Listen to Jeremiah's complaint in chapter 12:1-4:

> Righteous are You, O LORD, when I plead with You; yet let me talk with You about Your judgments. Why does the way of the wicked prosper? Why are those happy who deal so treacherously? 2 You have planted them, yes, they have taken root; they grow, yes, they bear fruit. You are near in their mouth but far from their mind. 3 But You, O LORD, know me; You have seen me, and You have tested my heart toward You. Pull them out like sheep for the slaughter, and prepare them for the day of slaughter. 4 How long will the land mourn, and the herbs of every field wither? The beasts and birds are consumed, for the wickedness of those who dwell there, because they said, "He will not see our final end."

Do you sometimes think like this? Are there times when you have wanted to talk with God about His Judgments and tell Him what to do or what you think about what He is doing? We discussed a similar idea in Chapter 13, but here, Jeremiah says what has come to the mind of many faithful Christians. Remember when God called Jeremiah, He told him, "Do not be afraid of their faces, for I am with you to deliver you" (1:8). And, throughout the New Testament, God has given us similar promises.

Now, let's look at God's answer, and notice that He doesn't get angry with Jeremiah for voicing his frustration. God answers Jeremiah with a mild rebuke, a warning, and encouragement. I think God's answer also demonstrates His confidence in Jeremiah to continue to fulfill his ministry. Figures 18.4, pages 1 and 2 illustrate what God is saying to Jeremiah.

> If you have run with the footmen, and they have wearied you, then how can you contend with horses? And if in the land of peace, in which you trusted, they wearied you, then how will you do in the floodplain of the Jordan? 6 For even your brothers, the house of your father, even they have dealt treacherously with you; yes, they have called a multitude after you. Do not believe them, even though they speak smooth words to you (12:5-6).

We might paraphrase God's answer like this, "If you are tired and ready to sit down and rest when you've just been racing with men, what will you do when things get much worse, when you have to race against horses? If you are having trouble standing on level ground, what will happen when you are in the thicket with wild animals?" Remember Jeremiah had been preaching with no success and was impatient. He wanted God to deal with the wicked people right now. If God did so, Jeremiah felt that he would be vindicated and could rest. However, the job isn't finished.

Jeremiah has more work to do, and it's going to get harder. So, God basically says, "Look up Jeremiah. Quit being distracted by what others are saying and doing. I have a more difficult work for you to do, and I trust you to do it."

I think it's important to remember that God doesn't put us in a race with horses until He has trained us with the footman. Every Christian will have challenges to their faith, but each trial we overcome fits us for a greater service. Like Jeremiah, we must continue to work until the job is finished. This is what God told Isaiah when he asked, "How long?" in Isa. 6:11.

Concluding Comments:

Often children wonder if God really exists. The history of the Jewish people, fulfilled prophecy, the coming of Jesus, and the existence of the church cannot be explained in any other way—God is! This is why I believe in holistic teaching, showing the shadows, pictures, the promises, the prophecies, and that they are fulfilled in Christ. Through his faith and devotion to Jehovah, Jeremiah saw the significance of Judah's captivity and deliverance, and he could face the future with confidence. As we look back and see that Jehovah did accomplish all He promised through Jeremiah, we, too, can face the future with confidence, knowing God is faithful (1 Cor. 1:9; 10:13).

A note to teachers:

I am including edited notes of a portion of a lesson I was asked to present at a ladies' day recently. The theme was from Jer. 29:11, "For I know the plans I have for you," declares the LORD, "plans to prosper you and not to harm you, plans to give you hope and a future" (NIV). I'm not sure if they were thinking about the popular way that scripture is used today, but I knew many in the audience would be, so I studied the context to make certain I presented the message God intended in these verses.

Remember that Jeremiah was preaching to people who were destined for captivity in Babylon. Two groups had already been taken, and false prophets were telling those left that their friends and relatives would be back in two years. Also, there were false prophets in with the captives, telling them the same thing. Jeremiah was commissioned by Jehovah to write a letter to the elders, priests, and prophets who had been taken to Babylon. In that letter, he reminds them that their captivity is God's doing (29:4). He tells them to build houses, plant gardens, marry and have children so they are not diminished in captivity (v.6). Note especially verse 10: "For thus says the LORD: 'After seventy years are completed at Babylon, I will visit you and perform My good word toward you, and cause you to return to this place.'"

With this background, what do we learn from Jer. 29: 11-14? Why was it written and preserved for us? [Rick Warren in The Purpose Driven Life has taken this out of context and along with others like Joel Osteen and Max Lucado, and has popularized it as God's answer to just about everything. Warren quotes Jer. 29:11 and says things like, "Wonderful things happen in your life as you begin to live it on purpose. God says 'I know what I am planning for you… I have good plans for you… I will give you hope and a good future'" (Warren 2002, p.31). His messages, like Osteen's, are on TV, YouTube and podcasts, and are often punctuated with similar statements about God's plan for you.] We see Jer. 29:11 on greeting cards and banners and in little tracts left in restrooms: "God loves you and has a plan for your life." Some of our preachers and teachers have jumped on this band wagon, too. It sounds good. It seems to be in harmony with the gospel – but if you examine closely, it sounds like a ME centered message—success in this life message.

Paul tells us in 1 Cor. 10:6-7 that the Old Testament contains examples for us. And, in Rom. 15:4, "Things written aforetime were written for our learning, that we through patience and comfort of the Scriptures might have hope." God was teaching His people in captivity about Himself, His plan, His purpose, and He is teaching us, too, so that we through "patience and comfort of the Scriptures might have hope."

God had a specific plan and purpose for Israel – that plan which He announced in the garden in <u>promise</u> in Gen. 3:15 and in <u>type</u> in Gen. 3:21 when He shed the innocent blood of an animal to provide a covering for sin. Often through the Old Testament, God refers to that divine covenant promise He made with Abraham and his descendants that "in your seed all nations of the earth will be blessed." You see, in Jer. 29:11 <u>God is not speaking to individuals</u>, <u>but to the nation</u> – to the nation in captivity who thought God had abandoned them and had forgotten His promises to them. The "future and hope" He planned for Israel, as He explains, is to bring them back to their land for that purpose—that desired end—to bring about the promise He had sworn to their fathers. Though the captives did not see it fully then, the remnant did return through God's work and grace. Yet, when we read Haggai, Zechariah, and Malachi, we see that the real situation was less than the ideal. In spite of that, there was the faithful remnant who waited for the kingdom of God, who desired the fruition of that "future and hope" in its truest sense. In the fullness of time, God visited His people and raised up a horn of salvation in the house of David when Mary wrapped her baby in swaddling clothes and placed Immanuel (God with us) in a manger in Bethlehem. From this small group—people like Mary, Joseph, Zacharias, Elizabeth, Simeon, Anna, the apostles and the 120 gathered in the upper room on Pentecost—the message of salvation, hope, and peace began to be proclaimed in "Jerusalem, Judea, Samaria, and the uttermost part of the earth" (Acts 1:8). On that first Pentecost after the resurrection, the mountain of the Lord's house was "established in the top of the mountains and exalted above the hills" (Isa. 2:1). And, on that day, all nations began to flow into it. The Mount Zion of Old Testament prophecy, the Spiritual Israel, the kingdom that will never be destroyed was their future and hope—that desired end.

And, that is also our future and hope! In Rom. 1:1-5 Paul said of the gospel that God "promised (*it*) before through His prophets in the Holy Scriptures, concerning His Son Jesus Christ our Lord, who was born of the seed of David according to the flesh, and declared to be the Son of God with power…, by the resurrection from the dead." This divine plan, this eternal purpose, this great drama of redemption is what gives us **a future and a hope today**! God was in Christ reconciling the world to Himself (2 Cor. 5:19). God has made us to sit in heavenly places in Christ, made both Jew and Gentile one body, fellow citizens, and members of His household (Eph. 2). THIS IS HIS PLAN FOR OUR FUTURE AND OUR HOPE!

Jeremiah 23:5-8

5 "Behold, the days are coming," says the LORD,
"That I will raise to David a Branch of righteousness;
A King shall reign and prosper,
And execute judgment and righteousness in the earth.
6 In His days Judah will be saved,
And Israel will dwell safely;
Now this is His name by which He will be called:

7 "Therefore, behold, the days are coming," says the LORD, "that they shall no longer say, 'As the LORD lives who brought up the children of Israel from the land of Egypt,' 8 but, 'As the LORD lives who brought up and led the descendants of the house of Israel from the north

Jeremiah 33:14-18

14 Behold, the days are coming,' says the LORD, 'that I will perform that good thing which I have promised to the house of Israel and to the house of Judah:

15 'In those days and at that time I will cause to grow up to David
A Branch of righteousness;
He shall execute judgment and righteousness in the earth.
16 In those days Judah will be saved,
And Jerusalem will dwell safely.
And this is the name by which she will be called:

17 "For thus says the LORD: 'David shall never lack a man to sit on the throne of the house of Israel; 18 nor shall the priests, the Levites, lack a man to offer burnt offerings before Me, to kindle grain offerings, and to sacrifice continually.'"

Question from Jeremiah 33:14:

What is the "good thing" Jehovah had promised to Israel and Judah?

Figure 18.1

OLD TESTAMENT

NEW TESTAMENT

Jeremiah 31:31-34

31 "Behold, the days are coming, says the LORD, when I will make a new covenant with the house of Israel and with the house of Judah -- 32 not according to the covenant that I made with their fathers in the day that I took them by the hand to lead them out of the land of Egypt, My covenant which they broke, though I was a husband to them, says the LORD. 33 But this is the covenant that I will make with the house of Israel after those days, says the LORD: I will put My law in their minds, and write it on their hearts; and I will be their God, and they shall be My people. 34 No more shall every man teach his neighbor, and every man his brother, saying, 'Know the LORD,' for they all shall know Me, from the least of them to the greatest of them, says the LORD. For I will forgive their iniquity, and their sin I will remember no more."

Heb 8:8-12

8 Because finding fault with them, He says: "Behold, the days are coming, says the LORD, when I will make a new covenant with the house of Israel and with the house of Judah -- 9 not according to the covenant that I made with their fathers in the day when I took them by the hand to lead them out of the land of Egypt; because they did not continue in My covenant, and I disregarded them, says the LORD. 10 For this is the covenant that I will make with the house of Israel after those days, says the LORD: I will put My laws in their mind and write them on their hearts; and I will be their God, and they shall be My people. 11 None of them shall teach his neighbor, and none his brother, saying, 'Know the LORD,' for all shall know Me, from the least of them to the greatest of them. 12 For I will be merciful to their unrighteousness, and their sins and their lawless deeds I will remember no more."

Figure 18.2

Distinctions Between The Two Covenants

Old Covenant

Given by Moses, son of Amram (Ex. 6:20; Deut. 31:24-26; Jn. 1:17)

National law to Israel (Ex. 19:3-8; Deut. 5:1-3; Neh. 8:1-3)

Animal sacrifices year by year (Lev. 16:1-34; Heb. 10:1-8)

Circumcision was binding (Gen. 17:9-14; Lev. 12:1-3; Jn. 7:22, 23)

Sabbath, covenant day to Israel (Ex. 20:8-11; 31:12-18; Deut. 5:12-15; Neh. 9:13, 14)

Giving through tithes (Lev. 27:30-32; Num. 18:25-29; Neh. 10:37-39)

Musical instruments used in worship (2 Chron. 29:25-28; Ps. 150:1-6)

Incense a part of worship (Ex. 30:8, 9; 31:11; Lev. 16:12, 13)

Looking to the coming of the Messiah (2 Sam. 7:12-16; Is. 7:14; 9:6, 7; Jer. 23:5, 6)

New Covenant

Given by Jesus Christ, Son of God (Heb. 1:1-4; 8:6-13; 13:20, 21)

International law to every creature (Mt. 28:18-20; Mk. 16:15, 16; Acts 1:8)

Christ, the sacrifice, once for all (Heb. 7:26-28; 9:11-15, 24-27; 13:15, 16)

Circumcision was not binding (Acts 15:1-11; Gal. 5:1-6).

First day is the special day under Christ (Acts 2:1-47; 20:7; 1 Cor. 16:1, 2; Col. 2:16).

Giving as one has prospered and purposed in his heart (Acts 2:42-44; 1 Cor. 16:1, 2; 2 Cor. 9:6-11)

Singing only of psalms, hymns, and spiritual songs in worship (1 Cor. 14:15; Eph. 5:19; Col. 3:16; Jas. 5:13)

Prayers to God in Christ's name in worship (Jn. 16:23; Eph. 5:20; Phil 4:6, 7; Rev. 5:8)

Living under Christ, who is the Messiah, and looking for His second coming (Mt. 1:1-25; 28:18-20; Acts 2:22-47; 3:13-26; 1 Thess. 4:16, 17; Rev. 21)

Figure 18.3

Racing Horses – Jeremiah 12

If you have run with the footmen, and they have wearied you,

Then how can you contend with horses?

Figure 18.4

For even your brothers... have dealt treacherously with you;.... Do not believe them, even though they speak smooth words to you. (v. 6)

Figure 18.4

Chapter 19
EZEKIEL AND GOD'S GLORY

*E*zekiel is one of the most fascinating prophets to introduce to children. They relate to his dramatic portrayals and remember the events of Israel's history during this period more readily than just seeing those events in the last part of 2 Kings and Chronicles. Also, Ezekiel teaches us much about God that is important for children and adults. Let's remember that Ezekiel was a young priest who was taken to Babylon along with the second and larger group including King Jehoiachin in 597 B.C. If you read about the good and bad figs in Jeremiah 24, you will see that God had this group taken to Babylon to preserve them. They are the best of the people, and from these, God will be able to find a remnant through whom He can work. Keep in mind that the people to whom Ezekiel is called to preach have heard Jeremiah's pleadings for repentance. They have rejected his warnings and are now suffering the consequences. Many are still thinking the captivity will be short and Jerusalem won't be destroyed. This is why God calls them rebellious and stubborn. It is Ezekiel's responsibility to prepare them for the destruction of Jerusalem and the temple, and to encourage them to trust Jehovah to bring about His purpose for them. Just as Babylon is Jehovah's instrument to discipline His people, so Ezekiel is His instrument to instruct and protect them.

If you aren't familiar with Ezekiel, take time to read the first 12 chapters before reading the rest of this chapter. I am including some story sheets I made for these chapters when I was teaching third and fourth graders. Feel free to copy these for your students or edit them in any way you find helpful for use with the children you are teaching. Some of these have activities for the children like fill-in-the-blanks, unscramble the words, and decode a puzzle. I will organize this chapter a little differently from the others. After discussing each main topic, I will include the story sheets and illustrations for that topic so you will have access to these in a more orderly fashion. When I first taught this, I didn't have good illustrations and had to improvise with the felt Bible figures, copying, reducing, adjusting, and filling in with my sketches. Roy's drawings will help you convey these concepts to children with ease. I plan to divide my discussion of these chapters like this:

Ezekiel's call – chapters 1-3

Getting the people's attention – chapters 4-7

God's glory leaves His temple – chapters 8-11

Go into captivity – chapter 12

Ezekiel's call:

I suggest you read all of chapter 1 to the children. One way to begin the class is to ask children to tell of something exciting they have seen recently. Then you can do like Granddaddy and say something like, "All of those are interesting, but you didn't see something as great and exciting as what Ezekiel saw!" When you end this reading with verse 28, before you read Ezekiel's response, you may want to ask if they remember the first rainbow in the Bible (Gen. 9:13-17) and what it represented. The rainbow about God's throne represents to Ezekiel the same thing—God is a promise-keeping God. Ezekiel needed that assurance because in the time which he lived it could seem like God had forgotten His promises to Israel.

Ezekiel's response to seeing God's glory, "So when I saw it, I fell on my face…" (v.28) should remind us of Isaiah's response to God in the vision in Isaiah 6. Remember that Moses saw God's glory in Ex. 33:17-23 & 34:6-9; Isaiah saw God's glory in Isaiah 6. Now we read that Ezekiel saw God's glory. Would you like to see God's glory? We can see more than they saw! (John 1:14; John 14:7-11; Heb. 1:1-3; Col. 1:15-18). You may want to review some of those scriptures with the children. Roy's illustration (figure 19.1) will help children visualize what Ezekiel saw. I have included a story sheet with activities for this lesson. This will help you explain the vision in words the children can understand, so I'm not going into great detail about the vision here. Don't be afraid to tell the children that some of the details in the vision like the colors, the placement of the wheels, and the movement of the cherubim are all just part of the picture to help us see how great, glorious and wonderful God is. Notice that Ezekiel didn't ask God about all those details. He just fell on his face, realizing he was in the presence of almighty God! This is a good time to speak with the children about our attitude in worship; we should be reverent in worship; we should not be doing things like passing notes, playing computer games, drawing pictures, etc. Teachers will use applications that are applicable to the age of the children.

Chapters 2 and 3 continue to tell us about Ezekiel's call. In chapter 2, God tells Ezekiel that his work will be hard, but he is not to be afraid. This sounds like what He said to Jeremiah earlier, doesn't it? However, God describes their opposition to him in rather graphic terms: "And you, son of man, do not be afraid of them nor be afraid of their words, though briers and thorns are with you and you dwell among scorpions; do not be afraid of their words or dismayed by their looks, though they are a rebellious house" (2:6). Would you like to live in briars and thorns with scorpions all about you? This was just God's way of telling Ezekiel how difficult and unpleasant his work would be.

Now, God tells Ezekiel to eat a scroll (2:9-3:3). What does this mean? God's messenger must always ingest God's word. It is not enough for teachers just to know the word. It must be a part of their lives. Listen to God in Ez. 3:10-11: "Son of man, receive into your heart all My words that I speak to you, and hear with your ears. And go, get to the captives, to the children of your people, and speak to them…" Don't overlook verse 14: "So the Spirit lifted me up and took me away, and I went in bitterness, in the heat of my spirit; but the hand of the LORD was strong upon me." Use figure 19.2 for this part of the lesson. The story sheet I referred to earlier also has this information in words the children can understand. The story sheet includes a "sub-lesson" relating to making God's word a part of our lives. That is an excellent application of God's calling Ezekiel.

The Glory of God – Ezekiel 1

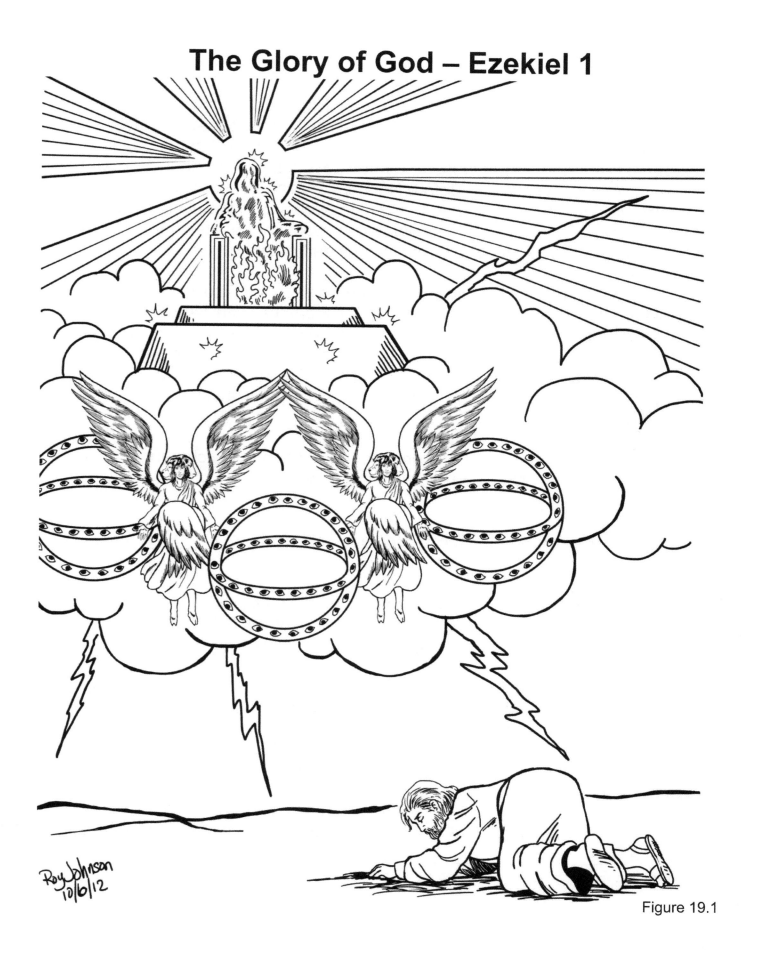

Figure 19.1

GOD CALLS EZEKIEL

Ezekiel was an interesting prophet. He preached to God's people right after Judah (the southern kingdom) was taken into captivity by Nebuchadnezzar, the king of Babylon. We would think that the people would listen to God's preacher after such a bad thing had happened. But, they didn't want to listen. Before Nebuchadnezzar had come to Jerusalem, false prophets had told the people that they would be in Babylon only a short time. They also said that Jerusalem would not be destroyed. The people listened to the false preaching instead of to the truth.

God sent Ezekiel to the people who were taken into Babylon. God told Ezekiel to warn the people and to tell them the truth. And the truth was that the captivity was going to be a long time (70 years) and that Jerusalem would really be destroyed. God asked Ezekiel to do many unusual things to get the people's attention and to teach the lessons God wanted them to learn. I like learning about Ezekiel because he is so unusual among the prophets.

Ezekiel had a very hard job. God called him a "watchman" of the people of Israel. What does a "watchman" do? _____
_____

God told Ezekiel that His people were _____ and
_____. (Ez. 2:4)

God told Ezekiel to preach to them even if they didn't listen. He said that even if they wouldn't obey, that at least they would know that a _____ had been among them. (Ez. 2:5)

God also told Ezekiel not to fear what the people might say or do to him. Read Ez. 2:6-7: Ezekiel was not to fear, even though _____ and _____ might be with him and even if he had to sit on _____. God said, "Speak _____ to them whether they listen or not, for they are _____.

In Ez. 2:8, God told Ezekiel to listen to what He was speaking and not to be _____ like the people of Israel.

Would you want to do the work Ezekiel had to do? _____ He knew from the beginning that his work would be very, very hard. He knew people wouldn't listen to him, that they would hate him, and that they would do lots of things to discourage him and try to make him quit.

Since Ezekiel's job was so difficult, God wanted him to know that he was not alone. God wanted Ezekiel to be certain that He was in control and that it was His Word that Ezekiel was speaking. God gave Ezekiel that assurance when He first called him to do this work of preaching to rebellious people. In Ezekiel chapter one, the prophet records his vision of the glory of God. We can only imagine what it must have been like to see God's wonderful greatness, power and glory. We have already studied Isaiah 6 where Isaiah saw God on the throne and all the glory about Him. Later, we learn that Daniel saw a glorious throne with the "Ancient of Days" sitting on it in Daniel 7:9-10. Then, when we read in Revelation 4 and 5, we see that John saw a similar scene of the glory of God.

It is not important to know what every little detail of Ezekiel's vision means. What is important is that we learn how great and glorious God is. We can learn that God is to be praised by all the creation. The faces of the cherubim ("living creatures") that Ezekiel saw suggests the strongest of certain animal groups -- lion (strongest wild animal); ox or bull (strongest of the domestic animals); eagle (strongest of the birds); and man (intelligent, the one God set to "have dominion over" things of the earth). The wheels with rims full of eyes suggest that God can go everywhere in all the earth and that He sees everything. Sometimes we use big words to explain these things about God, words like *omniscient, omnipresent, and omnipotent.* This is what God's vision represents—that He is all-knowing, everywhere, and all powerful. I like Ezekiel's picture, don't you?

Another important lesson we can learn from Ezekiel's vision is that even though God is great and glorious, He cares about His people in a very personal way. God wanted Ezekiel to know that he would not be doing this difficult work alone. God—the One worshipped by all the host of heaven and by all creation, the One who rules the whole universe—was going to be with Ezekiel. God would give him the words to speak. God would help him and encourage him even when the people wouldn't listen. Ezekiel

2

Figure 19.1

could know that as long as he did what God said, that God would reward him. God has made that same promise to us, too. Let's remember that and be a faithful servant like Ezekiel was.

One of the first things God asked Ezekiel to do was unusual: God asked him to eat a scroll! That doesn't seem like a very good lunch! Read Ez. 2:9 to find out what was written on the scroll: _____
_____

Let's read part of chapter 3 and fill in the missing words about Ezekiel and the scroll:

"Moreover He said to me, 'Son of man, _____ what you find; _____ this _____, and _____, _____ to the house of Israel.'
So I opened my _____ , and He caused me to _____ that
_____ .
And He said to me, 'Son of man, _____ your belly, and _____ your stomach with this _____ that I give you.' So I _____ , and it was in my mouth like _____ in _____."

Someone else in the Bible was told to eat a scroll. John (Revelation 10) ate a "little book." Here is part of chapter 10:1-2 and 8-11:

"I saw still another mighty angel coming down from heaven, clothed with a cloud. And a rainbow was on his head, his face was like the sun, and his feet like pillars of fire. He had a little book open in his hand.... Then the voice which I heard from heaven spoke to me again and said, 'Go, take the little book which is open in the hand of the angel who stands on the sea and on the earth.' So I went to the angel and said to him, 'Give me the little book.' And he said to me, 'Take and eat it; and it will make your stomach bitter, but it will be as sweet as honey in your mouth.' Then I took the little book out of the angel's hand and ate it, and it was as sweet as honey in mouth. But when I had eaten it, my stomach became bitter. And he said to me, 'You must prophesy again about many peoples, nations, tongues, and kings.'"

Figure 19.1

John ate a _____ that was sweet as _____ in his mouth, but _____ in his stomach. Ezekiel ate a _____ that was sweet as _____ in his mouth. He does not say that it was bitter in his stomach, but after he ate the scroll, God told him again that he was to preach to the people of Israel. God said the people were rebellious and would not listen to Ezekiel. Then, in Ez. 3:14-15, the prophet says, "So the Spirit lifted me up and took me away, and I went in <u>bitterness</u>, in the heat of my spirit; but the hand of the Lord was strong upon me. Then I came to the captives at Tel Abib, who dwelt by the River Chebar; and I sat where they sat, and remained there astonished among them seven days."

After eating the sweet scroll, Ezekiel went to the people in _____.
Was this scroll bitter in his stomach (bitter after he ate it)?_____
What happens to the food we eat? _____
Does it become a part of our bodies? _____ Does it help us grow?_____
Now, let's think about God's Word in the same way. If we study it, learn it and live by it, God's Word becomes a part of us. It is in our minds, guiding our lives. And, God's Word helps us grow spiritually. It helps us grow to be the kind of person God wants us to be.

Old Testament verses about God's Word as food:

Deut. 8:3b: "...that He might make you know that man shall not live by bread alone; but man lives by every word that proceeds from the mouth of the Lord."

Job 23:12b: "...I have treasured the words of His mouth more than my necessary food."

Psalm 119:103: "How sweet are Your words to my taste, sweeter than honey to my mouth!"

Jeremiah 15:16: "Your words were found, and I ate them, and Your word was to me the joy and rejoicing of my heart; for I am called by Your name, O Lord God of hosts."

Figure 19.1

New Testament verses about God's Word as food:

Matthew 4:4: "But He answered and said, 'It is written, "Man shall not live by bread alone, but by every work that proceeds from the mouth of God."'"

I Peter 2:2-3: "As newborn babes, desire the pure milk of the word, that you may grow thereby, if indeed you have tasted that the Lord is gracious."

The scroll was sweet to Ezekiel because of the promises God had made to him. But the scroll was bitter because it contained a message the people of Israel did not want to hear. God told Ezekiel to preach that message, anyway. God's Word is sweet to the person who obeys it. The Bible has many promises of special blessings for those who love God. But, God's Word can be bitter, too. Sometimes, people will not listen to us when we try to tell them about God and His plan of salvation. They may get angry and say bad things about us. So, when we teach God's Word and people don't want to hear it, the word is "bitter in our stomach." It is hard to preach God's Word and live as He wants us to when all our friends don't care about God and make fun of us for going to Church, studying the Bible and trying to do good things.

Figure 19.1

Ezekiel 2 & 3

"Son of man...
eat this scroll,
and go speak to
the house of Israel."

So I ate,
and it was in
my mouth like
honey in sweetness.

"Go...and speak
with My words..."
and I went in bitterness,
in the heat of my spirit.

Figure 19.2

GOD CALLS EZEKIEL – CHAPTER 2

Unscramble these words from our lesson in Ezekiel Chapter 2, then use the circled letters to make a secret message from our lesson.

RIPITS   __ __ __ __ Ⓞ

LEASRI   __ __ __ Ⓞ __ __

LILOUREEBS   __ __ __ __ __ __ Ⓞ __ __

SEGRESDANRTS   __ __ __ Ⓞ __ __ __ __ __ __ __

BORNUBTS   Ⓞ __ __ __ __ __ __ __

REAH   Ⓞ __ __ __

SUEFER   __ __ __ __ __ __

PTREHOP   __ __ __ __ __ __ __

DORWS   __ __ __ Ⓞ __

MISDAYED   __ __ __ Ⓞ __ __ __ __

LORCLS   __ Ⓞ __ __ __ __

SNOITATNEMAL   __ Ⓞ __ __ __ __ __ __ __ __ __

GMNOIURN   __ __ __ __ __ __ Ⓞ __

OEW   Ⓞ __ __

WHAT WAS EZEKIEL CALLED TO BE?

__ __ __ __   __ __ __ __ __ __ __ __

(You will find the answer in Ezekiel 3:17)

Use the two words that have no letters circled to complete this sentence that is Ezekiel's message to Israel and God's message to us, too:

DON'T __ __ __ __ __ __   GOD'S __ __ __ __ __ __ __ !

Figure 19.3

Getting the people's attention:

Ezekiel begins his work among the people with four symbolic actions that are designed to impress the people with the importance of his message. Three of these actions occur simultaneously, and I will discuss them in that manner. These cause the people to stop what they are doing, to watch him, to think about it, and to ask questions. God had been using Jeremiah with his object lessons, parables and discourses to get their attention. They had ignored him, laughed at him, and persecuted him. Now, He is using Ezekiel in an even more dramatic way to convince them. Jehovah will explain these actions in 5:5-17 and in 7:27. In chapter 6, He will reveal the root of their sins, which is idolatry.

First, God has Ezekiel draw a sketch of Jerusalem on a tile and set up armaments against it (4:1-3). Second, at the same time (v.7), he is to lie on his left side 390 days for the sins of Israel and on his right side 40 days for the sins of Judah. That seems horribly uncomfortable. How would he accomplish that? Verse 8 gives the answer, "I will restrain you so that you cannot turn from one side to another till you have ended the days of your siege." Jehovah will make it possible for him to do this seemingly impossible and painful task.

There are various explanations of the total number of days—430. I found Jim McGuiggan's to be the most reasonable. God told Ezekiel, "I have laid on you a day for each year" (v. 6). The whole nation had been in Egyptian captivity a total of 430 years (Ex. 12:40-41). Hosea had predicted the captivity of the Northern Kingdom by Assyria as Egyptian bondage, "Now He will remember their iniquity and punish their sins. They shall return to Egypt" (Hos. 8:13). Saying "430 years" to a Jew at that time brought to memory the slavery in Egypt, the most horrible and painful time in their history. Since Israel is already in captivity in Assyria and all of Judah is about to go into captivity in Babylon, 430 years would speak symbolically of a complete national bondage. And, this is exactly what happened, though many thought it wouldn't. Even those left in the land after Nebuchadnezzar's complete razing of the city and temple did not remain in the land. God left it desolate (McGuiggan 1979, 52-53). If you want to share this with the children, that's fine, but I would probably wait and see if they asked the reason for the 430 days of Ezekiel's ordeal, unless you are teaching children in fifth grade and above.

Third, what will Ezekiel eat during those 430 days? "Also take for yourself wheat, barley, beans, lentils, millet, and spelt; put them into one vessel, and make bread of them for yourself" (4:9). He is instructed to measure the bread each time he ate it and measure his water each time he drank. Now, here comes the difficult part—God first instructs him to cook the bread over human waste. Ezekiel, as a faithful priest, had never done anything that would defile himself, so he protests this action, and God gives him cow's waste instead.

God explains the meaning of these actions to Ezekiel:

Moreover He said to me, "Son of man, surely I will cut off the supply of bread in Jerusalem; they shall eat bread by weight and with anxiety, and shall drink water by measure and with dread, that they may lack bread and water, and be dismayed with one another, and waste away because of their iniquity (4:16-17).

You may want to purchase Ezekiel bread and bring it to class for the children to eat. Of course, we do not know if the exact proportion of ingredients were used in this bread as in Ezekiel's, but one thing we do know—it was not cooked like Ezekiel's! You will also find Roy's illustrations helpful.

The fourth symbolic action is in chapter 5, and it was accomplished after the days of the siege. In this dramatic demonstration, God has Ezekiel cut his hair with a sharp sword, weigh it and divide it into three main parts. He is to burn one part, strike one part with the sword, scatter one part to the wind, and keep a very small amount in his clothing. After instructing him, God explains to the prophet what his actions mean, "This is Jerusalem; I have set her in the midst of the nations and countries all around her. She has rebelled against My judgments by doing wickedness more than the nations…" (v.6). He continues to describe the wickedness of the people and His coming judgment. Listen to the last verse of chapter 5: "So I will send against you famine and wild beasts, and they will bereave you. Pestilence and blood shall pass through you, and I will bring the sword against you. I, the LORD, have spoken." This is a sad picture, but Jehovah is assuring Ezekiel that His judgments are righteous and just. You will find Roy's illustrations of this action very helpful, especially the pie chart that shows the division of Ezekiel's hair and beard and what it represents.

I usually just make a quick reference to chapter 6 for two basic concepts. First, Jehovah asks Ezekiel to preach to the mountains of Israel. This represents the leaders and rulers of the people. What is he to preach? Idolatry is their root sin, and God will destroy their idols and altars. He will also destroy the people who worship them, but he will spare a remnant who will remember Him in captivity. He wants Ezekiel to really get their attention, so he says, "Pound your fists and stamp your feet, and say…" (v. 11). The leaders of the people were guilty of leading them away from God and into idolatry.

Second, they had blatantly broken the first commandment: "You shall have no other gods before me" (Ex. 20:3-4). While God had sent his prophets with the same message for hundreds of years, they still trampled His holiness underfoot and turned to the gods of the nations around them. Finally, Jehovah shouts, "Enough!" The reason for His judgments is stated first in 6:7 – "… and you shall know that I am the LORD." This phrase is repeated over and over and over some 65-70 times in chapters 6 through 39. God's holiness will be vindicated. His justice will be executed. And, His purpose for Israel will still be accomplished.

EZEKIEL PLAYED WAR!

Ezekiel 4:1-8

God gave Ezekiel several unusual assignments. Each of these was designed to help His people know what was going to happen to Jerusalem and to them because of their sins. The people had been taken captive to the land of Babylon. But, false prophets had said, "You won't have to stay very long. Your stay will be easy—about a 2 year vacation. Since the temple is in Jerusalem and you are the people of God, He won't let anything really bad happen to you."

Ezekiel's job was to tell them the truth. And the truth was just this: "You have sinned against God. Because you have sinned and won't repent, God has sent you into Babylon for 70 years, not 2 years! Also, Jerusalem and the temple will soon be completely destroyed."

To illustrate God's message, He told Ezekiel to do a very dramatic thing where the people could see it. God told him to take a tile or "clay tablet" and draw the city of Jerusalem on it. Then, build a "siege wall" around it and set up battering rams about it. God told Ezekiel to "play war" against his tile that represented Jerusalem. In fact, Ezekiel had to do this every day for more than a year! God told him to lie on his left side 390 days for the sins of Israel (the Northern Kingdom) and to lie on his right side 40 days for the sins of Judah (the Southern Kingdom). Ezekiel had to do this where everyone could see it. God said it was a sign to the people—Jerusalem and the temple would be destroyed!

Read Ezekiel 4:7-8 and fill in the blanks. Put the circled letters in order on the next page and decode a secret message.

"Therefore you shall set your face _ _ Ⓞ _ _ _ the siege of

Ⓞ _ _ _ _ _ Ⓞ _ _ ; your _ _ Ⓞ shall Ⓞ _ uncovered, and you shall

_ Ⓞ _ _ _ _ _ Ⓞ against it. And surely I will _ _ _ Ⓞ _ _ Ⓞ _ you

so that _ _ Ⓞ cannot turn from one Ⓞ _ _ _ to Ⓞ Ⓞ _ _ _ _ _ till you

have _ _ Ⓞ _ _ the days of your _ _ Ⓞ _ _ .

Figure 19.4

Ezekiel's Tile of the
City of Jerusalem

$\overline{}$ $\overline{}$ $\overline{}$ $\overline{}$ $\overline{}$ $\overline{}$ $\overline{}$ $\overline{}$ $\overline{}$ $\overline{}$ $\overline{}$ $\overline{}$
1   2   3   4   5   6   7   8   9   10   11   12

$\overline{}$ $\overline{}$ $\overline{}$
13   14   15

                    $\overline{}$ $\overline{}$ $\overline{}$!
                     1   12   6

$\overline{}$ $\overline{}$ $\overline{}$ $\overline{}$ $\overline{}$ $\overline{}$ $\overline{}$ $\overline{}$ $\overline{}$
2   15   6   10   11   12   3   15   4

      $\overline{}$ $\overline{}$ $\overline{}$ $\overline{}$ $\overline{}$ $\overline{}$
      1   9   3   3   5   15

$\overline{}$ $\overline{}$ $\overline{}$ $\overline{}$ $\overline{}$ $\overline{}$ $\overline{}$ $\overline{}$ $\overline{}$!
14   15   11   8   6   13   7   15   14

Figure 19.4

Ezekiel 4:9

"Also take for yourself wheat, barley, beans, lentils, millet, and spelt; put them into one vessel, and make bread of them for yourself. During the number of days that you lie on your side, three hundred and ninety days, you shall eat it.

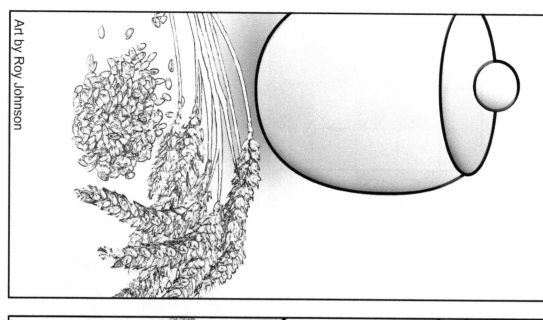

Art by Roy Johnson

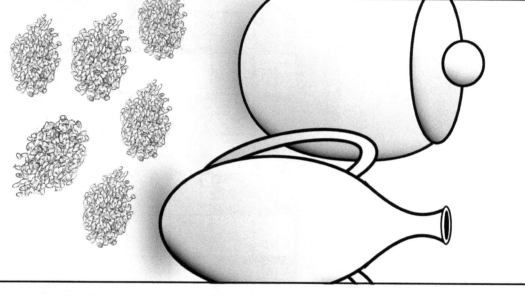

1

Figure 19.5

Ezekiel 4
"Defiled Bread"

Clues are on the next page.

Figure 19.5

Clues for "Defiled Bread" Crossword Puzzle

Across:

1. Ezekiel was to measure and drink this. (v. 11)

2. A grain that Ezekiel was to use to make his bread. (v. 9)

3. Ezekiel was to eat his bread by _____. (v. 10)

4. The children of Israel would eat (8 down) bread among the _____. (v. 13)

5. They would drink their water by (4 down) and with _____. (v. 16)

6. They would eat their bread by (3 across) and with _____. (v. 16)

7. Ezekiel told God he had never eaten abominable _____. (v. 14)

8. Ezekiel was to bake this over fire fueled with cow's waste. (vs. 9 & 12)

Down:

1. A grain Ezekiel was to use to make his bread. (v. 9)

2. A type of bean that Ezekiel was to eat. (v. 9)

3. Ezekiel was to eat only 20 ____ of food each day. (v. 10)

4. The children of Israel would drink their water by _____. (v. 11)

5. The reason all these bad things would happen to the children of Israel. (v. 17)

6. Ezekiel was to eat his bread as barley _____. (v. 12)

7. God said the people would lack bread and be _____. (v. 17)

8. The children of Israel would eat ____ bread among the (4 across). (v. 13)

9. Ezekiel was to measure his water and drink one-sixth of a ____. (v. 11)

Note to teachers: You can "white out" the verse numbers and make this a little more challenging for older students.

Figure 19.5

A Haircut with a Sword!
Ezekiel 5

"...take a sharp sword as a razor..."

"...take scales to weigh and divide the hair."

"You shall burn with fire one-third in the midst of the city..."

1

Figure 19.6

Ray Johnson
5/3/10

A Haircut with a Sword!
Ezekiel 5

"...then you shall take one third and strike around it with the sword..."

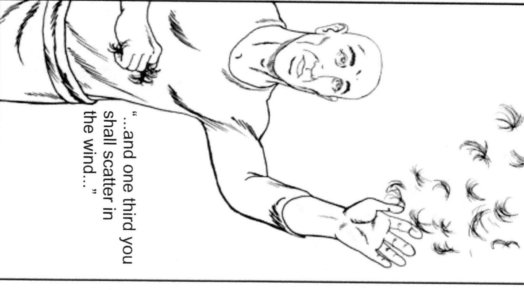

"...and one third you shall scatter in the wind..."

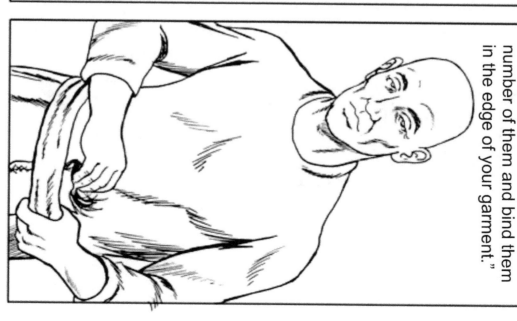

"You shall also take a small number of them and bind them in the edge of your garment."

Roy Johnson
6/1/10

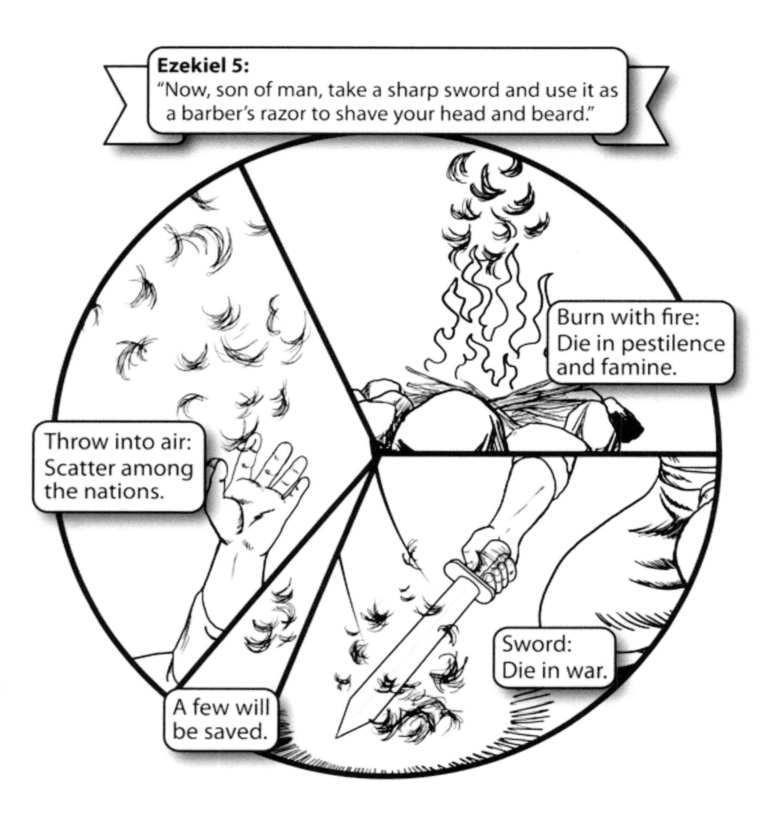

Figure 19.7

A Haircut with a Sword

After Ezekiel demonstrated that Jerusalem would be destroyed and that the people would eat "defiled food" among the Gentile nations, God asked him to do another very dramatic thing in the sight of all the people. This time, Ezekiel was told to go to the center of the city and shave his hair and beard. He could not use a regular barber's razor. God told him to use a sword. After he shaved his head, he had to weigh it on the scales and divide it into three parts. God told him to burn one third of his hair. He had to strike one third of his hair with the sword. Then, he had to throw one third of his hair into the wind and scatter it around. However, God told him to keep a very small amount of his hair and hold it inside his clothing.

What did all this mean? God told Ezekiel to tell the people the meaning. The part of his hair that he burned represented the fact that many of the people of Israel would die from "famine and pestilence." They would not have food to eat, and they would have horrible diseases and die. The part of his hair that he struck with the sword described how many would also die in the war that was coming because Nebuchadnezzar of Babylon was going to destroy the city of Jerusalem and kill many people. The hair that Ezekiel threw into the wind represented all the people that were taken to other nations, away from their homeland. In fact, the people to whom Ezekiel was preaching were some of those who had been scattered. They were among the first group of people that Nebuchadnezzar took to Babylon.

This all sounds really bad! Why would God let something so bad happen to His people? Actually, God was causing it to happen! Why? God tells Ezekiel the answer: His people had rebelled against Him. They would not keep His Law. They had followed the pagan gods of the nations around them. They had quit worshiping God in the way He had told them to, and they were even offering human sacrifices to the pagan gods! They had become worse than the nations around them! God had to punish them. He didn't want to, but He had to. And, it was for their good. He wanted them to learn that He is the One True God. He wanted them to

Figure 19.8

learn that they couldn't rebel against Him continually. He had sent His prophets to warn them and to beg them to give up the idols and the evil they were doing. They didn't listen to His prophets. Not only did they refuse to listen, they killed many of the prophets! God loved them. He warned them because He loved them, and He punished them because He loved them.

Remember that Ezekiel kept a small amount of his hair and put it inside his clothing, close to his body. This represented the few people who were still faithful to God. It demonstrated God's love and care for them. And, it demonstrated God's love and care for us. God was going to save and protect the people who were faithful to Him so He could work His purpose to send Jesus. Even when things seemed bad, God was working His purpose. His people had rebelled and had sinned against Him. However, that would not prevent God from fulfilling His promise to send Jesus. We should always remember that God had a plan and purpose even before He made the world.

Sometimes we might look at how God had to punish the people and think that He is mean. We should also remember that God is holy and God is love. He did not punish the people because He wanted to, but because He had to. If He let their continual sin and rebellion go unpunished, it would look like He didn't care how they lived. If they could "get away with anything", it would appear to them and the nations around them that God's Word was meaningless, too. God wanted them to learn that He is God; that His Word is important; and that He loved them too much to let them continue in sin. We can look at the people of Israel and their prophets and learn these same lessons. God loves us and He wants us to obey Him because this is best for us. Peter tells us in the New Testament in 2 Peter 3:9 that God doesn't want anyone to perish, but all to repent. It is not God's desire that anyone be lost, and His plan to send Jesus to save us is proof of His great love for us.

Figure 19.8

2

Unscramble these words and use them to fill in the blanks below:

ZARRO   CEALSS   REHET
RAW   ROWDS   RABED
TETACRS   MIFENA   TANNIOS

1. God told Ezekiel to shave his head and _____ using a sword
instead of a _____.
2. Ezekiel weighed his hair on _____ and divided it into
_____ parts.
3. He burned one third of his hair. This meant that part of God's people
would die from pestilence and _____.
4. He struck one third with the _____. This meant that one third of
the people would die in _____.
5. Ezekiel threw one third of his hair into the air. This meant that God
would _____ some of the people among the Gentile

_____.
QUESTIONS:
 Did Ezekiel keep any of his hair? _____   How much? _____
Where did he put it? _____
What did this mean? _____

These next words are a little harder. You will find 3 of them in Ezekiel 5:6
and 2 of them in verse 11. The other one is easy. When you unscramble
the words, use them to fill in the blanks in the next group of questions. Put
one letter in each space. Then, arrange the circled letters in order on the
next page and use them to decode a message about God.

LEBEDERL   BATETEDELS   SANBOOIMTIAN
KIDECW   RUDEEFS   VELI

Figure 19.8

Reasons God had to punish His people:

1. They were O _ OO _ _ and _ _ O _ _ .

2. They had O _ O _ _ O _ _ against Him.

3. They _ _ OO _ O _ to obey Him.

4. They had done O _ O _ _ _ O _ _ _ things.

5. They had practiced the _ _ OO _ O _ _ O _ _ O of the other nations.

Put the circled letters in order below:

1	2	3	4	5	6	7	8	9

10	11	12	13	14	15	16	17	18

Use the number code on the letters above to make words that describe God:

___ ___ ___ ___
7 14 4 10

___ ___ ___ ___ ___ ___ ___ ___
15 10 5 2 17 8 9 7

___ ___ ___ ___
3 17 16 11

___ ___ ___ ___ ___ ___ ___ ___ ___ ___ ___ ___ ___ ___ ___ ___ ___ .
1 13 16 12 18 13 7 7 12 14 6 10 18 13 4 10 11

4   Figure 19.8

A trip to Jerusalem in a vision:

Ezekiel needs assurance that Jehovah's judgements are justified, so God took him by the hair of his head in a vision to Jerusalem. As you read chapter 8, you see the horrible things the people were doing. They brought idols into the temple, and the elders of Israel burned incense to idols in secret. Women were "weeping for Tammuz" (8:14) who was probably the Sumerian god of food and vegetation; mourning was a part of the ritual worship. That's not all! At the door of the temple, between the porch and the altar, men had their backs to the temple and were facing the east, worshiping the sun! (8:16). Because of these abominations, Jehovah says, "Therefore I also will act in fury. My eye will not spare nor will I have pity; and though they cry in My ears with a loud voice, I will not hear them" (8:18).

Chapter 9 is one that people have taken out of context and developed all kinds of strange doctrines about the man with the writer's inkhorn. This is still a part of the vision in Jerusalem. The cry goes out for those "who have charge over the city" to come with deadly weapons. Six men came, each holding a battle-ax. Then one appeared who was "clothed in linen and had a writer's inkhorn at his side." These all stood beside the bronze altar (9:1-2). Much discussion has been given to whether the man with the inkhorn was one of the six or a seventh, distinct from them. It doesn't matter; the meaning is the same.

The glory of God is at the threshold of the temple, and He tells the man with the inkhorn to go through the city and "put a mark on the foreheads of the men who sigh and cry over all the abominations that are done within it" (v. 4). The others are told to "Go after him through the city and kill; do not let your eye spare, nor have any pity" (v. 5). As Ezekiel watches this vision of destruction, his tender, loving heart is aching for his people and he cries out, "Ah, Lord God! Will You destroy all the remnant of Israel…" (v. 8). God assures Ezekiel that though it seems extreme to him, He must do this because of their great wickedness. Something important that we learn about God is He knows those who are faithful to Him and will protect them in His judgments. The people with the mark on their foreheads in this vision represent the faithful few—the righteous remnant.

Chapters 10 and 11 are probably the most pitiful and distressing in Ezekiel's book. The man clothed in linen from chapter 9 now is told, "Go in among the wheels, under the cherub, fill your hands with coals of fire from the cherubim, and scatter them over the city" (v. 2). Thus, the destruction came from Jehovah, not from man. Jehovah was using Nebuchadnezzar as the instrument of His judgment. In the rest of chapter 10, Ezekiel describes the glory of God much like he did in chapter 1. The chapter ends with the glory of the LORD departing from the temple (vs. 18-19). How sad! They had defiled the temple with idols, and He could no longer dwell there. [Remember that God's glory filled the tabernacle (Ex. 40:34) and Solomon's temple (1 Kings 8:11).] Jehovah had to desert His temple and His city (11:22-23) because they had no use for Him, no place for Him in their lives and in their hearts.

A very good application here is that Paul in the New Testament tells us that we are God's temple and His Spirit dwells in us and warns us: "Do you not know that you are the temple of God and that the Spirit of God dwells in you? If anyone defiles the temple of God, God will destroy him. For the temple of God is holy, which temple you are" (1 Cor. 3:16-17). Good teachers will think of appropriate applications of this concept depending on the age and maturity of their children.

Ezekiel is again overwhelmed with the fury of God's judgments and cries out, "Ah, Lord God! Will You make a complete end of the remnant of Israel?" (11:13). God is sensitive to his concern and gives him assurance that though He has scattered Israel "far off among the Gentiles… yet I shall be a little sanctuary for them in the countries where they have gone" (11:16). He will bring them back to their land and bless them according to His word. Ezekiel can now return from the vision with the confidence that God has not fully rejected His people and will continue to work His purpose through them. He will not abandon them in the foreign lands, for He is the LORD of heaven and earth, the God of all nations.

God's people committed "great abominations."
Ezekiel 8

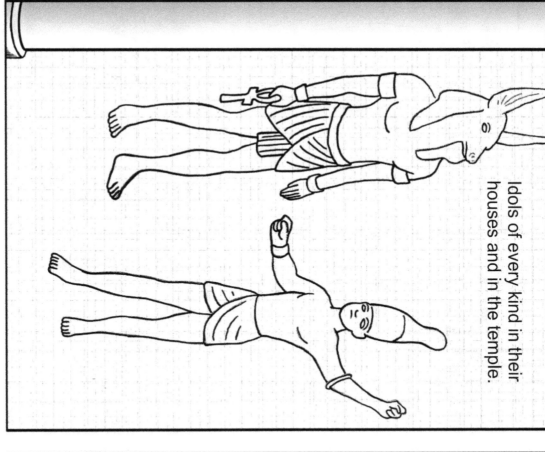

Idols of every kind in their houses and in the temple.

Women weeping for Tammuz.

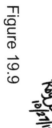

Figure 19.9

Idol Worship at God's Temple – Ezekiel 8:5-16

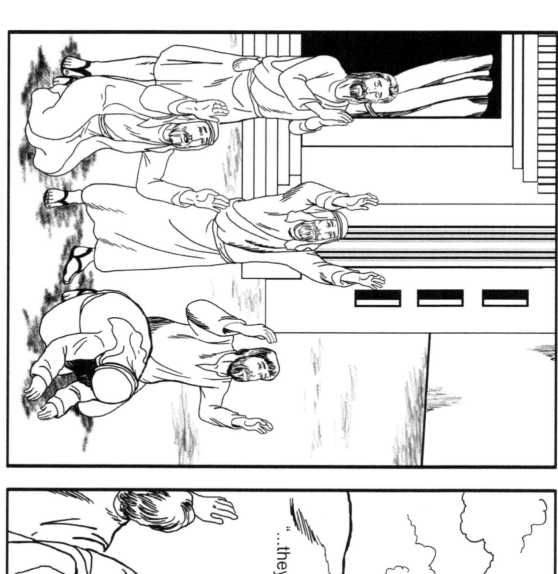

"...they were worshiping the sun toward the east."

Figure 19.9

God Preserves the Righteous when He Destroys the Wicked

Ezekiel 9

"And suddenly six men came from the direction of the upper gate, which faces north, each with his battle-ax in his hand."

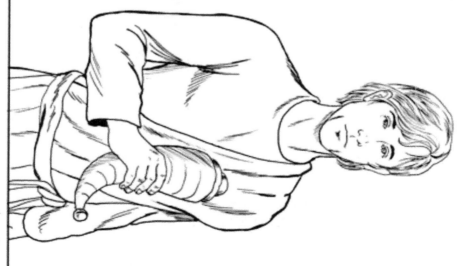

"One man among them was clothed with linen and had a writer's inkhorn at his side..."

Figure 19.10

1

The Righteous Are Marked in the Vision
God Preserves the Faithful in Judgment

Ezekiel 9:3-4
And He called to the man clothed with linen, who had the writer's inkhorn at his side; 4 and the LORD said to him, "Go through the midst of the city, through the midst of Jerusalem, and put a mark on the foreheads of the men who sigh and cry over all the abominations that are done within it."

2

Figure 19.10

God's Glory Leaves His Temple!

Ezekiel 10:18-19

Then the glory of the LORD departed from the threshold of the temple and stood over the cherubim. 19 And the cherubim lifted their wings and mounted up from the earth in my sight. When they went out, the wheels were beside them; and they stood at the door of the east gate of the LORD's house, and the glory of the God of Israel was above them.

Figure 19.11

Another symbolic action – Go into captivity:

The people are still stubborn and do not believe all Ezekiel has been telling them through these actions. They are certain Zedekiah will remain on the throne, Jerusalem will be spared and the temple will not be destroyed. No wonder God calls them "a rebellious house." In chapter 12, God calls upon Ezekiel to demonstrate the captivity of the people left in the land and, especially, the captivity of Zedekiah. This was a very important message to get across to the people, because six times in verses 3 through 6, Ezekiel is told to do this "in their sight."

That evening at twilight, Ezekiel packed his things, dug through the wall and carried his possessions on his shoulder in the sight of the people. There was one additional element in this dramatic presentation—he covered his face so he could not see the ground. Ezekiel portrayed a blind man groping for his way, going into captivity. What did all this mean? Would the people ask him about it, or were they tired of his actions?

The next morning, God tells Ezekiel what he is to say to the people—this action is a sign and it concerns the "prince in Jerusalem." The prince will carry his belongings on his shoulders and have to dig through the wall to leave. That's an ignoble task for a king, but he had rebelled against God and against Nebuchadnezzar and must pay the price. Also, God says Zedekiah will die in Babylon, though he will not see it. We learn the meaning of that from 2 Kings 25:7: "Then they killed the sons of Zedekiah before his eyes, put out the eyes of Zedekiah, bound him with bronze fetters, and took him to Babylon."

If the king is not spared, what hope is there for all the people? This is the unspoken question God answers in 12:16, "But I will spare a few of their men… that they may declare all their abominations among the Gentiles wherever they go. Then they shall know that I am the LORD." The pagan nations looked upon Jehovah as a national god of Israel. If a nation was captured and subjugated, that meant the god of that nation was weaker than the god of the nation who conquered them. The Jews who were in the distant lands of the Gentiles would tell the people why they were there. Jehovah was not weak. He had given them into the hands of their enemies to punish them for their sins. When they declare this to their captors, the heathen nations will "know that I am the LORD." This corresponds to Isa. 26:9, "For when Your judgments are in the earth, the inhabitants of the world will learn righteousness." Remember Jehovah had promised earlier through Isaiah that He would also bring the captives back to their land under Cyrus. All of this is designed to convince His people that He is Lord of heaven and earth. It is also a demonstration to pagan nations that there is no God but Jehovah.

Personally, I find it difficult to see how anyone who honestly reviews the history of the Jews from Egypt onward can reject the God of the Bible. I also think it is important to remind our students of the definition of faith. Atheists and agnostics will laugh at us and call us closed-minded, irrational, and ignorant. They say we just "believe in a mystical fairy tale"—that we just accept the Bible and God as true without evidence. This is not the faith I have, and it is not the faith God requires. He does not ask us to shut our eyes, disregard all reason, park our brains, and make a "leap of faith." Right here in Ezekiel, He is giving us evidence. The history of the Jewish people was not happenstance.

Go Into Captivity! – Ezekiel 12:1-16

"Therefore, son of man, prepare your belongings for captivity, and go into captivity by day in their sight."

"Dig through the wall in their sight, and carry your belongings out through it. In their sight you shall bear them on your shoulders and carry them out at twilight; you shall cover your face, so that you cannot see the ground, for I have made you a sign to the house of Israel."

Figure 19.12

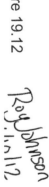

Roy Johnson
19.12

GO INTO CAPTIVITY!
EZEKIEL 12: 1-13

In Jerusalem and in Babylon, false teachers were telling the people that captivity would be short, and that only a few of them would actually go into Babylon as captives. Ezekiel had to preach the Word of God to people who were already in Babylon. They were among the second group that Nebuchadnezzar took to his kingdom of Babylon. They should have known that most of the people were going to be taken to Babylon, because they were there! But, they were sure their king Zedekiah would not be taken to Babylon. God had Ezekiel "act out" going into captivity. God told him to cover his face so he couldn't see the ground. Then He told Ezekiel what that meant. He said that the king would go into Babylon, yet he would not see it. That is exactly what happened. We read in 2 Kings 25:5-7 that Nebuchadnezzar's army captured Zedekiah and his sons: "Then they killed the sons of Zedekiah before his eyes, put out the eyes of Zedekiah, bound him with bronze fetters, and took him to Babylon."

Answer these questions from Ezekiel 12: 1-13:

1. The people of Israel had eyes, but did _____ _____; they had ears, but did _____ _____ . (Verse 2)

2. They were r_____. (Verse 2)

3. God told Ezekiel to prepare his _____ for _____ and to go into captivity in _____ sight. (Verse 3)

1

Figure 19.13

4. God told him to _____ through the _____ in their _____. (Verse 5)

5. Ezekiel had to carry his things on his _____ and cover his _____ so that he could not see the _____. (Verse 6)

6. When the people asked what he was doing, God told Ezekiel to tell them: "This burden concerns the _____ in _____, and all the house (people) of _____. (Verse 10)

7. Ezekiel said to the people, "I am a _____ to you. As I have done, so shall they be carried away into _____. (Verse 11)

8. He also told them, "The prince who is among them shall bear his _____ on his shoulders at _____, and go out. They shall _____ through the _____ to carry them out through it. (Verse 12)

9. The prince (King Zedekiah) would go to Babylon, but he would not _____ it. He would _____ in the land of Babylon. (Verse 13)

THE FALSE PROPHETS WERE WRONG! ZEDEKIAH DID GO INTO CAPTIVITY! ZEDEKIAH WAS BLINDED WHEN NEBUCHADNEZZAR HAD HIS EYES PUT OUT! GOD'S TRUE PROPHETS—JEREMIAH AND EZEKIEL—TOLD THE TRUTH, BUT THE PEOPLE WOULDN'T LISTEN.

LET'S BE SURE TO LISTEN TO GOD'S WORD!

Figure 19.13

Concluding Comments:

This completes the lessons from the first half of Ezekiel that I have taught to children up to about sixth grade. There are two more lessons that I'm including here which are not appropriate for younger children, but would be good for junior high and above. Teachers should use good judgment in deciding to teach these lessons and in the wording they choose.

In chapter 16 Jehovah describes His relationship with the nation of Israel and Judah. The imagery is of a man finding a newborn baby that has been discarded and left to die. The man saves the baby, nurtures her and protects her. Later, as she comes of age, he loves her, marries her, and gives her fabulous jewels and clothing—whatever she desires. What a beautiful love story! However, she spurns his love, goes out to other men, and gives his gifts to them in exchange for their sexual favors. The ingratitude and immorality of Judah is pictured in very graphic terms. You can just read and summarize this for your students or have them read it together. I have included Roy's illustration of this scenario in the Appendix – Figure A.6 – in case you would like to illustrate the lesson.

The application for us today is obvious—the church is described as Jesus' wife or bride (Eph. 5:20-32). In that context, Paul describes the relationship similar to Ezekiel. Jesus' love for the church is sacrificial, benevolent, and holy. In response to that love, we should be thankful for the gift of salvation and all spiritual blessings, and return that love in obedient service in His kingdom. Unfaithfulness to Jesus is like a wife being unfaithful to a benevolent, gracious husband.

In Chapter 24, there is a parable and a sign. The parable of the boiling caldron assures the people that Nebuchadnezzar, who had begun the siege of Jerusalem (vs. 1-2), will completely destroy the people, the temple, and the city. The sign, beginning in verse 15, is harder to understand. God tells Ezekiel, "Behold, I take away from you the desire of your eyes with one stroke; yet you shall neither mourn nor weep, nor shall your tears run down" (v. 16). Now, this really got the people's attention! The other signs had not touched Ezekiel personally, but this one hit him directly in his home and heart—the wife he loved and cherished died. Yet, he did as God commanded. When the people asked him, Ezekiel delivered the message from God, "Behold, I will profane My sanctuary, your arrogant boast, the desire of your eyes, the delight of your souls… And you shall do as I have done; you shall not cover your lips nor eat man's bread of sorrow" (vs. 21-22). Additionally, God tells Ezekiel that he will be mute until the day a man escapes from Jerusalem and brings news that the city has been destroyed. Then, he will speak. Thus, in these two ways, Ezekiel now becomes the sign to the people.

This sign strikes at the heart of the prophet, but he doesn't lash out at God or question His methods. Instead, "the next morning I did as I was commanded" (v.18). We may be prone to question God about this, but the one whom it affected most humbly submitted. He was living in desperate times. In the past, God had asked Hosea to marry a harlot who bore children that were not his. Hosea learned God's anguish from his experience. Jeremiah's family plotted against him, and he had to give up those close family ties to continue as God's servant. God never promised Ezekiel, Hosea, or Jeremiah that service to Him would be easy. In fact, He said much the opposite. Should we be surprised when we have to suffer loss in His service?

Chapter 20
EZEKIEL'S MESSAGE AFTER THE FALL OF JERUSALEM

Jehovah had told Ezekiel in the last verse of chapter 24 that he would not have a message for the people—that he would be mute—until the day when one who escaped Jerusalem tells him of the city's destruction. We read in 33:21 that a messenger came "in the twelfth year of our captivity, in the tenth month, on the fifth day of the month… and said, 'The city has been captured!'" Ezekiel, again, had a message for his people. (You will notice that chapters 25-32 discuss the fate of the nations around Israel.)

At first, Ezekiel's job was to prepare the captives for the destruction of Jerusalem and the temple. Now, he must give them hope for the future. There is a good lesson for older students in chapter 34— selfish shepherds (leaders) had been the downfall of Israel. Now, God will gather His sheep and "I will establish one shepherd over them, and he shall feed them—My servant David…" (v. 23). This is clearly a Messianic prophecy, fulfilled in Jesus, the Good Shepherd (John 10). In this same context, Jehovah declares, "I will make a covenant of peace with them, and cause wild beasts to cease from the land; and they will dwell safely…" (v. 25). Does this remind you of Isaiah's picture of God's holy mountain in chapter 11? Also, remember Jeremiah's new covenant. Ezekiel is using similar figurative language to describe the same event—the Messiah's reign.

How will this be accomplished, since both Israel and Judah are in captivity and scattered throughout the nations? Their land is desolate and unproductive. God answers that question by sending Ezekiel to a valley filled with dry bones. He asks the prophet, "Can these bones live?" (v. 3). Ezekiel obeys the command to prophecy to the dry bones, and when he does, they come together with sinews and flesh over them, but with no life in them. Then, God commands him to prophecy to the breath, and when he does, the men come alive as a great army. I have included a story sheet that explains for children, but the explanation is rather clear. God will give His people their land, and they shall become alive through His work and through obedience to His Word. Figures 20.1, pages 1 and 2 illustrate this event. I also have a story sheet for preaching to the dry bones, figure 20.2, pages 1 and 2.

After this experience, God tells Ezekiel to get two sticks. Write on one, "For Judah and for the children of Israel, his companions;" and write on the other, "For Joseph, the stick of Ephraim and for all the house of Israel, and his companions." Now, again, this is a demonstration before all the people. When Ezekiel joins the two sticks, they become one stick in his hands. Then, when the people ask what it means, Ezekiel is commanded to say, "Thus says the Lord God: 'Surely I will take the children of Israel from among the nations, wherever they have gone... and I will make them one nation in the land... David My servant shall be king over them...'" (37:21-24).

All of this is Messianic. Let's notice how chapter 37 ends:

David My servant shall be king over them, and they shall all have one shepherd; they shall also walk in My judgments and observe My statutes, and do them. Then they shall dwell in the land that I have given to Jacob My servant, where your fathers dwelt; and they shall dwell there, they, their children, and their children's children, forever; and My servant David shall be their prince forever. Moreover I will make a covenant of peace with them, and it shall be an everlasting covenant with them; I will establish them and multiply them, and I will set My sanctuary in their midst forevermore. My tabernacle also shall be with them; indeed I will be their God, and they shall be My people. The nations also will know that I, the LORD, sanctify Israel, when My sanctuary is in their midst forevermore (37:24-28).

I have prepared a story sheet and two side-by-side scripture sheets that will help you illustrate the Messianic imagery in this passage as it is fulfilled in the New Testament.

It is important to establish the Messianic context in which Ezekiel is speaking, because this impacts the rest of his book. We have allowed Ezekiel's message to be shrouded in mystery and complexity because of the false teachings that are touted on TV, the internet, and by door-to-door evangelists. This is especially true of these last chapters.

I have had children ask me about Gog in chapters 38-39, though I've never prepared a special lesson for them. When you read all the imagery of this humongous army from all over the known world, riding horses, wearing magnificent armor, and wielding swords, it's an amazing and frightening sight. The army of Gog comes into their land to overtake it, but God destroys them completely, protecting His people.

For decades in America, at least, preachers have tried to make Gog an amalgamation of various nations of the day—Russia, China, Eurozone, and now Iran or ISIS. If the world continues, a new theory will arise with a new timetable. We have seen Hal Lindsey's predictions of Jesus' return in the 1980's come to naught. Other theories have come and gone as well. Now, the pundits are saying they can't be sure of an exact date, but they know it will be soon and that Ezekiel's prophecy of Gog relates to what is going on in our world today.

I don't want to write a treatise on millennialism, because we don't need that to understand what Ezekiel was telling God's people then and what that means to us today. Now that Ezekiel is giving the people hope for the future when the Messiah comes, we can see how they would need assurance that destruction and captivity would never occur under His reign. Ezekiel could have said directly, "When the Messiah comes, those who are in His kingdom will be absolutely victorious. Nothing can harm them." However, in the style characteristic of much of his writing and of the other prophets, God reveals victory in terms of a great battle that Israel wins. The enemy is larger and fiercer than any they have faced before, and he comes with greater force than all of them combined. How will they withstand such an army? God destroys their enemy decisively and immediately! Does that give you the idea that those in the Messiah's kingdom are safe? Listen to how Paul expresses that concept:

> Yet in all these things we are more than conquerors through Him who loved us. For I am persuaded that neither death nor life, nor angels nor principalities nor powers, nor things present nor things to come, nor height nor depth, nor any other created thing, shall be able to separate us from the love of God which is in Christ Jesus our Lord (Rom. 8:37-39).

How is it possible to be "more than conquerors?" The Messiah has destroyed the works of our worst enemy—Satan—and delivered us "who through fear of death were all our lifetime subject to bondage" (Heb. 2:15). Therefore, as long as we remain in His kingdom and are faithful to Him, we have the victory.

Chapters 40-48 describe a new temple and a new city under the Messiah's reign. There is a new city where the Messiah's throne will be established, and a new temple in that city where the High Priest will officiate. Ezekiel uses the language of the old order in a highly figurative way to describe the sacrifice and worship in the new. I have not taught this to children in great detail, but I have read through these chapters, just "hitting the highlights" as we go, and reminding them of Isaiah's fabulous city in chapter 60. I usually tell them that Ezekiel was a priest, so he focuses more on the temple in this new city, whereas Isaiah was just telling us about the grandeur of the city where Jehovah dwells. Homer Hailey has an easy to follow discussion of these chapters in The Messiah in Prophecy to the Messiah on the Throne if you are teaching older children and want to go into greater detail.

However, there are some things that are important for children of all ages. First, let's go back to a statement in Ezekiel 21 that sheds light on this section:

Now to you, O profane, wicked prince of Israel, whose day has come, whose iniquity shall end, thus says the Lord GOD:

"Remove the turban, and take off the crown;

Nothing shall remain the same.

Exalt the humble, and humble the exalted.

Overthrown, overthrown,

I will make it overthrown!

It shall be no longer,

Until He comes whose right it is,

And I will give it to Him" (21:25-27).

Jeconiah (Coniah) was taken to Babylon with the first group of captives. Zedekiah, blinded and humiliated, was taken with the last. Thus, the crown had been removed from the physical kingdom. Nebuchadnezzar completely destroyed the temple, and so the turban was removed from the physical kingdom. Truly, "nothing shall remain the same." The new order will be different from the old. Notice verse 27: "It shall be no longer, until He comes whose right it is, and I will give it to Him." The crown and turban, symbols of the king and priest, would be given to the One "whose right it is." And, it would be given by almighty God. Jesus, the Messiah, serves as both king and priest under the new covenant as we have mentioned previously. Figure 20.5 is a chart I prepared that will help you teach this concept to children. We will see this idea of king and priest again sixty to seventy years later in the prophecy of Zechariah.

Second, recall that God's glory left the physical temple in Jerusalem in chapter 10. In this new temple, Ezekiel says, "And behold, the glory of the LORD filled the house of the LORD; and I fell on my face" (44:4). It is worth remembering that God's glory filled the tabernacle after it was completed (Ex. 40:34), and His glory filled Solomon's temple (1 Kings 8:11). However, we do not read of God's glory filling the temple when it was rebuilt by Zerubbabel and the remnant who returned to Jerusalem. Thus, the temple Ezekiel is describing is not that temple. Also, according to Jesus' prediction, it was destroyed in 70 A.D. by the Roman army. This new temple is where God's glory dwells in Christ (Heb. 1:3; Eph. 1:22-23).

Third, and probably most important, the description of the temple and city ends with, "and the name of the city from that day shall be: THE LORD IS THERE" (48:35). I love that! The LORD is there! If I can't understand all the imagery Ezekiel is using, if I can't figure out everything about this city and temple, this one thing I can know—this is the city where Jehovah dwells! This is the same city Isaiah called "The City of the LORD, Zion of the Holy One of Israel" (Isa. 60:14). Where does Jehovah dwell? Of the church, Paul says in Ephesians 2:22, that we are "a dwelling place of God in the Spirit." Don't you want to live in that city?

Concluding Comments:

There are other great lessons in Ezekiel, but these are my favorites. I hope they become yours, too. Also, I hope you have seen that all the mystery about Ezekiel is caused by men and not by this great prophet of God. As you can see, Ezekiel is a man of conviction, imagination, creativity, courage, and perseverance, and is a tremendous example of service to God in difficult times. Ezekiel gives us hope that Jehovah will fight for us if we just remain true to Him.

The Dry Bones Live – Ezekiel 37:1-14

"Prophesy to these bones, and say to them, 'O dry bones, hear the word of the LORD!'"

"As I looked, the sinews and the flesh came upon them, and the skin covered them over, but there was no breath in them."

RoyJohnson
11/11/12

The Dry Bones Live ⇨ A Remnant Shall Return!

"Prophesy to the breath, 'Come O breath, and breathe on these slain, that they may live.'"

"And breath came into them and they lived, and stood upon their feet, an exceedingly great army."

I will put My Spirit in you, and you shall live, and I will place you in your own land. Then you shall know that I, the LORD, have spoken it and performed it," says the LORD'" (Ezekiel 37:14)

Figure 20.1

2

PREACH TO THE BONES
EZEKIEL 37: 1-14
THE POWER OF GOD'S WORD

This is an interesting vision, too. God showed Ezekiel a whole great big valley full of dry bones. There was no life in the bones. They were just dead and dried up. Then God told Ezekiel to preach to them. When he did, the bones came together and muscle and skin came onto them! Then Ezekiel saw them as a great army! But, they had no life. They were just standing there. God told Ezekiel to preach to the "breath" and to call it from the wind. When he did, breath came into the great army and they were alive!

What did all this mean? The people of Israel had not obeyed God. They had worshipped idols and had lived very, very bad lives. God had to send Nebuchadnezzar from Babylon to destroy their land, the city of Jerusalem and the temple. Also, Nebuchadnezzar took many of the people away from their homes to live in Babylon. God used this vision to show Ezekiel that the people would not stay in Babylon. God promised to bring them back to their home in the land of Israel. He also promised they would build their temple again. It would be like being dead (dry bones) and then coming back to life.

How would God do this? The people would have to hear and obey God's word. That's why God told Ezekiel to preach to the dry bones. While they were in Babylon for 70 years, they learned their lesson. They changed their minds and repented. God brought them back to their home just like He promised.

God's word is powerful! We must obey His word for it to have power in our lives. Paul says in the New Testament that people who are not Christians are "dead in their sins." They are "made alive in Christ" when they obey God's word. (Col. 2:13)

Figure 20.2

QUESTIONS

1. What did Ezekiel see in the valley?_____

2. What did God tell him to do? _____

3. What happened to the bones? _____

4. What caused life to come into them?

_____

_____

5. Who did the bones represent? _____

6. What did the vision mean? _____

7. How would this happen? _____

8. Is God's word powerful? _____

9. Is it important to obey His word? _____

What does each of these scriptures tell us about God's Word?

Luke 4:32: _____

Mark 13:31: _____

John 6:63: _____

John 6:68: _____

John 12:48: _____

Hebrews 4:12: _____

Romans 1:16: _____

God's Eternal Purpose in the Sign of Two Sticks
Ezekiel 37:15-28

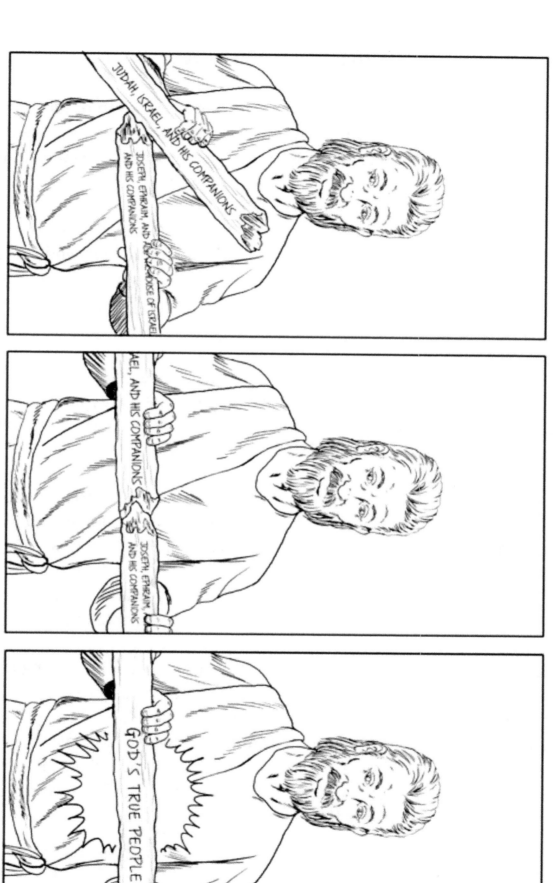

"My tabernacle also shall be with them; indeed I will be their God, and they shall be My people"
(Ezekiel 37:27)

Figure 20.3

GOD'S PROMISE AND TWO STICKS

As we have been learning about Ezekiel and his work to preach to God's people, we see that he had a difficult job. He had to preach a message that was not popular. The people had sinned, and they had to suffer the consequences of their sin.

God had a plan to send Jesus into the world even before He made the world. He knew man would sin and that he would need to be saved from sin. When God's people were so sinful, it seemed like God could not fulfill His purpose. However, God gave Ezekiel the assurance that He was going to fulfill all His promises to His people.

We have already seen one way God helped Ezekiel know that His people would return to their land. That was in the vision of the valley of dry bones. When Ezekiel preached to those dry bones, they became alive! They even became as a great army! This is in Ezekiel chapter 37.

Also in chapter 37, God gives Ezekiel another picture of His plan to bring the people of Israel back to their land and to send Jesus. God told him to take two sticks. On one, he was to write: "Judah, Israel and his companions." On the other, he was to write: "Joseph, Ephraim and all the house of Israel and his companions." Then God told Ezekiel to hold the two sticks in his hand and they would become one stick. Ezekiel had to do this so the people could see.

God explained the meaning of this. He said that He would bring the people back from all the nations where they had been scattered and they would be one people. This was first fulfilled when Ezra and Nehemiah came back to Judah and Jerusalem and rebuilt their city and the temple. However, the last few verses relate to a greater time, when a king like David will rule over God's kingdom forever. This is a promise of Jesus. He is the "King of Kings." It is also a promise of Jesus' Church. The Church is the people over whom God rules.

Figure 20.3

The Sign of Two Sticks
Ezekiel 37:15-28

For _____ and the children of _____, his companions.

'For _____ the stick of _____, and for all the house of _____, his companions

---

GOD'S TRUE PEOPLE

This prophecy is fully fulfilled in Jesus, the Messiah.

Ezekiel 37:24-28
"David My servant shall be king over them, and they shall all have one shepherd; they shall also walk in My judgments and observe My statutes, and do them. ...27 My tabernacle also shall be with them; indeed I will be their God, and they shall be My people. 28 The nations also will know that I, the LORD, sanctify Israel, when My sanctuary is in their midst forevermore.""

John 10:11
"I am the good shepherd. The good shepherd gives His life for the sheep."

Romans 2:28-29
For he is not a Jew who is one outwardly, nor is circumcision that which is outward in the flesh; 29 but he is a Jew who is one inwardly; and circumcision is that of the heart, in the Spirit, not in the letter; whose praise is

Galatians 4:26-2
7"... but the Jerusalem above is free, which is the mother of us all."

OLD TESTAMENT

Ezek 37:24-28
4 "David My servant shall be king over them, and they shall all have one shepherd; they shall also walk in My judgments and observe My statutes, and do them. 25 Then they shall dwell in the land that I have given to Jacob My servant, where your fathers dwelt; and they shall dwell there, they, their children, and their children's children, forever; and My servant David shall be their prince forever. 26 Moreover I will make a covenant of peace with them, and it shall be an everlasting covenant with them; I will establish them and multiply them, and I will set My sanctuary in their midst forevermore. 27 My tabernacle also shall be with them; indeed I will be their God, and they shall be My people. 28 The nations also will know that I, the LORD, sanctify Israel, when My sanctuary is in their midst forevermore."'"

NEW TESTAMENT

Luke 1:30-33
30 Then the angel said to her, "Do not be afraid, Mary, for you have found favor with God. 31 And behold, you will conceive in your womb and bring forth a Son, and shall call His name JESUS. 32 He will be great, and will be called the Son of the Highest; and the Lord God will give Him the throne of His father David. 33 And He will reign over the house of Jacob forever, and of His kingdom there will be no end."

Heb 8:8-11
"Behold, the days are coming, says the LORD, when I will make a new covenant with the house of Israel and with the house of Judah -- 9 not according to the covenant that I made with their fathers in the day when I took them by the hand to lead them out of the land of Egypt; because they did not continue in My covenant, and I disregarded them, says the LORD. 10 For this is the covenant that I will make with the house of Israel after those days, says the LORD: I will put My laws in their mind and write them on their hearts; and I will be their God, and they shall be My people.

2 Cor 6:16
For you are the temple of the living God. As God has said:

"I will dwell in them
And walk among them.
I will be their God,
And they shall be My people."

Ezekiel 21:26-27

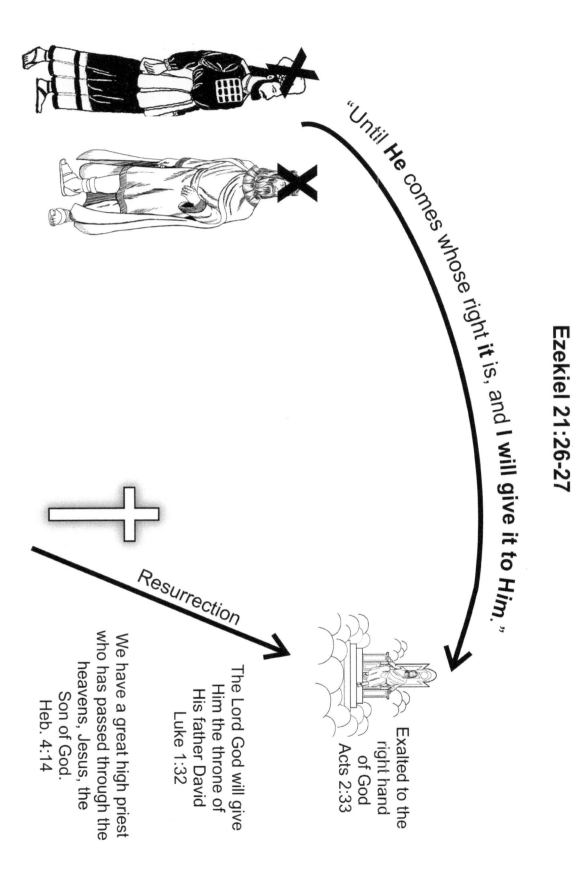

"Until **He** comes whose right **it** is, and I will give it to **Him**."

Remove the turban (priest)
Take off the crown (king)

©Chart by Sarah Fallis
Art by Roy Johnson

Resurrection

Exalted to the
right hand
of God
Acts 2:33

The Lord God will give
Him the throne of
His father David
Luke 1:32

We have a great high priest
who has passed through the
heavens, Jesus, the
Son of God.
Heb. 4:14

**Jesus is both priest and king.
He wears the turban and crown.**

Figure 20.5

Chapter 21
A DREAM OF AN IMAGE AND A VISION OF FOUR BEASTS

My first introduction to the weakness of our published curriculum materials for children was in early 1969 when Gary was preaching for a congregation in northeast Texas. I had taught Bible classes previously, but I was free to work up my own lessons. This congregation was using some material from a respected publisher, and I was following the outline because that was what the elders had chosen for the classes. I was also teaching junior high mathematics during the week, so Saturday was usually my time to do intense preparation for my Sunday class. I remember clearly one special lesson—Daniel 2 for fifth and sixth grades. The main focus of the lesson was: Daniel could interpret Nebuchadnezzar's dream because he studied hard in school. There was a picture of a young Daniel sitting in a school desk, and the application we were supposed to make was children should work hard in school and obey their teachers so they could be like Daniel.

You can imagine my reaction! I could not believe anyone would write something for a children's class that was so out of harmony with what the Bible actually says: "But there is a God in heaven who reveals secrets..." (Dan. 2:28). I taught the lesson correctly, but I wondered how many novice teachers may have taught "obey your teachers" as the focus of that lesson. However, I wasn't satisfied. I felt my students really were not getting the message of the Bible from that curriculum and from my dutifully following it as my elders had indicated. This event caused me to look more critically at the materials. I am happy to report that apparently someone complained to the publisher of that material, because all the future lessons for children dealing with Daniel 2 have been biblically correct. A few years later, I saw Daniel 2 as a lesson for Vacation Bible School or as a lesson in a series on Daniel in the typical chronological format for Bible class materials. However, remembering how Granddaddy had interested me in the prophets, I decided to work toward that goal with children and also to help teachers see ways they could incorporate those messages in their teaching.

This chapter deals with the familiar dream of Nebuchadnezzar and with the less familiar vision of Daniel in chapter 7. These are parallel accounts, as you will see. You remember from Daniel 2 Nebuchadnezzar had a troubling dream. He called all his magicians and astrologers to give him the dream and interpretation, but they could not. The king issued a decree to kill all the wise men in the kingdom, including Daniel, but Daniel prayed and then asked to see the king. He correctly identified the dream and gave the interpretation.

Let's review the dream: Nebuchadnezzar saw an image with head of gold, breast and arms of silver, belly and thighs of brass, and legs and feet of iron and iron mixed with clay. A stone was cut out and hit the image in the feet, destroyed it completely, and became a great mountain, filling all the earth. The interpretation dealt with the future kingdoms as Daniel tells Nebuchadnezzar in verse 38, "…you are this head of gold." The kingdoms following Babylon are Persia, Greece, and Rome. The climax of the prophecy is in verse 44: "And in the days of these kings (*the fourth kingdom*) the God of heaven will set up a kingdom which shall never be destroyed; and the kingdom shall not be left to other people; it shall break in pieces and consume all these kingdoms, and it shall stand forever."

As the included story/lesson sheets indicate, Jesus was born, lived, died and rose from the dead during the time when Rome ruled the world. The church was established and the gospel was preached throughout the Roman Empire during the first and second centuries. Thus, confirming Daniel's prophecy. It is also interesting to read in Luke 3:15 when John the Baptizer was preaching the people were in expectation, wondering if he were the Christ. Why were they expecting the Christ at that time? They knew Daniel's prophecy, and they knew they were living in the time of that fourth kingdom.

One Wednesday, after we had studied Daniel 2 and the children were interested in his prophecy, I decided to teach chapter 7. If you aren't familiar with that chapter, please read it before you continue. I began by telling them I was going to read something that was very different from the things we'd read, but that was also an interesting vision God revealed to Daniel. As I read chapter 7, I could see their interest and curiosity coming to the surface. I had made drawings of the four beasts of verses 1-8, but they were definitely not as good as those Jodie Boren did for us later. The children critiqued my drawings, but they were even more interested in what all these beasts meant. So, we reviewed Nebuchadnezzar's dream from chapter 2 and then made the parallel application.

Like Daniel, they were really interested in the fourth beast, the one we named "Big, Bad and Ugly." I didn't go into detail about the emperors of Rome and exactly who the "little horn" was; it was enough for them to know that the horn was a very bad emperor who wanted people to worship him instead of God and who persecuted Christians because they would not worship him. We spent two or three class periods on chapter 7, but the children were definitely "getting it." During that time, I had asked Jodie Boren to draw the beasts. He sent me copies, and the children critiqued those as well. I had to send "Big, Bad and Ugly" back for revisions; they didn't think his first rendition was fierce enough. I have all of these and the explanation with them at the end of this chapter.

I can't close this chapter without relating this incident: After we studied Daniel 7, Jordan, a fourth grader, came to class a little early one Wednesday evening. He said, "Mrs. Sarah, I was reading in Revelation that John saw something kind-of like Daniel saw. What does that mean?" I walked to the timeline on our wall and stood where Daniel was and said, "Jordan, Daniel was here, over 500 years before Jesus was born. He's looking this way into the future. In what order did he see the beasts?" He quickly answered, "The lion, the bear, the leopard with 4 heads, and 'Big, Bad and Ugly.'" I said, "That's right." Then, I walked to the end of the timeline for John's position in history and said, "Now, John is here, looking back this way," as I pointed back toward all the previous history. I asked, "In what order did he see the beasts?" He paused and thought and then he said, "Backwards!" I said, "That's right!" He replied, "Well, that makes sense!" and sat down.

Now, some may say a fourth grader doesn't need to know about the four beasts of Daniel 7. A fourth grader needs to know to tell the truth, to obey his parents, to obey God, etc. Yes, those are important for any child to know. But, look at what Jordan learned—he learned God's Word makes sense! That lesson will undergird his faith when he is hit with atheistic ideas from professors, friends, or the media. That lesson will keep him anchored in the Word when he is challenged by world religions and other "sacred books." We all need that lesson—God's Word makes sense.

Concluding comments:

There are many false teachings from the book of Daniel floating around in the religious world. I remember studying with some women who were going door-to-door in San Antonio teaching that Daniel's prophecy related to sometime in the then 20th century. They told me the head of gold was Assyria. When I protested and said what Daniel said—that it was Babylon. They said it couldn't be Babylon; it had to be Assyria. As they continued, I saw why they wanted it to be Assyria. They did not want the fourth kingdom to be Rome. They were trying to make a part of that image into the European Common Market and another part into Russia. The only way their theory would hold was if the head of gold in the image was Assyria.

While that may sound a bit outlandish, it is still a popular teaching. However, there is another more subtle teaching on this that is touted by some very respected scholars and is taught in some Christian Universities. We need to fortify our children relating to this because they may be influenced by professors or teachers who espouse this more subtle and "plausible" doctrine. "Most scholars, however, understand the kingdoms to be Babylon, Media, Persia, and the Hellenistic realms… the visions of chapters 7-12 concern the Hellenistic kingdoms and nothing later… and Greek ideas of four successive kingdoms were Babylon, Media, Persia, and Greece" (Hamilton 2009, 656). While Hamilton stands by this interpretation of the four kingdoms, he does admit that Media never dominated Israel, which presents a problem for this theory. What he overlooks is, "The leadership of the Median chieftains was of short duration. A certain Cyrus, king of Anshan, in Elam, overthrew their power, and assumed the headship of both Medes and Persians… Cyrus soon built up an empire more extended than any… ruler before his time" (Myers 1904, 88).

Why would any Bible professor want the four great kingdoms to exclude Rome? That answer is simple—they do not want the kingdom that God established to be the church of Christ of the New Testament. The evidence is so clear if the fourth kingdom of both Daniel 2 and 7 is Rome that the only way around it is to somehow discredit the clarity of the prophecy. Also, listen to Hamilton's explanation of the fourth beast of Daniel 7: "Coins from Alexander the Great and his immediate successors portrayed a ruler wearing a horned crown, and such an image may have triggered the author's imagination here" (Hamilton 2009, 660). So these pagan images "triggered" Daniel's imagination? Are we to conclude that Daniel 7 is just a product of his imagination? This is the kind of "double speak" some scholars are trying to ingrain in young, fertile minds. It undermines the credibility of the Bible and places human scholarship above the divine authorship. The true Bible scholar sits in judgment under the Word, not in judgment on the Word.

Daniel 2:24-45

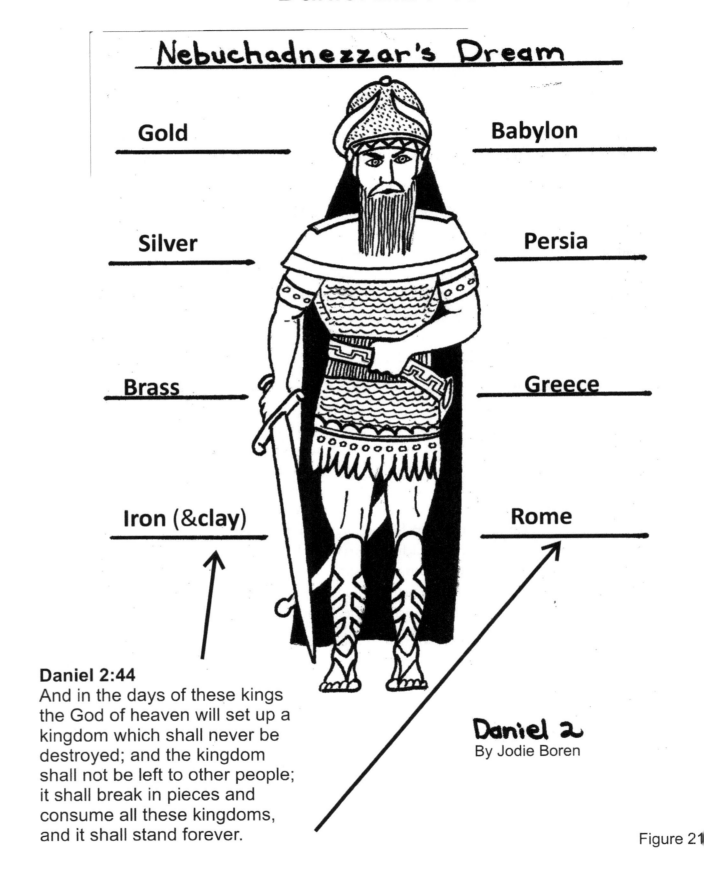

Nebuchadnezzar's Dream

Gold

Silver

Brass

Iron (&clay)

Babylon

Persia

Greece

Rome

Daniel 2:44
And in the days of these kings the God of heaven will set up a kingdom which shall never be destroyed; and the kingdom shall not be left to other people; it shall break in pieces and consume all these kingdoms, and it shall stand forever.

Daniel 2
By Jodie Boren

Figure 21

Daniel's Vision of Four Great Beasts
Daniel 7

- "I saw in my vision by night, and behold, the four winds of heaven were stirring up the Great Sea. 3 And four great beasts came up from the sea, each different from the other. 4 The first was like a lion, and had eagle's wings.

- **Dan 7:2-4**

- I watched till its wings were plucked off; and it was lifted up from the earth and made to stand on two feet like a man, and a man's heart was given to it.
- **Dan 7:4**

Figure 21.2

Daniel's Vision Continued
Daniel 7

- "And suddenly another beast, a second, like a bear. It was raised up on one side, and had three ribs in its mouth between its teeth. And they said thus to it: 'Arise, devour much flesh!'
- **Dan 7:5**

- "After this I looked, and there was another, like a leopard, which had on its back four wings of a bird. The beast also had four heads, and dominion was given to it."
- **Dan 7:6**

Figure 21.2

Daniel's Vision Continued
Daniel 7

BIG, BAD & UGLY

- "After this I saw in the night visions, and behold, a fourth beast, dreadful and terrible, exceedingly strong. It had huge iron teeth; it was devouring, breaking in pieces, and trampling the residue with its feet. It was different from all the beasts that were before it, and it had ten horns. I was considering the horns, and there was <u>another horn, a little one, coming up among them,</u> before whom three of the first horns were plucked out by the roots. And there, **in this horn, were eyes like the eyes of a man, and a mouth speaking pompous words.**

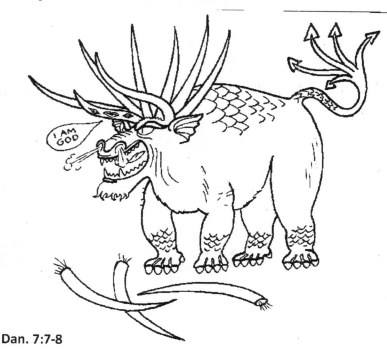

Dan. 7:7-8

Judgment on "BIG, BAD & UGLY"

- "I watched then because of the sound of the **pompous words** which the horn was speaking; I watched till the beast was slain, and its body destroyed and given to the burning flame. As for the rest of the beasts, they had their dominion taken away, yet their lives were prolonged for a season and a time."

(Color in fire destroying "Big, Bad & Ugly)

Figure 21.2

Daniel's Vision – The Interpretation
Daniel 7:15-28

Four kings (kingdoms) – same as chapter 2

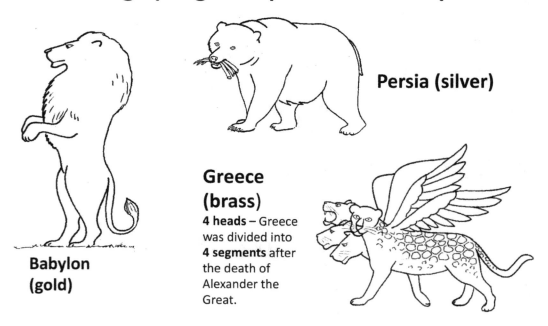

Persia (silver)

Greece (brass)
4 heads – Greece was divided into **4 segments** after the death of Alexander the Great.

Babylon (gold)

Verse 19 – Daniel: "I want to know the truth about **BIG, BAD & UGLY**!"

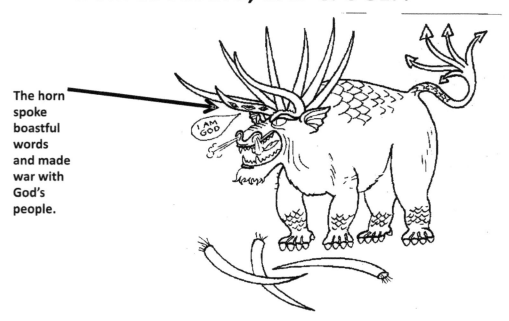

The horn spoke boastful words and made war with God's people.

I AM GOD

Figure 21.3

The Interpretation, Continued

Dan 7:23-25

- The **fourth beast** shall be a **fourth kingdom** on earth, which shall be different from all other kingdoms, and shall devour the whole earth, trample it and break it in pieces. The **ten horns are ten kings** who shall arise from this kingdom. And another shall rise after them; he shall be different from the first ones, and shall subdue three kings. He shall **speak pompous words** against the Most High, **shall persecute the saints** of the Most High, and shall intend to change times and law. Then the saints shall be given into his hand for a time and times and half a time.

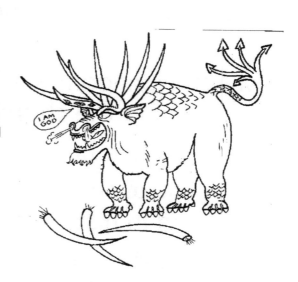

BIG, BAD & UGLY DOESN'T WIN!!
Dan. 7:26-27

- But the court shall be seated, and they shall take away his dominion, to consume and destroy it forever. Then the kingdom and dominion, and the greatness of the kingdoms under the whole heaven, shall be given to the people, the saints of the Most High. **His kingdom is an everlasting kingdom, And all dominions shall serve and obey Him**.'

★Christians—"the saints of the Most High"—are the winners!

Figure 21.3

History facts & Bible facts

- **Rome** was the great kingdom when Jesus was born, lived, was crucified and rose from the dead.

- **Rome** was the kingdom when the gospel was first preached and the church established.

- Some **Roman** rulers persecuted Christians.

- **Rome** was destroyed; it only exists today in dusty ruins and in history books.

- **God's kingdom (the Church) is alive and well today! It will never be destroyed!!!**

These are some scriptures that tell us the above facts are true:
Luke 1:5
Luke 2:1-2
Matthew 27:1-2, 11-26
Acts 12
Acts 23:23-35
Acts 24-28
1 Peter 1:6-8
1 Peter 3:13-17

Figure 21.3

DANIEL 2

Unscramble the words from our lesson.

DLGO   __ __ __ __

SARSB   __ __ __ __ __

LAYBBON   __ __ __ __ __ __ __

SEIARP   __ __ __ __ __ __

VILERS   __ __ __ __ __ __

CREEEG   __ __ __ __ __ __

RION   __ __ __ __

MORE   __ __ __ __

LACY   __ __ __ __

1. Put a star * by the kingdom that Nebuchadnezzar ruled.
2. Underline in blue the kingdom/kingdoms that Daniel lived in.
3. Draw a ring around the kingdom of which Esther was queen.
4. Highlight in yellow the kingdom that ruled the world when Jesus was born.
5. Underline in red the kingdom that ruled when the apostles began preaching the gospel and the Church was established.
6. Put a star * by the material that represented Nebuchadnezzar's kingdom.
7. Put a small circle by the material that represented Esther's kingdom.
8. Put a small square by the material that represented the kingdom that ruled when God would set up His kingdom.

1

Figure 21.4

WHEN WILL GOD SET UP HIS KINGDOM THAT WILL NEVER BE DESTROYED?
WHAT DOES THE BIBLE SAY?

I. WHEN JESUS WAS BORN: "And it came to pass in those days that a decree went out from Caesar Augustus that all the world would be registered" (Luke 2:1).
Which one of the 4 kingdoms had Caesar Augustus as its ruler?_____

II. WHEN JESUS DIED: "When morning came, all the chief priests and elders of the people plotted against Jesus to put Him to death. And when they had bound Him, they led Him away and delivered Him to Pontius Pilate the governor" (Matthew 27:1-2).
Which one of the 4 kingdoms had an emperor who appointed Pontius Pilate to be governor of Judea and Jerusalem? _____

III. AFTER THE CHURCH WAS ESTABLISHED: "After these things Paul departed from Athens and went to Corinth. And he found a certain Jew named Aquila, born in Pontus, who had recently come from Italy with his wife Priscilla (because Claudius had commanded all the Jews to depart from Rome); and he came to them" (Acts 18:1-2).
Which one of the 4 kingdoms had Claudius as ruler? _____

IV. THE CHURCH OF CHRIST IS HIS KINGDOM: "He (Jesus) said to them, 'But who do you say that I am?' Simon Peter answered and said, 'You are the Christ, the son of the living God.' Jesus answered and said to him, 'Blessed are you...and I also say to you that you are Peter, and on this rock I will build My church and the gates of Hades shall not prevail against it. And I will give you the keys of the kingdom of heaven...'" Jesus used the words "church" and "kingdom" to mean the same thing. And, since the Church began when _____ ruled the world, we know the Church is the kingdom that Daniel prophesied about.

Figure 21.4

WHEN WILL GOD'S KINGDOM COME AND WHAT WILL IT BE LIKE?

Daniel 2 and 7:

When Nebuchadnezzar, king of Babylon, had a dream that none of his wise men could interpret, God sent Daniel to tell him what it meant. You may remember learning about this dream before. We will review the facts from Daniel chapter 2.

In his dream, Nebuchadnezzar saw a great image. Read Daniel 2:32-33 and fill in these blanks:

The image's head was of fine _____.

Its chest and arms were made of _____.

The image's belly and thighs were made from _____.

Its legs were of _____, its feet partly of _____and partly of _____.

The king also saw a stone that was cut without hands, and the stone struck the image in the feet and broke them in pieces. Then the whole image -- the silver, gold and brass were crushed together and became like chaff (dust) that was blown away by the wind. However, that stone became a great mountain and filled the whole earth (Daniel 2:34-35).

Daniel told the king that God was showing him what would happen to all the great kingdoms from the time of Babylon until God's kingdom would come. Daniel said that the parts of the image represented four great kingdoms that would rule that part of the world. Read verse 38. What king and kingdom is the head of gold?

King _____ and _____

From history, we learn that the other three kingdoms were:

_____, _____ and _____.

Figure 21.5

Daniel said that when the last kingdom (Rome) ruled the world, God would set up His kingdom. Read Daniel 2:44:

"And in the days of these kings the _____ of heaven will set up a _____ which shall never be _____: and the kingdom shall not be left to other people; it shall break in pieces and consume all these kingdoms, and it shall stand _____."

We can read from Luke chapter 2, where Luke tells us about the birth of Jesus. In verse one, he tells us "...that a decree went out from Caesar Augustus that all the world should be registered..." From history, we learn that Caesar Augustus was the emperor (king) of the Roman Empire until 14 AD. Daniel's prophecy is being fulfilled when Jesus is born during the rule of Augustus!

Daniel tells us more of what God's kingdom would be like in Daniel 7:13-14. Before verse 13, Daniel tells about a beast with horns and that one of the horns was speaking "pompous" words -- being proud and self-important. The great beast is killed because of what the horn was doing and saying. (When we have time to study this more, we will learn that this horn was one of the Roman emperors who tried to destroy Christians.) As this scene occurs, Daniel says: "I was watching in the night visions, and behold, One like the Son of Man, coming with the clouds of heaven! He came to the Ancient of Days, and they brought Him near before Him. Then to Him was given dominion and glory and a kingdom, that all peoples, nations, and languages should serve Him. His dominion is an everlasting dominion, which shall not pass away, and His kingdom the one which shall not be destroyed."

Who is the "Son of Man"? _____ (Matt. 16:13)

What was He given? _____ and _____

and a _____.

Who should serve Him? All _____,_____,

and _____.

Figure 21.5

In Mark 16:15, Jesus told His disciples to go into all the _____ and preach the gospel to _____ _____.

Daniel chapter 2 and chapter 7 tell us about the same kingdoms of the world, but in different ways. Let's see how they match:

Daniel 2	Daniel 7	Kingdom
Head of gold	_____	Babylon
_____	Bear with 3 ribs	Persia
Belly & thighs of brass	Leopard with 4 heads	_____
Legs/feet of iron/clay	"Big/Bad/Ugly"	_____

In Daniel chapter 2, a stone was cut out, without _____ and struck the image in its _____. The image fell, and all of it—the gold, silver, brass, iron and clay were crushed together. They became like _____ and the wind blew them away. Then that stone became a great _____ and filled all the _____. In Daniel chapter 7, the "little horn" on "Big-Bad-Ugly" was saying _____ words. And he was also making _____ with the saints (God's people—Christians.) Because of that, God judged him. Daniel said the "Big - Bad- Ugly" beast was _____ and its body was _____ and given to the _____ _____ (Verse 11). After "Big-Bad-Ugly" was destroyed, Daniel saw the "Son of Man" who was given an everlasting _____. Look at Daniel 7:14 to see how this kingdom is described: "Then to Him was given _____ and _____ and a_____. that all

Figure 21.5

and _____ should serve Him. His dominion is an

everlasting dominion, which shall not _____ _____, And His

kingdom the one which shall not be _____."

In both these visions, God told Daniel what they mean. Today there
are many people who try to scare us and tell us these visions mean
something about what will happen in our lifetime. They say Daniel's visions
are about things that will happen sometime soon in our world. But we want
to believe what God said! God's messenger told Daniel that the 4 beasts
were 4 great kingdoms, that because of the boastful words of that little horn
the 4th kingdom would be forever destroyed, and that God's kingdom
would be established during the time the 4th great kingdom ruled the world.
Daniel's vision in chapter 7 and Nebuchadnezzar's dream in chapter 2
were both fulfilled when Jesus was born, when He lived, when He died for
our sins, when He arose from the dead, and when His disciples preached
the gospel. His church is the kingdom of Old Testament prophecy! The
church of Christ is the kingdom that Daniel saw!

Daniel's prophecies prove that God had a plan before He made the
world and that He worked all through the Old Testament to make that plan
happen. He showed the prophets visions and pictures of the plan, but they
did not fully understand it. When Jesus came, He fulfilled all those
prophecies perfectly. And when He died, that was God's plan. Today, you
and I can be a part of God's plan if we will obey Him.

Figure 21.5

Chapter 22
SEVENTY WEEKS

Daniel's prophecies are of particular interest because they answer more clearly the question, "When will Jesus come?" When the Jews finally realized Jeremiah and Ezekiel were right—captivity was going to be a long time—they became interested in what would occur after their captivity had ended. God chose to reveal this to Daniel. As we noted in chapters 2 and 7, God tells Daniel about four great kingdoms that will arise on the earth and about the eternal kingdom of the Messiah that will never be destroyed. The other visions from chapters 8 through 12 concern more detail about the time from the fall of Babylon to the coming of the Roman domination and the destruction of Jerusalem. Much of what God reveals to Daniel in this chapter deals with events in the time between the testaments, so we have to go to secular history, to the record of the Maccabees, and to Josephus to see the fulfillment of these events.

Following is a brief summary of chapter 8:

The vision: A ram with 2 horns is standing by the river; it is strong, pushing in every direction. Out of the west, a he-goat with a notable horn between his eyes comes toward the ram so fast that he doesn't even touch the ground. He is very strong and magnifies himself exceedingly, but the great horn is broken off and 4 horns come up in its place. Then, a little horn comes forth out of one of the 4 horns and also becomes very great (verse 10). This horn magnified itself even to the point of taking away the continual burnt-offering, taking over the sanctuary, and casting down the truth to the ground. "Because of transgression, an army was given over to the horn to oppose the daily sacrifices; and he cast truth down to the ground. He did all this and prospered" (8:12). This abomination of desolation and trodding under foot should continue for 2300 days (vs. 13-14).

The interpretation: The ram with 2 horns is the Medo-Persian Empire (note ch.7 – bear with side raised up). The he-goat with a great horn is Greece under Alexander the Great. When he died, Greece was divided into 4 parts (note ch.7 – leopard with 4 heads). Who is the horn that rises up from one of the 4 and magnifies himself? Note Gabriel's description of that ruler and of that time:

And in the latter time of their kingdom, when the transgressors have reached their fullness, a king shall arise, having fierce features, who understands sinister schemes. His power shall be mighty, but not by his own power; he shall destroy fearfully, and shall prosper and thrive; he shall destroy the mighty, and also the holy people.

Through his cunning he shall cause deceit to prosper under his rule; and he shall exalt himself in his heart. He shall destroy many in their prosperity. He shall even rise against the Prince of princes; but he shall be broken without human means. And the vision of the evenings and mornings which was told is true; therefore seal up the vision, for it refers to many days in the future (Dan. 8:23-26).

Most reputable commentators agree this king is Antiochus Epiphanes, who ruled over Syria, one of the four parts of the Greek Empire, between 175-163 B.C. He was a strong devotee of the Hellenistic culture, and determined to cement his kingdom into a unit by imposing Greek culture and Greek gods upon all his subjects. From history and the record of the Maccabees, we learn that Antiochus conquered Jerusalem, set up an image in the temple, desecrated the worship by offering swine flesh on the altar, and encouraged the Greek soldiers to bring "religious prostitutes" into the temple area and carry on licentious worship, with its pagan orgies. To further enforce his purpose, he forbade the Jews to circumcise their children, to observe the Sabbath, and to possess a copy of the scriptures, which he sought to destroy. He also appointed a high priest who was favorable to the Hellenistic movement, built a stadium in Jerusalem, and encouraged the Jewish youth to participate in the gymnastic exercises in the nude, as practiced by the Greeks. Laws pertaining to these matters were enforced with the utmost cruelty.

The twenty-three hundred days (v. 14) probably refer to this period (171-165). It seems that the angel's statement that what Daniel had heard concerning the number of days 'is true' (v. 26) was to impress the fact that the number was not a symbolic number, but a period of time of some 6 years and a little over. This was the length of time that the temple was desecrated. With the overthrow of the Syrian supremacy in Jerusalem by the Maccabees, the temple was cleansed and the worship re-dedicated. Out of this grew 'the feast of the dedication' mentioned by John (Jn. 10:22) (Hailey 1985, 256).

Why this vision at this time since it related to some events far into their future? God was preparing His people for the trying days of the reign of Antiochus, and assuring them that his power would be broken by Jehovah. **The fulfillment of prophecies such as this is powerful evidence that the Bible is inspired by God.** During Babylonian captivity, the Jews needed to know that God still ruled in the kingdoms of men. Also, the fulfillment of this prophecy helped prepare the people for the coming of Christ. I referred to Luke 3 in the previous chapter, but it is noteworthy again "Now as the people were in expectation, and all reasoned in their hearts about John, whether he was the Christ or not…" (Luke 3:15-16). Why were they expecting the Christ at that time? In captivity, they were learning the truth of Isaiah's declaration: "Remember the former things of old, for I am God, and there is no other; I am God, and there is none like Me, declaring the end from the beginning, and from ancient times things that are not yet done, saying, 'My counsel shall stand, and I will do all My pleasure'" (Isa. 46:9-10). Figures 22.1 and 22.2 illustrate this conflict if you choose to teach it to your students. Since it involves historical details unfamiliar to younger students, it is probably best for 6th grade and above.

I have enjoyed teaching chapter 9, the seventy weeks prophecy, to children in 3rd and 4th grades. Since it involves the coming of Christ and His work of redemption, I think it is important for them to understand this prophecy. While it does involve some historical details, these are familiar to them. It is helpful to have a little review of the chronology of Daniel before I deal with chapter 9. Nebuchadnezzar's dream in chapter 2 occurs shortly after the arrival of the first group of captives in 606 B.C.; the vision of chapter 7 is in the first year of Belshazzar (553), and the vision of chapter 8 is in the third year of his reign (551). The events of chapter 9 are "In the first year of Darius the son of Ahasuerus, of the lineage of the Medes, who was made king over the realm of the Chaldeans" (9:1) (539).

Daniel realized that Jeremiah's prophecy of 70 years captivity was approaching its fulfillment. His response was a prayer of confession and a plea for mercy for the nation: "…for we do not present our supplications before You because of our righteous deeds, but because of Your great mercies" (Dan. 9:18). In answer to his prayer, Gabriel is sent with the message of the seventy weeks prophecy.

> Seventy weeks are determined for your people and for your holy city, to finish the transgression, to make an end of sins, to make reconciliation for iniquity, to bring in everlasting righteousness, to seal up vision and prophecy, and to anoint the Most Holy.
>
> Know therefore and understand, that from the going forth of the command to restore and build Jerusalem until Messiah the Prince, there shall be seven weeks and sixty-two weeks; the street shall be built again, and the wall, even in troublesome times.
>
> And after the sixty-two weeks Messiah shall be cut off, but not for Himself; and the people of the prince who is to come shall destroy the city and the sanctuary. The end of it shall be with a flood, and till the end of the war desolations are determined. Then he shall confirm a covenant with many for one week; but in the middle of the week He shall bring an end to sacrifice and offering. And on the wing of abominations shall be one who makes desolate, even until the consummation, which is determined, is poured out on the desolate (9:24-27).

There are at least three views of this prophecy. The first is the premillennial view which has various renditions, but extends the prophecy to "modern times" corresponding to world conditions involving the nation of Israel depending on if the expositor is living in 1950, 1980, 2000, or 2015. It is chronological, using the concept of a year in prophecy equals a day, but it usually begins in 445 B.C. when Nehemiah led a group back to Jerusalem. Why 445? That date fits their theory of a church age gap. There are a few other theories that begin with 457 and end with a gap. I have an advertisement in my files for a seminar conducted in 1999 by a premillennial group that applied this prophecy to "surviving the year 2000." We have passed 2000, and none of the things they predicted have occurred, so I will dispense with all these views of a prophetic gap involving the church, the rapture, and tribulation. We should not let such sensational teaching rob us of the message of Daniel and keep us from studying this prophecy or any other.

The second view is non-millennial, but has some things in common with the premillennial view. Both of these use the same technique in interpreting the seventy weeks—a day equals a year. In Numbers 14:33-34, God tells Israel they will wander in the wilderness forty years, a year for each day they spied out the land. Also, in Ezekiel 4:6, God tells Ezekiel to lie on his side for the sins of Israel and Judah, a day for a year. However, nowhere in the context of Daniel 9 are we told to use this formula, so I never have thought about doing so since it isn't mentioned by Gabriel or by Daniel. This theory has appeal, though, because of 2 Chron. 36:21 which states the purpose of the 70 years of captivity: "… to fulfill the word of the LORD by the mouth of Jeremiah, until the land had enjoyed her Sabbaths. As long as she lay desolate she kept Sabbath, to fulfill seventy years." If it is true that Israel never observed the Sabbath for the land, then 490 years would be the sum of 70 missed Sabbath years. I realize there are many good Bible teachers who hold to this view, but the first time I heard this explanation of the year for a day, I was skeptical, thinking, "How do I know to use a year for a day?" This one point caused me to reject this theory even before studying Daniel 9 more in-depth to teach children.

I have always looked at the seventy weeks prophecy as a figurative timeframe. First of all, as I mentioned above, the context gives me no clue to use the year/day method of interpretation. Second, the decree by Cyrus makes more sense as a starting point. Why? God had announced in Isaiah 44 that Cyrus would issue a command that Jerusalem and the temple would be built (v.28). This would serve as proof that God declares "the end from the beginning" (Isa. 46:10). Then, in Ezra 1:2 and 2 Chron. 36:22, Cyrus issues that decree in 536 B.C., which is exactly 70 years from the first date of the captivity, fulfilling Isaiah 44 and 45. Cyrus' decree may not fit the year/day method, but it definitely fits the prophetic context. Gabriel also tells Daniel, "At the beginning of your supplications the command went out, and I have come to tell you…" (9:23).

Using the seventy weeks as figurative and the decree of Cyrus as the beginning point, made this prophecy easy to explain to children. By this time, they were accustomed to prophecies having figurative language. The two charts (figures 22.3a and 22.3b) help illustrate what Gabriel is telling Daniel. I prepared these several years ago for 3rd and 4th graders, and Jodie Boren graciously did the artwork for the charts. I also illustrated this on the timeline in our classroom.

In 2013, I was teaching some of these prophecies to my Ladies' Bible Class at the Bridgewood church of Christ in Fort Worth, Texas. Since I was teaching adults, I thought I'd better check with "scholars" about this prophecy. I found that Homer Hailey, Jim McGuiggan, and Don Simpson agreed with the figurative seventy weeks. I'm sure there are others, but this was enough to convince me I hadn't short-changed the children just because it is easier to understand the prophecy this way.

What about the details of the prophecy? I'm including two sets of charts for you to use. One is just a copy of power point slides (Figure 22.4) with scripture references for the fulfillment. This would be good for older children. The other is a set of 4 charts that have selected scriptures quoted for the fulfillment (Figure 22.3, pages 1-4). These are good for younger students and would work nicely in a notebook if you are having them make a notebook of the prophecies. When I taught this to the children, I had the details of the prophecy on colored strips of paper and put each on the bulletin board as we discussed "what will happen when Jesus comes, and what will He do?" I had the students read the New Testament passages and we discussed how those fulfilled what Gabriel told Daniel.

Concluding Comments:

Children are usually familiar with Daniel as one of the great servants and prophets of God. They enjoy learning something new and different about him, and this is why I've enjoyed sharing these lessons with them. Sometimes when I have taught these lessons, I've asked the children to tell me what they know about Daniel, or I ask them if they know about the fiery furnace or the lion's den or the handwriting on the wall. This gives me an idea of where to begin. Since most of those lessons are usually covered in a chronological curriculum, I have chosen to omit those in this book.

Kings of Media & Persia
Dan. 8:20

Kingdom of Greece
Large horn – Alexander the Great
Dan. 8:21

Figure 22.1

Alexander the Great
conquered
Media/Persia
Dan. 8:6,7,20,21

Greece divided
into 4 parts
after
Alexander
Dan. 8:22

A little horn out of
1 of the 4 grew great,
opposed sacrifice, etc.
is destroyed by God.
Dan. 8:9-12,25
Antiochus Epiphanes
of Syria (history)

Figure 22.2

Daniel 9:24-27

Prophecy	Fulfillment
Finish transgression; make end of sin (v.24).	But this Man, after He had offered one sacrifice for sins forever, sat down at the right hand of God (Heb.10:12), For He Himself is our peace, who has made both one, and has broken down the middle wall of separation, 15 having abolished in His flesh the enmity, that is, the law of commandments contained in ordinances, so as to create in Himself one new man from the two, thus making peace, 16 and that He might reconcile them both to God in one body through the cross, thereby putting to death the enmity. 17 And He came and preached peace to you who were afar off and to those who were near. (Eph. 2:14-17)
Bring in everlasting righteousness (v.24).	But now the righteousness of God apart from the law is revealed, being witnessed by the Law and the Prophets, 22 even the righteousness of God, through faith in Jesus Christ, to all and on all who believe. For there is no difference; 23 for all have sinned and fall short of the glory of God, 24 being justified freely by His grace through the redemption that is in Christ Jesus, 25 whom God set forth as a propitiation by His blood, through faith, to demonstrate His righteousness, because in His forbearance God had passed over the sins that were previously committed, 26 to demonstrate at the present time His righteousness, that He might be just and the justifier of the one who has faith in Jesus (Rom. 3:21-27).

Figure 22.3

1

Prophecy	Fulfillment

Prophecy

Make reconciliation
for iniquity (v.24).

Anoint the most
Holy (v. 24).

Fulfillment

, 20 and by Him to reconcile all things to Himself, by Him, whether things on earth or things in heaven, having made peace through the blood of His cross.

21 And you, who once were alienated and enemies in your mind by wicked works, yet now He has reconciled 22 in the body of His flesh through death, to present you holy, and blameless, and above reproach in His sight -- 23 if indeed you continue in the faith, grounded and steadfast, and are not moved away from the hope of the gospel(Col. 1:20-23).

27 "For truly against Your holy Servant Jesus, whom You anointed, both Herod and Pontius Pilate, with the Gentiles and the people of Israel, were gathered together 28 to do whatever Your hand and Your purpose determined before to be done (Acts 4:27-28).

8 But to the Son He says:

"Your throne, O God, is forever and ever; A scepter of righteousness is the scepter of Your kingdom.
9 You have loved righteousness and hated lawlessness;
Therefore God, Your God, has anointed You
With the oil of gladness more than Your companions."

2

Figure 22.3

Prophecy	**Fulfillment**
Jerusalem rebuilt (v. 25).	15 Now the temple was finished on the third day of the month of Adar, which was in the sixth year of the reign of King Darius (Ezra 6:15).

Now the leaders of the people dwelt at Jerusalem; the rest of the people cast lots to bring one out of ten to dwell in Jerusalem, the holy city, and nine-tenths were to dwell in other cities (Neh.11:1). |
| Anointed one cut off (v. 26). | Now from the sixth hour until the ninth hour there was darkness over all the land. 46 And about the ninth hour Jesus cried out with a loud voice, saying, "Eli, Eli, lama sabachthani?" that is, "My God, My God, why have You forsaken Me?"

47 Some of those who stood there, when they heard that, said, "This Man is calling for Elijah!" 48 Immediately one of them ran and took a sponge, filled it with sour wine and put it on a reed, and offered it to Him to drink.

49 The rest said, "Let Him alone; let us see if Elijah will come to save Him" (Matt. 27:45-49) |
| Destroy the city and sanctuary (v. 26). | Then Jesus went out and departed from the temple, and His disciples came up to show Him the buildings of the temple. 2 And Jesus said to them, "Do you not see all these things? Assuredly, I say to you, not one stone shall be left here upon another, that shall not be thrown down" (Matt. 24:1-2). |

Figure 22.3

3

Prophecy	**Fulfillment**

Make a firm covenant with many (v. 27).

24 And He said to them, "This is My blood of the new covenant, which is shed for many. 25 Assuredly, I say to you, I will no longer drink of the fruit of the vine until that day when I drink it new in the kingdom of God" Mark 14:24-25)

To seal up vision and prophecy (v.24).

Then He said to them, "These are the words which I spoke to you while I was still with you, that all things must be fulfilled which were written in the Law of Moses and the Prophets and the Psalms concerning Me." 45 And He opened their understanding, that they might comprehend the Scriptures.

46 Then He said to them, "Thus it is written, and thus it was necessary for the Christ to suffer and to rise from the dead the third day, 47 and that repentance and remission of sins should be preached in His name to all nations, beginning at Jerusalem. 48 And you are witnesses of these things" (Luke 24:44-48).

God, who at various times and in various ways spoke in time past to the fathers by the prophets, 2 has in these last days spoken to us by His Son" (Heb. 1:1-2).

Figure 22.3

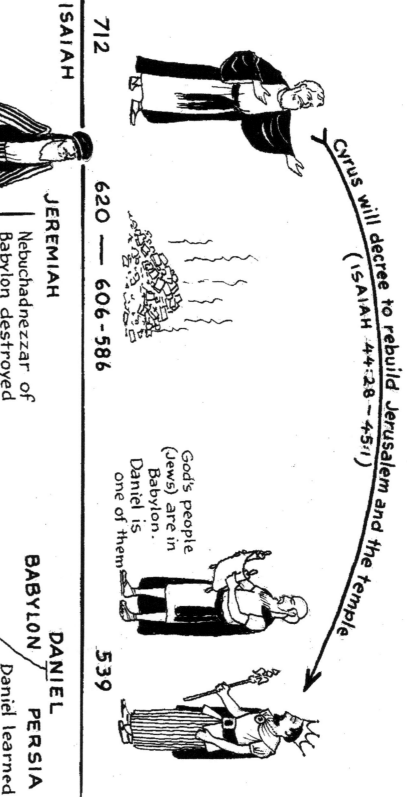

Daniel and the 70 weeks

Figure 22.3a

Art by Jodie Boren

©Chart design by Sarah Fallis

712

ISAIAH

Jerusalem

Cyrus will decree to rebuild Jerusalem and the temple

(ISAIAH 44:28 — 45:1)

620 — 606-586

JEREMIAH

Nebuchadnezzar of Babylon destroyed Jerusalem and took the people captive in 3 groups, beginning in 606 and ending in 586 when he burned the city.

"CAPTIVITY WILL BE 70 YEARS"

(JEREMIAH 25:11-12)

God's people (Jews) are in Babylon. Daniel is one of them.

539

DANIEL

BABYLON   PERSIA

Daniel learned that captivity was near its end. He prayed and asked God to fulfill His promise. God answered his prayer by saying "70 more 7's must happen..."

Daniel's Vision of 70 Weeks

Cyrus commands to build Jerusalem

539 B.C.

©Chart design by Sarah Fallis

Art by Jodie Boren

God's promises will be fulfilled in 70 7's weeks

7 WEEKS | 62 WEEKS | 1 WEEK

Jerusalem is rebuilt in troublesome times (EZRA and NEHEMIAH)

MESSIAH
* Will die for others
* Will make a firm covenant
* Will cause O.T. sacrifices to end

JERUSALEM WILL BE MADE DESOLATE

God's plan is complete

DAN. 9:24

Figure 22.3a

Daniel—The Seventy Weeks Prophecy
Daniel 9:24-27

Prophecy

- Finish transgression; make end of sin.
- Bring in everlasting righteousness.
- Make reconciliation for iniquity.
- Anoint the most Holy.
- Anointed one cut off.

Fulfillment

- Heb. 10:12; Eph. 2:14-17

- Rom. 3:21-31; 2 Cor. 5:21

- Col. 1:20 - 23; Heb. 2:17.

- Acts 4:26-27; Heb. 1:8-9
- Isa. 53:8; Acts 8:32-33

~~~ Continued...

Prophecy

- Destroy the city and sanctuary.
- Make a firm covenant with many.
- To seal up vision – the vision is completed by the fulfillment of these events.

Fulfillment

- Matt. 24:1-34

- Matt. 26:28; Mark 14:24; Heb. 8:8-13.
- Luke 24:44; 1 Pet. 1:9-12; Heb. 1:1-2; Rev. 19:10.

Figure 22.4

DANIEL 9:24 AND GOD'S PLAN

"Seventy weeks are determined for your people and for your holy city,

To finish the _____,

To make an end of _____,

To make reconciliation for _____,

To bring in everlasting _____,

To seal up _____ and _____,

And to anoint the _____ _____."

Transgression, sin, and iniquity are all words that mean sin, or disobeying God. Jesus made an end of sin, finished transgression, and made reconciliation for iniquity when He died on the cross. Jesus also made us righteous through His death. That is, He made it possible for us to be right with God. Read the verses below and see that this is what Paul said about Jesus and His death.

Romans 5:8 -- "But God demonstrates His own _____ toward us, in that while we were still _____, Christ died for _____."

2 Corinthians 5:21 -- "For He (God) made Him (Jesus) who knew no _____ to be _____ for us, that we might become the _____ of God in Him."

God's plan involved sealing prophecy. Jesus fulfilled all Old Testament prophecy as we have been learning. After He came, there is no more prophecy to be fulfilled. It is "sealed" or finished in Jesus and His work.

Read Matthew 5:17 -- "Do not think that I came to _____ the Law or the _____. I did not come to destroy but to _____."

Jesus is the Most Holy One, and was anointed at His baptism (Luke 4:18).

Figure 22.5

Background for Haggai, Zechariah, and Malachi

Haggai, Zechariah, and Malachi are the prophets during the rebuilding of Jerusalem and the temple, with Haggai and Zechariah being the earliest of the three (520, 518 B.C.). Both returned from Babylon under Zerubbabel in 536. When the group first returned, they restored the altar of sacrifices to Jehovah and laid the foundation of the temple. However, the people grew lackadaisical and more interested in their possessions than in finishing the temple, so God called on Haggai and Zechariah to admonish them and encourage them to continue.

Haggai's message had a single theme—build the temple. His style is simple and direct. Within about three weeks after his first message, the people began work and finally completed the temple in less than five years. An essential characteristic of his message is that it is from Jehovah, not from himself. Twenty-six times in thirty-eight verses, Haggai uses phrases similar to "thus says Jehovah" or "the word of the LORD." This appeal to divine authority caused the people to pay attention and respond to his message.

Haggai was assisted by Zechariah, a prophet who was also a priest like Jeremiah and Ezekiel before him. Zechariah's book is considered by many as the most difficult to interpret because it is filled with visions and symbols. However, there are some very important lessons we can learn from his work. While the visions and figurative language may present problems, we can know that his prophecy, like all the others, is fulfilled in Christ and the preaching of the gospel into the entire world (Luke 24:44-46).

Malachi is the last of the prophets, and his work is dated at about 445-432 B.C. His is the final voice until John the Baptizer comes preaching a message of repentance. In fact, Malachi ends his book with the announcement of God's messenger coming who is like Elijah and will turn many back to Jehovah.

Figure 23.0

Chapter 23
THE MESSIAH IN ZECHARIAH

Zechariah is the most Messianic of the Minor Prophets, and his pictures of the Messiah are the focus of this chapter. He presents Christ as a king, different from most earthly rulers, as He enters the holy city riding on a donkey that has never been ridden. Zechariah's picture of the Messiah moves quickly to His true mission—the salvation of His people. Most of his prophecies center in the crucifixion of Jesus. He is the rejected shepherd, sold for the price of a wounded slave, and pierced for His sheep who would be scattered. Through His death, a fountain for sin and cleansing is open for all.

Zechariah has one dramatic picture of the Messiah that reaches back to the shadowy picture of Melchizedek in Genesis 14, forward through the 110th Psalm, and extends into the future in the New Testament book of Hebrews. This is one of my favorites to teach to children because of its all-encompassing theme.

> Then the word of the LORD came to me, saying: "Receive the gift from the captives -- from Heldai, Tobijah, and Jedaiah, who have come from Babylon -- and go the same day and enter the house of Josiah the son of Zephaniah. Take the silver and gold, make an elaborate crown, and set it on the head of Joshua the son of Jehozadak, the high priest. Then speak to him, saying, 'Thus says the LORD of hosts, saying:

> "Behold, the Man whose name is the BRANCH!

> From His place He shall branch out,

> And He shall build the temple of the LORD;

> Yes, He shall build the temple of the LORD.

> He shall bear the glory,

> And shall sit and rule on His throne;

> So He shall be a priest on His throne,

> And the counsel of peace shall be between them both.'"

> "Now the elaborate crown shall be for a memorial in the temple of the LORD for Helem, Tobijah, Jedaiah, and Hen the son of Zephaniah. Even those from afar shall

come and build the temple of the LORD. Then you shall know that the LORD of hosts has sent Me to you. And this shall come to pass if you diligently obey the voice of the LORD your God" (Zech. 6:9-15).

"Behold the Man whose name is 'the BRANCH!'" This echoes both the messages of Isaiah and Jeremiah centuries earlier. Isaiah had called the Messiah the Branch of Jehovah, emphasizing His divine nature, and Jeremiah referred to Him as a Branch unto David, emphasizing His human nature. Now, Zechariah combines the two natures in the statement, "Behold the Man whose name is 'the BRANCH!'" Surely, those leaders present with Zechariah remembered the words of Isaiah and Jeremiah and knew he was speaking of the Messiah. Notice, also, that Zechariah says of this crowned priest, "Behold the **Man**" not, "Behold the men." Why is this important? A popular doctrine floating around in Bible and theology departments at universities is that the Jewish leaders expected two Messiahs—a priestly one and a kingly one. And, since they did, Jesus is the kingly Messiah and John the Baptist is the priestly Messiah. I have seen this theory presented as a "possible explanation of the concept of a priest and king in the Old Testament" in books written for Bible teachers. Zechariah dispenses with that theory before it was even imagined by using the singular "the Man."

Zechariah's preaching had been centered on rebuilding the temple in Jerusalem. In chapter 4, Jehovah tells the people that as Zerubbabel has laid the foundation, he will also place the capstone, completing the temple by the grace and power of God. As the news of renewed work on the temple reaches the captives remaining in Babylon, three men come with gifts of gold and silver so those who are still in Babylon can help in building the temple. However, Jehovah has a different purpose for their gift of gold and silver. He tells Zechariah to take that gift and make an "elaborate crown"—a two-tiered crown—of the gold and silver and go to the house of Josiah, the son of Zephaniah. There, with the three from Babylon watching, he is to set the crown on the head of Joshua, the high priest and announce, "Behold the Man whose name is the BRANCH!" (6:12).

Now to see the significance of this action, we need to remember Ezekiel had prophesied in 21:26 that the turban (symbol of the high priest) and the crown (symbol of the king) would be removed "until He comes whose right it is, and I will give it to Him" (21:27). (You may want to refer back to Figure 20.5 from Ezekiel.) Jeremiah had foretold that none of Coniah's seed would sit on the throne ruling in Jerusalem (Jer. 22:28-30). Yet, he had also stated that David would never lack a man sitting on his throne and the priests would never lack one to offer sacrifice continually (33:17-18). The priesthood had been restored after the captives returned from Babylon; Joshua was the high priest of the family of Aaron according to the law. However, the kingship had not been restored; Zerubbabel was a descendent of David and Coniah, but he was only governor—an honored position, but not ruling on the throne as king. Since the temple was almost finished and the priesthood restored, the people may have been looking for the throne to be restored as well. Jehovah has Zechariah demonstrate the true nature of the temple, the priesthood, and the Messiah. In this picture, God not only dispels false hopes, but He focuses their attention back to His eternal purpose which involved a perfect sacrifice, perfect priest, and perfect king.

How could both of Jeremiah's prophecies about the king and priest be fulfilled? The answer is in Ezekiel's prophecy—"until He comes whose right it is." Notice the statement is singular, "until **He** comes whose right **it** is." The crown and turban belonged to two distinct people from two distinct tribes under the law. Now, according to Ezekiel, those are combined into one official position, occupied by one person—the Messiah. He will wear both the crown and turban; He will be both priest and king. This concept of One who is both priest and king was first introduced as a shadow of Jesus in the Old Testament in the person of Melchizedek who received tithes from Abram and blessed him (Gen. 14:18-20). This obscure meeting of Abram and Melchizedek would hardly be noticed except for the clearly Messianic Psalm 110. In verse 4 of that Psalm, David reaches back to that shadowy figure in Genesis and announces, "The LORD has sworn / And will not relent, / 'You are a priest forever / According to the order of Melchizedek.'" Then, the writer of Hebrews takes the truths in these four Old Testament verses and builds the majestic doctrine of Jesus as priest and king in a new spiritual kingdom, under a new covenant, officiating in the real Most Holy Place, and reigning on God's throne which is David's throne of prophecy (1Kings 2:10-12; 1 Chron. 29:23).

There are five things that describe the mission of "the BRANCH" in these verses:

1. **"From His place, He shall branch out…"** When Jesus was born, the house of David was in a state of decay. No one had occupied the throne since Babylonian captivity. From this lowly beginning, the world-wide kingdom of the Messiah would be established. This is in harmony with Isaiah's prophecy that He would grow up "as a root out of dry ground" (Isa. 53:2).

2. **"And He shall build the temple of the LORD…"** This phrase is stated twice in verses 12 and 13, so it must be of primary importance. Jesus said He would build His church on the fact of His deity that Peter had just confessed (Matt. 16:13-18). The New Testament teaches plainly that the Church is the true temple of the LORD—a spiritual temple, built of living stones on Christ, the Chief Cornerstone. (Eph. 2:21-22; 1 Pet. 2:5).

3. **"He shall bear the glory, and shall sit and rule on His throne."** The writer of Hebrews confirms this prophecy of Jesus as he says of Him, "…who being the brightness of His glory and the express image of His person, and upholding all things by the word of His power, when He had by Himself purged our sins, sat down at the right hand of the Majesty on high…" (Heb. 1:3). In this one verse, the writer tells us Jesus completed His mission and is now ruling on His throne. This is a death blow to the popular doctrine that Jesus will come back to the earth and rule on an earthly throne in Jerusalem. If that had been His purpose, wouldn't God have inspired the writer to tell us so?

4. **"So He shall be a priest on His throne…"** In the first gospel sermon, Peter proclaimed that Jesus is "exalted to the right hand of God" (Acts 2:33) and has been made "both Lord and Christ" (Acts 2:36). Then, in Hebrews 4:14-16, the writer tells us that Jesus is our "great High Priest who has passed through the heavens."

5. **"And the counsel of peace shall be between them both."** In the office of both king and priest, the BRANCH will provide peace for all who put their trust in Him. This peace was prophesied in Isaiah 2, 9 and 11. In each of those prophecies, it is evident the peace is not world peace between nations, but peace in God's Holy Mountain.

Jesus told His disciples just before His crucifixion, "Peace I leave with you, My peace I give to you; not as the world gives do I give to you. Let not your heart be troubled, neither let it be afraid" (John 14:27). Paul discusses extensively the peace that Jesus brings in Ephesians 2—Jesus is our peace; He made peace; and He preached peace.

Jehovah wanted this event to be remembered until it was fulfilled, so He directed Zechariah to take the crown and place it in the temple as a memorial. A memorial is something that helps us remember an important event or person. These men as well as generations following until the Messiah came could look at this crown in the temple and remember God's promise. It was like the stones the people of Israel set up at Gilgal as a memorial to God's work in bringing them across the Jordan into the Promised Land (Joshua 4).

The crown was a memorial that Jews who had been scattered into other nations would have a part in building the temple. It was also a memorial that the Gentiles would participate in the building: "Even those from afar shall come and build the temple of the LORD. Then you shall know that the LORD of hosts has sent Me to you. And this shall come to pass if you diligently obey the voice of the LORD your God" (Zech. 6:15). It is interesting to notice that a common theme through all the prophets is the worldwide nature of the kingdom of the Messiah. Amos 9:11-12 comes to mind, "'On that day I will raise up the tabernacle of David, which has fallen down, and repair its damages; I will raise up its ruins, and rebuild it as in the days of old; that they may possess the remnant of Edom, and all the Gentiles who are called by My name,' says the LORD who does this thing."

How do you teach this to children? Remember they love pictures. I have used the "Bible in felt" material and made a crown of gold and silver pipe cleaners to illustrate the symbolic crowning of the high priest. Jodie Boren's illustration is good if you are having the children make a notebook. You may want to place it on the timeline in your classroom as well. I also think it is important to illustrate on the timeline the concept of king and priest as it is developed through scripture. When I taught this to children, I printed the five important things about the Messiah on colored paper and put them on the bulletin board as I discussed them. The accompanying side-by-side scripture sheet will also help the children remember the important parts of Zechariah's prophecy. Neal Pollard outlined this section of scripture around the concept of "The Crown" using words that all begin with P. This would be easy for children to memorize:

1. IT SHALL BE PRECIOUS (11a)
2. IT SHALL BE PLACED (11b)
3. IT SHALL BE PREEMINENT (12-13)
4. IT SHALL BE PRINCELY (13a)
5. IT SHALL BE PRIESTLY (13b)
6. IT SHALL BE OF PEACE (13c)
7. IT SHALL BE PURPOSEFUL (14-15)

Concluding Comments:

In my first book, I dealt with Genesis 14, Psalm 110, and Hebrews 7, showing the undeniable evidence that the Bible is from God and not from man. I did not add the evidence from the prophets to that discussion, since I would be presenting it here. As I'm writing this, I'm amazed at the magnitude of the evidence God has given us. Look at this priest and king concept from a timeline perspective, dates are approximate: Melchizedek blesses Abram (2080 B.C.); David adds significance to the event as a shadow of the Messiah (1000 B.C.); Jeremiah prophesies of the perpetual nature of the king and priest (600 B.C.); Ezekiel says the crown and turban will be removed until the Messiah comes (580 B.C.); Zechariah symbolically crowns the high priest, naming the priest/king figure "the BRANCH" (520 B.C.); and the writer of Hebrews uses all of this to explain the concept of the priesthood of Jesus (70 A.D.). No "sacred book" of any world religion has this amount of internal evidence. I have included a chart of this timeline for the students' notebooks.

I remember as a teenager questioning the inspiration of the Bible, asking questions like, "How can I know for certain the Bible is from God?" Granddaddy's answer was always focused on this type of evidence. He would couple with that how the Bible had been attacked through the centuries, but still endures today. When I think of all the voices our children are hearing today from atheists, agnostics and leaders of world religions, I see a tremendous need for us to show them the marvelous internal evidence from shadow to substance, from picture to promise to prophecy to fulfillment. I know I've said it previously, but I must say it again: God does not ask us to take a leap of faith. He gives us evidence on top of evidence that He is and that His Word is truth.

A note to teachers:

In Matthew 27:3-10, the action by Judas and the counsel in dispensing with the thirty pieces of silver is spoken of as fulfilling "that which was spoken through Jeremiah the prophet, saying…" (vs. 7-10). On his *Christian Courier* website, Wayne Jackson discusses this in detail in an article entitled, "Did Matthew Blunder?" Burton Coffman gives a shorter explanation, noting that "'Jeremiah' was the name of a larger grouping of the Hebrew scriptures which contained both Jeremiah and Zechariah, along with other books including all the minor prophets" (Coffman 1968, 469). Astute students may ask about that, so we need to be prepared to answer.

The Messiah in Zechariah

Prophecy

Fulfillment

Price agreed upon.

30 pieces of silver.

Zechariah 11:12-13

12 Then I said to them, "If it is agreeable to you, give me my wages; and if not, refrain." So they weighed out for my wages thirty pieces of silver.

13 And the LORD said to me, "Throw it to the potter" -- that princely price they set on me. So I took the thirty pieces of silver and threw them into the house of the LORD for the potter.

Cast into the house of the LORD

For the potter.

Matt. 26:14-16

Then one of the twelve, called Judas Iscariot, went to the chief priests 15 and said,"What are you willing to give me if I deliver Him to you?" And they counted out to him thirty pieces of silver. 16 So from that time he sought opportunity to betray Him.

Matt. 27:3-8

Then Judas, His betrayer, seeing that He had been condemned, was remorseful and brought back the thirty pieces of silver to the chief priests and elders, 4 saying, "I have sinned by betraying innocent blood."

And they said, "What is that to us? You see to it!"

5 Then he threw down the pieces of silver in the temple and departed, and went and hanged himself.

6 But the chief priests took the silver pieces and said, "It is not lawful to put them into the treasury, because they are the price of blood." 7 And they consulted together and bought with them the potter's field, to bury strangers in. 8 Therefore that field has been called the Field of Blood to this day.

Figure 23.1

Prophecy

Zechariah 9:9-10

9 Rejoice greatly, O daughter of Zion!
Shout, O daughter of Jerusalem!
Behold, your King is coming to you;
He is just and having salvation,
Lowly and riding on a donkey,
A colt, the foal of a donkey.
10 I will cut off the chariot from Ephraim
And the horse from Jerusalem;
The battle bow shall be cut off.
He shall speak peace to the nations;
His dominion shall be 'from sea to sea,
And from the River to the ends of the earth.'

Zechariah 12:10

And I will pour on the house of David
and on the inhabitants of Jerusalem
the Spirit of grace and supplication;
then they will look on Me whom they
pierced. Yes, they will mourn for Him
as one mourns for his only son, and
grieve for Him as one grieves for a
firstborn.

Fulfillment

Matthew 21:1-9

Now when they drew near Jerusalem, and
came to Bethphage, at the Mount of Olives,
then Jesus sent two disciples, 2 saying to
them, "Go into the village opposite you, and
immediately you will find a donkey tied, and
a colt with her. Loose them and bring them
to Me. 3 And if anyone says anything to
you, you shall say, 'The Lord has need of
them,' and immediately he will send them."

4 All this was done that it might be fulfilled
which was spoken by the prophet, saying:

5 "Tell the daughter of Zion,
'Behold, your King is coming to you,
Lowly, and sitting on a donkey,
A colt, the foal of a donkey.'"

6 So the disciples went and did as Jesus
commanded them. 7 They brought the
donkey and the colt, laid their clothes on
them, and set Him on them. 8 And a very
great multitude spread their clothes on the
road; others cut down branches from the
trees and spread them on the road. 9 Then
the multitudes who went before and those
who followed cried out, saying:

"Hosanna to the Son of David!
'Blessed is He who comes in the name of
the LORD!'

John 19:33-37

34 But one of the soldiers pierced His
side with a spear, and immediately
blood and water came out. 35 And he
who has seen has testified, and his
testimony is true; and he knows that he
is telling the truth, so that you may
believe. 36 For these things were done
that the Scripture should be fulfilled,
"Not one of His bones shall be
broken."   37 And again another
Scripture says, "They shall look on Him
whom they pierced."

Figure 23.1

2

Prophecy	Fulfillment

Revelation 1:5

Zechariah 13:1

5 and from Jesus Christ, the faithful witness, the firstborn from the dead, and the ruler over the kings of the earth. To Him who loved us and washed us from our sins in His own blood,

"In that day a fountain shall be opened for the house of David and for the inhabitants of Jerusalem, for sin and for uncleanness.

Acts 22:16

16 And now why are you waiting? Arise and be baptized, and wash away your sins, calling on the name of the Lord.'

Matt. 26:48-51

48 Now His betrayer had given them a sign, saying, "Whomever I kiss, He is the One; seize Him." 49 Immediately he went up to Jesus and said, "Greetings, Rabbi!" and kissed Him.

Zechariah 13:6-7

6 And one will say to him,
'What are these wounds between
your arms?' Then he will answer,
'Those with which I was wounded
in the house of my friends.'

50 But Jesus said to him, "Friend, why have you come?"

Mark 14:27

7 Awake, O sword, against My Shepherd,
Against the Man who is My Companion,"
Says the LORD of hosts.
"Strike the Shepherd,
And the sheep will be scattered;

Then Jesus said to them, "All of you will be made to stumble because of Me this night, for it is written:

'I will strike the Shepherd,
And the sheep will be scattered.'

3

Figure 23.1

Zechariah 6:9-15

Joshua
High Priest

Zechariah

Heldia, Tobijah, Jedaiah

Figure 23.2a

Zechariah 6:9-15

"Behold the man whose name is **'the Branch!'**"

Joshua
High Priest

Zechariah

Heldia, Tobijah, Jedaiah

Figure 23.2b

FULFILLED PROPHECY
PROOF THAT THE BIBLE
IS FROM GOD!

Abram
and
Melchizedek
Gen. 14:16-18
2080 B.C.

David:
Messiah-
priest like
Melchizedek
Psalm 110:4
1000 B.C.

Jeremiah:
perpetual
king/priest
Jer. 33:17-18
600 B.C.

Ezekiel:
crown & turban
removed
Ezek. 21:26-27
580 B.C.

Zechariah:
crowns
high priest
"the BRANCH"
Zech. 6:9-15
520 B.C.

Jesus is
priest like
Melchizedek
Heb. 7
70 A.D.

Dates are approximate,
but in harmony with
most scholars.

Figure 23.3

THE BRANCH
ZECHARIAH 6

Time: After Cyrus made the decree for the Jews to return to Israel to build their temple and the city of Jerusalem, many people had returned to Jerusalem.

Events: When the people returned, they were glad and wanted to rebuild the city of Jerusalem and the temple. They soon began to think about themselves instead of God. They built their own houses and made sure their houses were nice. After all, they had come home from the foreign land of Babylon, and they wanted nice homes in Jerusalem. They quit building the temple, and they quickly forgot about how God had allowed them to come back home and what their true purpose was.

Prophets: God sent Haggai and Zechariah to preach to the people and to encourage them to continue building the temple. A man named Zerubbabel led the people in rebuilding the temple. It was a good temple, but God used Haggai to remind them that He had a greater plan then just for them to come back to live in Jerusalem and rebuild their physical temple. God's plan involved a temple greater than the one they were building (the Church) and a person who would build the temple who was greater then Zerubbabel (Jesus). You can read this in Haggai 2:7-9.

Picture of Jesus: God told Zechariah to take three men – Heldai, Tobijah, and Jedaiah – to the house of Josiah. These three men had just recently come from Babylon to Jerusalem. Then God told Zechariah to take a crown and place it on the head of Joshua who was the High Priest. He was to say, "Behold the man whose name is the Branch..." This is a picture of Jesus. He would be both a king and a priest. God told Zechariah to put the crown in the temple as a memorial. A memorial is just something to help us remember. The crown would be something to help the people remember that God would fulfill His promise to send Jesus who would build the real temple of God.

Figure 23.4

Read Zechariah 6:12-15 and answer these questions:

In verse 13, Zechariah describes what this One whose name is The Branch would do:

He shall _____ the temple of the Lord.

He shall bear the _____.

He shall sit and _____ on His _____.

He shall be a _____ on His _____.

"And the counsel of _____ shall be between them both."

In verse 15, Zechariah tells them (and us) that others that are not Jews will be a part of God's people:

"Even those from _____ shall _____ and _____ the _____ of the Lord."

In the New Testament, we learn that Jesus is the One that Zechariah was talking about. Read the verses below and you will see that the same thing is said about Jesus that Zechariah said about "The Branch."

Jesus said in Matthew 16:18: "And I also say to you that you are Peter, and on this rock I will _____ My _____ and the gates of Hades shall not prevail against it. And I will give you the keys of the _____ of heaven...."

When Jesus was born, the angels sang, "_____ to God in the highest, and on earth _____, goodwill toward men!" Luke 2:14

From Hebrews 4:14, we learn: "Seeing then that we have a great high _____ who has passed through the heavens, _____ the Son of _____, let us hold fast our confession."

Before He went back to heaven, Jesus told His disciples in Mark 16:15-16: "Go into all the _____ and preach the _____ to every _____. He who believes and is baptized will be _____, but he who does not believe will be condemned."

Figure 23.4

Chapter 24
THREE INTERESTING LIFE LESSONS

As we have seen, the prophets described the Messiah and His kingdom in vivid pictures and figurative language the people of their day could understand and relate to. Jehovah was teaching His people about a kingdom and priesthood that would transcend all earthly thrones and temples. They were like spiritual children, and He taught them with visual aids and illustrations that captured their interest and ignited their imaginations. And, like the parables of Jesus, these word pictures and graphic demonstrations hid the truth from the worldly and profane, and revealed the truth to the faithful remnant who desired the fruition of God's plan. The prophets also addressed the sinful, corrupt ways of the people of God in a similar manner, describing the moral, social, and religious condition in picturesque language that is still appealing today. Many of these lessons, like Hosea, Ezekiel 16 and 23, Habakkuk, and much of Amos are for more mature students. I have had the privilege of teaching these lessons in a ladies' class setting, but I would not teach them to children. I would like to challenge you to study the prophets' messages on these themes because you will come to see sin as "exceedingly sinful" (Rom. 7:13), and you will have a greater sense of gratitude for the magnificent love, mercy, kindness, and grace of God. I have put Roy's illustrations for Hosea 1-3 and Ezekiel 16 in the Appendix if you want to use them for older students. There are three lessons from the prophets that deal with worship, giving and forgiveness that I have taught to children, and I'm sharing those in this chapter.

Lesson 1 – Worship God hates: Children need to learn about worship and what proper worship involves. I have seen little story books and puppet scripts for teaching children as old as 10 about worship, but Amos, Isaiah, and Malachi tell us a lot more about worship than those stories. It is interesting that these men prophesied to God's people at different times throughout their history. Apparently Israel and Judah had not learned the purpose and nature of true worship. It is something that must be taught through all generations and modeled in our worship as well.

Let's start with Amos who preached to the Northern Kingdom before Isaiah began his ministry in Judah. Amos said that when Israel came with their tithes and sacrifices, they were actually sinning, because they were doing this as a show or pretense. Instead of giving their freewill offerings in secret, they were loudly announcing their giving, bringing honor to themselves (Amos 4:4-5). They enjoyed going to the feasts, seeing their friends, and putting on a show of how religious they were. That's why God says, "I hate, I despise your feast days, and I do not savor your sacred assemblies. Though you offer Me burnt offerings and your grain offerings, I will not accept them... Take away from Me the noise of your songs..." (5:21-24). Look at the contrast Amos presents—the people were having a great time going to worship, but God said, "Take it away! I hate it! It is just noise, burnt animals and smoke!" (vs. 21-24, paraphrased).

You may remember that Jeroboam, the first king of Israel after the division of the kingdom, set up images of calves at Dan and Bethel for the people to worship, declaring that it was too difficult to go back to Jerusalem to observe the feasts God had ordained there (1 Kings 12:28). This was actually a political expediency, because he didn't want the people going back to Jerusalem since that might cause them to want to be unified again. Since Elijah had preached in Israel about 100 years before Amos came on the scene, there were still a few who had not been swept totally into idolatry by the leadership of Jeroboam, and later by Ahab and Jezebel who introduced Baal worship throughout Israel. However, even these few were being affected by the materialism and idolatry. They were pretending to worship Jehovah, but their worship was a sham because their lives were full of selfishness, greed, corruption, and exploiting the weak and poor.

The conditions were not much better in Judah. The city of Jerusalem and the temple were near. They were going to the right place at the right time, offering the right sacrifices. However, Jehovah said, "To what purpose is the multitude of your sacrifices to Me?" (Isa. 1:11). They were offering even more than He had required, but He says, "I don't like them, and I've had enough!" (v. 11, paraphrased). Jehovah said when they came to the temple, they were just trampling His courts; they weren't there to worship from the heart. He goes on to tell them their festivals are annoying to Him; in fact, He says, "My soul hates" them (Isa. 1:14).

Why would God hate their worship and be tired of it? Jehovah answers the same way in both Amos and Isaiah. The best summary of His admonition is in Isa. 1:16-17: "Wash yourselves, make yourselves clean; put away the evil of your doings from before My eyes. Cease to do evil, learn to do good; seek justice, rebuke the oppressor; defend the fatherless, plead for the widow." God hates worship that is a cover for a sinful life or that is trying to buy His favor or impress Him. You see, the people were doing exactly what God through Moses had commanded them not to do. Moses told them when they came into the Promised Land, they were not to inquire about how the pagans worshiped their gods and decide to worship Jehovah in that way (Deut. 12:29-31). Those who worshiped Baal, Molech and other idols were trying to gain their favor through the sacrifices they offered. They thought they would have better harvests and make more money if they kept their gods happy and satisfied. They attributed any calamity to the gods' disfavor and immediately tried to bargain with the god by even offering their children as a sacrifice. In essence, they were trying to buy their gods' favor.

Jehovah had designed worship to help His people see their need for Him. In Psalm 50:7-15, He assures Israel He doesn't need their sacrifices. In offering the sheep, goats, bulls and rams to God, they were not feeding Him as the pagans were their gods. He did not need their sacrifices. They did. The blood sacrifices were a reminder of sin, repentance, forgiveness, and humility before God. The true worshipper brought his sacrifice to the priest, transferred his sins to that sacrifice, and the priest mediated the process. All of this was a reminder that "without the shedding of blood, there is no remission" (Heb. 9:22), and pointed to "the Lamb of God who takes away the sin of the world" (John 1:29). Those sacrifices also reminded them of God's grace, having provided a way for them to be forgiven. True worship under the Old and New Covenants is a motivation to become more like Jehovah, to become that holy nation He spoke of on Mt. Sinai to Israel and in 1 Peter 2:9 to Christians today. It is universally true that we become like the God (or god) we worship.

After the people returned to Judah and Jerusalem, rebuilt the temple, and began worshiping God according to the Law, we would think they would do so with their whole heart since they had been so long without the temple and priesthood. For a while, they did, but then they settled into just "going through the motions" of worship. They were also offering the lame and sick of their flocks to God, instead of giving Him the best. God said they sneered at Him and at worship, and they complained about having to make offerings and attend the feasts. They decided it was just too much trouble to worship God! (Mal. 1:12-14). They had done what the generations before had done—they had perverted the purpose and nature of worship.

What can we and children learn about worship from these messages? The people in Amos' time enjoyed putting on their religious show; the people in Isaiah's time brought more sacrifices than God had commanded, and the people in Malachi's time had become bored and tired of worship. Each of these responses to worship demonstrates a lack of knowledge of God. The people knew what sacrifices He required. They weren't offering pigs, buzzards, or lizards to Him. They knew the Law, but they didn't know the Giver of the Law. Some people today try to impress others with loud, proper singing, or with their long, eloquent prayers, or with how much they give or do in the church. Others may come to worship out of a sense of duty or habit, not worshiping with their hearts and minds, giving God what is left over of their money and time.

Another thing we learn is that we should not seek to worship like others around us. I've read about Bible professors attending Buddhist and Hindu retreats to learn about meditation, so they can teach their students. I've read of others who have joined in Muslim worship to learn more about prayer, and still others who join in Pentecostal miracle services to learn how the Holy Spirit works. This is doing exactly what Moses told God's people not to do. We are not to worship God the way other people worship. The children in your class may have friends who are using rock bands and "praise dancing" in worship. They may wonder why we don't engage in those things. They need to know the New Testament is a sufficient guide to how we worship and that God hates worship that is not in harmony with His revealed will. He hates worship that is done to put on a show, entertain us and make us feel good. He hates worship that is done from rote by bored worshipers. And, He hates worship that is not partnered with a godly life.

Lesson 2 – Bags with holes: This lesson relates to the lesson about worship, especially relating to those who were giving the lame, weak, and blind of their flocks to God. In Haggai's short book, he admonishes the people who have stopped building the temple, and says boldly, "Consider your ways!" (1:5, 7). They had become complacent and more interested in building their own houses, furnishing them with finery, and caring for their things than in finishing the temple. Because they have not put God first in their lives and have not taken care of His temple, Haggai says they earn "wages to put into a bag with holes" (1:6). Look at the picture—it's not very smart to put your money in a holey bag!

Children need to learn to give with the right motive and for the right purpose. We give today with a joyful heart to build up God's spiritual temple in the entire world. I enjoy illustrating this lesson, too. I have a cloth bag with several holes in it. I have used "play money" and sometimes real money from Gary's change box. Either one gets the point across. I come in with the bag, talking about how much money I'm making in my job and from things I've sold. I put the money in the bag and skip around the room, swinging the bag and bragging about how much money I have. The children see the lesson immediately! They usually tell me how dumb I am to think I'm getting money when most of it spills out onto the floor. Then, we read from Haggai 1:5-11 and discuss how foolish it is not to give to God.

In connection with this, I ask them if it is right to steal from a friend, an enemy or a stranger. Of course, they answer that it isn't right. Then, I ask if it is right to steal from God, if it is possible to steal from God, and how could a person steal from God? Those questions take us to Malachi 3:8-10, "Will a man rob God? Yet you have robbed Me! But you say, 'In what way have we robbed You?' … Bring all the tithes into the storehouse…" How had they robbed God? They were not giving to God as He had commanded.

God asks them to, "…try Me now in this…If I will not open for you the windows of heaven and pour out for you such a blessing that there will not be room enough to receive it" (3:10). This scripture, along with Luke 6:38 and other similar ones, has been used by the "health and wealth" teachers to mean, for example, if we give $10 to God, He will give us more money back. These scriptures don't teach that at all. First of all, even children can see that if I give $10 or whatever amount in the hope that I'll get more back, I'm not giving with the right motive. Second, this concept is not in harmony with all the other scriptures on giving. However, we do need to help children see that when they are gracious and generous, people will respond to them in loving and kind ways and they will be blessed. I have included a short story sheet and puzzle for you to use if it is appropriate for the age you are teaching.

Lesson 3 – A picture of God's forgiveness: Zechariah 3:1-5 has a beautiful vision (or picture) of forgiveness. It is a picture that is easy for children to understand, but it is also profound in the truths it communicates. There are three main characters in this vision—Satan, Joshua (high priest), and the LORD (or the Angel of the LORD):

> Then he showed me Joshua the high priest standing before the Angel of the LORD, and Satan standing at his right hand to oppose him. And the LORD said to Satan, "The LORD rebuke you, Satan! The LORD who has chosen Jerusalem rebuke you! Is this not a brand plucked from the fire?"

> Now Joshua was clothed with filthy garments, and was standing before the Angel. Then He answered and spoke to those who stood before Him, saying, "Take away the filthy garments from him." And to him He said, "See, I have removed your iniquity from you, and I will clothe you with rich robes."

And I said, "Let them put a clean turban on his head." So they put a clean turban on his head, and they put the clothes on him. And the Angel of the LORD stood by.

Notice the drama that is played out in this vision. Satan is the adversary, the accuser, who would prevent God from accepting Joshua, the priesthood, and the nation. As we learn from the beginning in Genesis 3, Satan has always tried to thwart God's purpose, to deceive people, to give them a skewed impression of God. Throughout Israel's history, Satan has deceived kings, priests, and other leaders of the people until their sin was so horrible, they had to be disciplined and punished. The Northern kingdom was taken captive by Assyria and scattered throughout the nations. Satan laughed! He had won that round. Then, Judah followed her sister into idolatry until there was no remedy except captivity. Satan laughed again as Nebuchadnezzar set fire to the city and left the temple in ruins! He thought he had won. But, God kept sending His prophets and preserved a remnant who did return to rebuild Jerusalem and the temple. One thing we might admire about Satan is that he doesn't quit; he doesn't give up.

Now, as the Jews have returned home, Satan still has some in his grasp. It is possible that Zechariah needs to know that God's ultimate will is going to prevail. Satan will not win! In this vision, Joshua has on filthy garments, and Satan is accusing him, pointing to his filthy clothing and sinful state. Notice God's answer, "The LORD rebuke you Satan! The LORD who has chosen Jerusalem rebuke you! Is not this a brand plucked from the fire?"(v.2). Jehovah is saying that He has brought His people through trials and captivity for His purpose. Satan would try to destroy that thought, though. He would overthrow the throne of grace, leaving God as a God of judgment and condemnation, only! Jehovah will not let that happen. He calls for Joshua's filthy garments to be removed and says, "See, I have removed your iniquity from you, and I will clothe you with rich robes" (v. 4). And, Zechariah adds, "Let them put a clean turban on his head" (v. 5). A powerful, beautiful picture of God's grace!

Satan misjudged God's grace, and many people today do the same. This picture of grace and forgiveness was in view of God's eternal purpose, His drama of redemption. He had brought His people back into the land and had preserved a remnant so He could bring Christ into the world "in the fullness of time" (Gal. 4:4). There was greater grace on the horizon—"For I am bringing forth My Servant the BRANCH" (Zech.3:8). Satan may accuse, he may deceive, but he cannot frustrate God's eternal purpose! This is the message of the last book of the Bible—Revelation—Christians win!

Notice that this picture is in harmony with other pictures of God's grace, especially in Isaiah. Isaiah 64:6 tells us our righteousness is worthless, like filthy rags, but Isaiah 61:10 says God clothes us with garments of salvation and robes of righteousness. Wouldn't you like to wear those beautiful clothes? In the New Testament, Paul tells us how we are clothed with salvation and righteousness: "For you are all sons of God through faith in Christ Jesus. For as many of you as were baptized into Christ have put on Christ" (Gal. 3:26-27). God clothes us with Christ, with salvation and with righteousness when we submit to Him in baptism.

I have used the "Bible in Felt" to illustrate this vision. There is a gray angel-like figure that represents Satan, and I use another angel-like figure to represent "the angel of the LORD." You may want to use that or just use a bright piece of felt and write the word "Jehovah" or "angel of Jehovah" on it. I always explain to children that we don't know what Satan or the angel of Jehovah looked like, but we're just using these figures to represent them so we can get an idea of the vision Zechariah saw. I usually put a figure representing Zechariah low on one side of the story board and have another different color piece of felt large enough to depict the vision on the main part of the board. I use some gray felt (you could use brown or another "dirty" color) to represent Joshua's dirty clothes. I cut the clothing and a turban from that and also mark it with black, brown, and red markers to make it look really dirty. This way, I can illustrate Joshua, the high priest, with filthy clothing, then remove it and show Joshua with the proper clean high priest's clothing.

An important lesson is that God forgives, and He forgives completely. However, we do have to remain faithful to Him in order to receive the crown and robes of eternal life (Rev. 2:10). In fact, in Zech. 3:6-10, Jehovah instructs Joshua that if he will continue to be obedient, then he will be blessed. Notice that the coming of the BRANCH **is not** dependent on Joshua's faithfulness, but his personal blessing **is** dependent on his faithfulness.

Concluding Comments:

As I complete this final chapter, I'm filled with mixed emotions. The prophets have been my friends since I was a child as I explained in Chapter 1, and I hope this introduction to my friends has helped you want them to be your friends, too. Each had a unique personality God could use to accomplish His purpose. I said at the beginning this is not an exhaustive commentary on the prophets, but just a collection of my favorite lessons to teach children. It has been a labor of love and a journey down memory lane. I have seen myself as a small child sitting in Granddaddy's lap with his open Bible, then later as a preteen lying on a quilt looking at the stars and listening to him quote from these giants of faith, and finally as a teenager firing question after question to him about how can we really know the Bible is true. Even now as I sit here at the computer I can faintly hear his deep bass voice saying, "Sarah, always remember that God knows the end from the beginning. His purpose will stand and His promises are sure. You can trust Him because He has proved Himself to be God. Fulfilled prophecy is the key."

BAGS WITH HOLES!
ROBBING GOD!

Would you put your money in a bag with holes in it? _____

Would you rob God? _____

These are two important questions that we need to answer. The people of Israel put their money in bags with holes. They also robbed God. How did they do that?

You remember that they were in Babylon in captivity for 70 years, just like Jeremiah and Ezekiel had said. They had sinned against God. While they were in Babylon, they realized they had sinned, and they repented. God let them go back to their home land. They were supposed to go back and build the city and the temple.

Ezra and Nehemiah were leaders of the people when they went back home to Israel. They began building the city of Jerusalem. And, they began rebuilding the temple. Zerubbabel was also a leader in building the temple. The temple was important because it was the place where they worshipped God.

The people also began building their houses. They needed houses to live in, and it wasn't wrong to build them. The problem was that they stopped working on the temple. In fact, they built very nice houses for themselves. They began to want more and more nice things for themselves. And, they left God's House unfinished.

God sent his prophets to them -- Haggai, Zechariah and Malachi. When they preached to the people, they repented and built the temple.

We can learn that we must put God first in our lives. It is important to give to God first. If we don't, it is like putting our money in bags with holes. We think we have lots of things, but we really don't have anything! And, when we don't give to God first, we are actually robbing Him.

Figure 24.1

QUESTIONS
(Hag. 1:6-12 questions 1-7)
(Mal. 3:8-10 questions 8-10)

1. The people had planted ___ ___ ___ ___, but they reaped
___ ___ ___ ___ ___(○). (H. vs. 6)

2. They would ___ ___ ___ and ___ ___(○)___ ___, but they were not
(○)___ ___ ___ ___ ___. (H. vs. 6)

3. They had clothes to wear, but they were not ___ ___(○)___. (H. vs. 6)

4. They were putting their money in ___ ___(○)___ with
___ ___ ___ ___ ___. (H. vs. 6)

5. God told them to: "Consider your ___ ___ ___(○)!" (H. vs. 7)

6. He said they had little because they had not built the
___ ___ ___ ___ ___ ___. (H. vs. 9)

7. When the people heard this, they listened to the prophet Haggai and to
Zerubbabel, and they ___ ___ ___ ___(○) the temple. (H. vs. 12)

8. Malachi told the people that they had robbed God. How? By not
___ ___(○)___ ___ ___ to Him first. (M. vs. 8)

Figure 24.2

9. God made them a promise that He would "Open for you the

___ ___ ___ Ⓞ ___ ___ ___ of heaven and pour out a great blessing

on them. (M. vs. 10)

10. The blessing God would give them would be so great that they would

not have ___ Ⓞ ___ ___ enough to receive it! (M. vs. 10)

Put the circled letters in order at the bottom of the page. Use them for the
puzzle on the next page.

___ ___ ___ ___ ___ ___ ___ ___ ___ ___
1   2   3   4   5   6   7   8   9   10

Figure 24.2

DON'T PUT YOUR MONEY IN BAGS WITH HOLES!

Luke 6:38
38 Give, and it will be given to you: good measure, pressed down, shaken together, and running over will be put into your bosom. For with the same measure that you use, it will be measured back to you.

Matthew 6:19-21
Do not lay up for yourselves treasures on earth, where moth and rust destroy and where thieves break in and steal; 20 but lay up for yourselves treasures in heaven, where neither moth nor rust destroys and where thieves do not break in and steal. 21 For where your treasure is, there your heart will be also.

2 Corinthians 9:7
 7 So let each one give as he purposes in his heart, not grudgingly or of necessity; for God loves a cheerful giver.

3

Figure 24.2

OTHER WAYS TO ROB GOD

We can rob God in other ways, not just in giving little of our money. Let's think about some other ways we can rob God:

What about our time?

What about our brains?

What about our abilities (talents)?

What about our attitude?

Jesus said in Luke 6:38: "Give, and it will be given to you; good measure, pressed down, shaken together and running over, will be put into your bosom. For with the same measure that you use, it will be measured back to you."

God always gives us more than we give Him!

Figure 24.3

Appendix

Some additional material that you may find useful is included here. I have already noted that I placed two versions of the shadow of Jesus illustrations and the illustrations for Hosea chapters 2-3 and Ezekiel 16 in the Appendix.

Several years ago when I was teaching third and fourth grades, the children asked how we got the Bible. That prompted me to write the short explanation under that title. I tried to write it on a level that would be understandable by children of that age, and I wrote in 14 point so children could easily read it. We copied it and put it in their notebooks. I've included the edited version, and if you want to copy it for the children's notebook, please do. I hope you find it helpful. There is much good material available on this topic, and if you are teaching older children, you may want to use other material or write something you think is appropriate.

How We Got The Bible

When I think about how we got the Bible, I think of something Jesus said, something Paul said, and something Peter said. These are all in the New Testament.

Peter talked about the Old Testament, especially about the prophets, and he said, "For the prophecy came not in old time by the will of man; but holy men of God spoke as they were moved by the Holy Spirit." (II Peter 1:21) Peter tells us that the Bible is not from men. Men did not "make it up." The Bible came from God. How? He says that these "holy men of God" (that's people like Moses, David, Isaiah, Jeremiah, and all the other prophets) spoke the words that God directed them to speak by the Holy Spirit.

Now, let's look at what Jesus told His apostles. In John chapter 16, He told His apostles that He would not be with them physically much longer. He said: "But now I go My way to Him that sent Me…" (John 16:5) That is, He was going back to God. Then, He promised to send them the Holy Spirit that He calls a "Comforter" in verse 7. Then, in verse 13, He said, "…when He, the Spirit of truth is come, He will guide you into all truth…" Jesus promised that the Holy Spirit would guide the apostles in their preaching and teaching and in what they would later write.

Paul was an apostle who became a Christian later than the others like Peter, Andrew, James and John. He wrote much of the New Testament. He wrote all the letters from Romans through Philemon; and he may also have been the writer of Hebrews. In Ephesians 3:3-4, he tells how he was able to write God's words, and he tells us that what he wrote was not something he made up. "How that by <u>revelation</u> He made known unto me the mystery; (as I <u>wrote</u> before in few words, whereby, when you <u>read</u>, you may understand my knowledge in the mystery of Christ.)"

Let's think about what Paul said here. I underlined the words revelation, wrote and read. Those are the words that tell us how we got the Bible. You see, what is true about how Paul got what he wrote is also true of all the other Bible writers. Let's look at these words:

REVELATION – God made the word known to Paul by the Holy Spirit. We don't know exactly how God did that, but the Old Testament prophets say things like, "His words were in my mouth…" or "Hear the word of the Lord…" or "The Lord spoke by me…" Some way, God put His words into the minds of these men so they could speak it just the way He wanted them to and so they could write exactly what He wanted written.

WROTE – Paul and other "holy men" wrote God's words. Moses wrote the first 5 books of the Old Testament. Samuel wrote some of the books we call "history." David wrote the Psalms. Solomon wrote most of Proverbs. Ezra and Nehemiah wrote the books that are named for them, and all the prophets wrote the books that have their names on them. Jeremiah also wrote Lamentations. God used about 40 men to write His word. They lived at different times and in different places. The Old Testament books were written in the Hebrew language. The New Testament was written in Greek.

READ – We learn about God and His will for us by reading what these men wrote. And Paul said that when we read what he wrote we can understand and know what he knew! Now, we have to do more than just casually read. We have to study and learn, because some of the things Paul wrote are difficult to understand. If by reading what Paul wrote we can understand what Paul knew and understood, that is true of all the other books of the Bible, no matter who wrote them.

Since we don't live in the time that these books were written, we have to learn things about the customs and culture of the people of that time. This is where the study of archeology helps us. People have gone to these countries and have found the ruins of the cities and towns that the Bible tells us about.

Also, we don't know how to read Hebrew and Greek. So the Bible has been translated into many different languages. Let's get a simple idea of how that happened. We do not have the original words on the original paper that Paul or any of the other Bible writers wrote. We have copies of those original books. Remember the "scribes" that are referred to in the New Testament? These were men who copied the words of the Old Testament so there could be copies for people to read. Now, they didn't have the printing press or Xerox machines like we do today, so there were few copies of God's word, but there were enough copies for people to read and learn. The Old Testament was also translated into Greek before Jesus was born. That way, people who didn't know the Hebrew language could read God's word. The Bible has been translated into English many different times. The invention of the printing press in 1440 (that's 560 years ago) made it possible to print more and more Bibles.

There is a word we use to describe God's work in the world and especially in our lives. That word is providence. What does it mean? Look at the part I underlined – "provide." That word means, then, that God provides what we need. He works through events like the invention of the printing press, good roads for travel, education that helps people learn other languages, and things like that. God has used all these events and many more to provide the Bible for us. He has guided men to write it, and He has protected it and preserved it through all time by His providence. We can know when we read a good and accurate translation of the Bible that we are reading what God wants us to know.

There is a promise about His word in the Old and New Testaments. This promise helps us know that we can depend on God's word. In Isaiah 40:8 and I Peter 1:24-25, we read the same promise:

"The grass withers, the flower fades; but the word of our God shall stand forever."

The Sign of Jonah

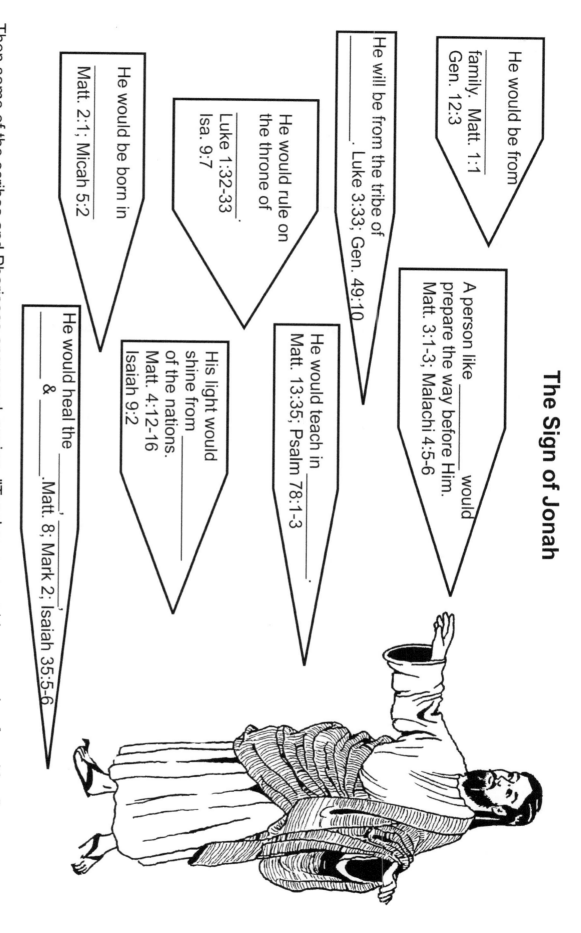

He would be from _____ family. Matt. 1:1 Gen. 12:3

A person like _____ would prepare the way before Him. Matt. 3:1-3; Malachi 4:5-6

He will be from the tribe of _____. Luke 3:33; Gen. 49:10

He would rule on the throne of _____. Luke 1:32-33 Isa. 9:7

He would be born in _____ Matt. 2:1; Micah 5:2

His light would shine from _____ of the nations. Matt. 4:12-16 Isaiah 9:2

He would teach in _____. Matt. 13:35; Psalm 78:1-3

He would heal the _____ & _____. Matt. 8; Mark 2; Isaiah 35:5-6

Then some of the scribes and Pharisees answered, saying, "Teacher, we want to see a sign from You." 39 But He answered and said to them, "An evil and adulterous generation seeks after a sign, and no sign will be given to it except the sign of the prophet Jonah. 40 For as Jonah was three days and three nights in the belly of the great fish, so will the Son of Man be three days and three nights in the heart of the earth." Matt. 12:38-41

The "sign of Jonah" was Jesus' _____!

Figure A.1

THE SIGN OF JONAH
Jonah 1-3

Some facts you remember about Jonah:

Jonah was a ___ ◯ ___ ___ ___ ___ ◯. God told him to go

preach to the people of ___ ◯ ___ ___ ___ ___ ___ . Jonah tried to run

away and got on a ◯ ___ ___ ___ going to Tarshish. God caused a great

___ ___ ◯ ___ ◯, AND THE SAILORS THREW Jonah into the___ ___ ◯.

Then God prepared a great ◯ ___ ___ ___ that swallowed Jonah. He was in

the fish___ ◯ ___ ___ ◯ days and three nights. When Jonah repented and

___ ___ ___ ◯ ___ ◯ the fish spit him out on dry land. Then he went and

preached to the people of Nineveh.

Write the circled letters in order below. Then use the number code to reveal the sign of Jonah.

___ ___ ___ ___ ___ ___ ___ ___ ___ ___ ___ ___
 1   2   3   4   5   6   7   8   9 10 11 12

Jesus would be ___ ___ ___ ___ ___ ___   ___ ___ ___ ___   ___ ___ ___
                1   7   3   4 10 12   8   1   5   6   2   9 10

___ ___ ___ ___   ___ ___ ___ ___ ___   ___ ___ ___ ___ ___
12 10   7 12   7   8   2 10   1   2   9   1 10 10

___ ___ ___ ___ .
12   7 11   4

Now, read Matthew 12:38-41 and Matthew 16:1-4.

Figure A.2

"(Jesus)..was fordained before the foundation of the world, but was manifest (made known) in these last times for you."

1 Peter 1:18-20

OLD TESTAMENT

NEW TESTAMENT

Old Testament ".. shadow of things to come.
But the body is Christ."

Col. 2:17

"For the law is a shadow of good things to come..."

Hebrews 10:1

Figure A.3

Jesus' Shadow is in the Old Testament Prophets

Acts 3:24-26

Yes, and all the prophets, from Samuel and those who follow, as many as have spoken, have also foretold these days. 25 You are sons of the prophets, and of the covenant which God made with our fathers, saying to Abraham, 'And in your seed all the families of the earth shall be blessed.' 26 To you first, God, having raised up His Servant Jesus, sent Him to bless you, in turning away every one of you from your iniquities."

Figure A.4

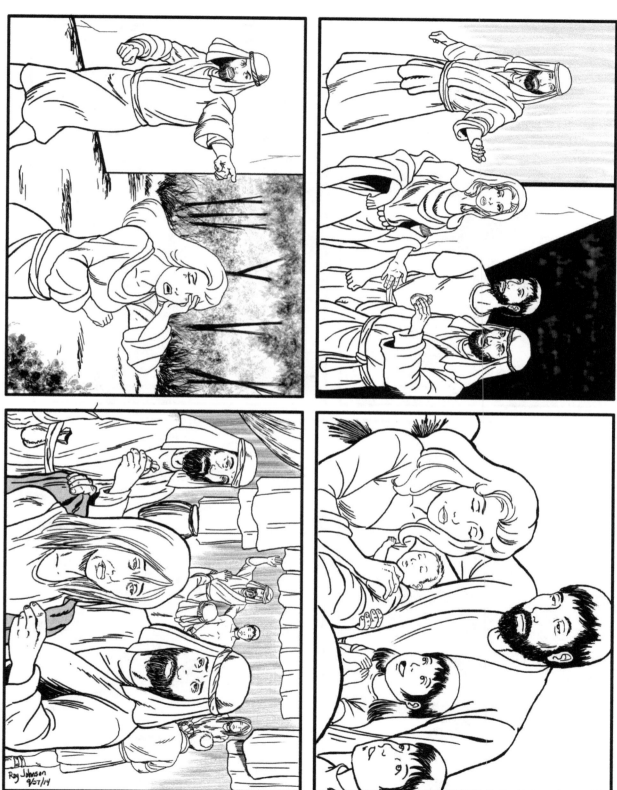

Hosea 1 - 3

Figure A.5

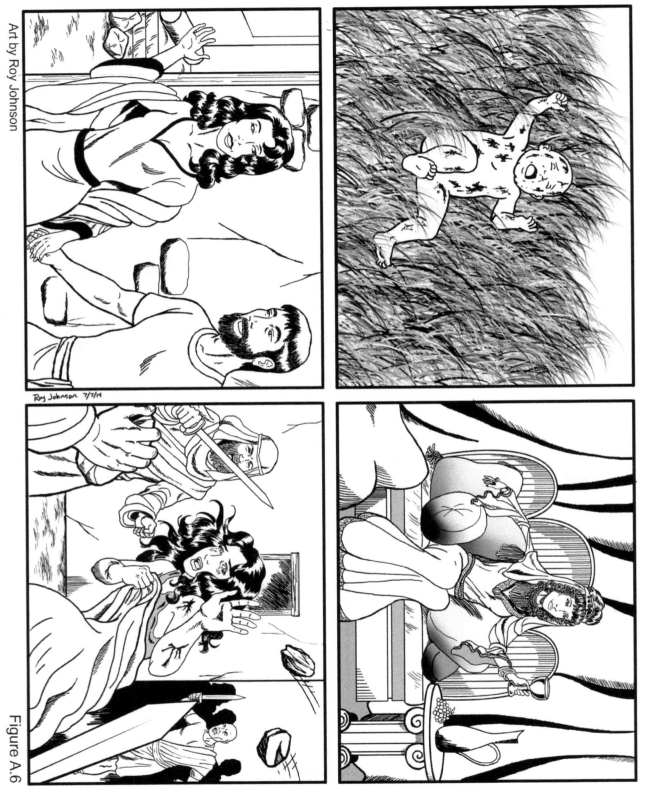

Art by Roy Johnson

Roy Johnson 7/7/14

Figure A.6

Suggestions for Teachers

Several good teachers have read this material pre-publication and have made observations about how this could be used to teach effectively and help children remember the lessons. Creative teachers will think of many other ways to use this material and help their children learn these great lessons. These are offered to stimulate your thinking:

1. Use the pictures to create flash cards. Write the name of the prophet or something interesting about the prophet on the opposite side of the card. You may want to use the list of questions at the end of Chapter 2. If you do, please note that some of these are not covered in this book. In the first grouping, numbers 2, 3, 5, 10, 12, 18, and 19 are not covered in this book; numbers 8 and 11 are referred to, but there is no picture to accompany them. In the second grouping, numbers 1, 3, 13, and 20 are not referenced, and numbers 4 and 21 are referred to, but there is no picture.

2. Use the pictures to make a matching game. This can be an activity for various ages, depending on how difficult you make the questions/facts about the prophets.

3. Other resources for puzzles and activities for learning are available on www.puzzlemaker.com. I used this website frequently when I was teaching this material, but I can't include those because they are for classroom use, only.

4. I referred to the side-by-side scripture sheets in Chapter 1. I found this to be very effective to help the children see the unity of God's Word.

5. Include the approximate date the prophet spoke and the date his prophecy was fulfilled on the scripture sheets or on the timeline in the classroom. For younger children, you may want to include the number of years until the prophecy was fulfilled.

Works Cited

Barfield, Kenny. 1995. *The Prophet Motive*. Nashville, TN: The Gospel Advocate Company.

Barnes, Albert. 1837. *Notes on the Bible*. StudyLight.org.

Bruce, F. F. 1961. The Epistle to the Ephesians. Old Tappan, NJ: Fleming H. Revell.

Coffman, James Burton. 1975. *Commentary of Matthew*. StudyLight.org.

Dawkins, Richard. 2008. *The God Delusion*. Boston, MA: Houghton Mifflin Company: A Mariner Book.

Hailey, Homer. 1972. *A Commentary on the Minor Prophets*. Grand Rapids, MI: Baker Book House.

Hailey, Homer. 1982. *From Creation to the Day of Eternity*. Las Vegas, NV: Nevada Publishing House.

Hailey, Homer. 1985. *A Commentary on Isaiah*. Grand Rapids, MI: Baker Book House.

Hailey, Homer. 1985. *Hailey's Comments, Volume I*. Las Vegas, NV: Nevada Publications.

Hailey, Homer. 1995. *The Messiah of Prophecy to the Messiah on the Throne*. Louisville, KY: Religious Supply, Inc.

Halley, Henry H. 1965. *Halley's Bible Handbook*. Grand Rapids, MI: Zondervan Publishing House.

Hamilton, Mark; Willis, John T., editors. 2009. *The Transforming Word*. Abilene, TX: Abilene Christian University Press.

Jamieson-Fausset-Brown. *Bible Commentary*. Gospel Advocate WORDsearch7.

Keesee, Dayton. 2011. *Truth for Today Commentary: Jeremiah 1-25*. Searcy, AR: Resource Publications.

Keesee, Dayton. 2011. *Truth for Today Commentary: Jeremiah 26-52 and Lamentations*. Searcy, AR: Resource Publications.

Kelcy, Raymond C. 1972. *The Letters of Peter and Jude*. Austin, TX: R. B. Sweet Company.

Kaiser, Walter C., Jr. 1995. *The Messiah in the Old Testament*. Grand Rapids, MI: Zondervan Publishing House.

Krakauer, Jon. 2004. *Under the Banner of Heaven*. New York, NY: Random House, Anchor Books.

McGuiggan, Jim. 1979. *The Book of Ezekiel*. Lubbock, TX: Montex Publishing Company.

Morgan, G. Campbell. 1912. *Living Messages of the Books of the Old Testament*. New York, NY: Fleming H. Revell Company.

Myers, Philip Van Ness. 1904. *Ancient History*. Boston, MA: Ginn & Company. (I found this first edition of Myer's *Ancient History* on Amazon.com when I began this book. It was the history text my grandfather used when he was in school, and I wanted to refer to it in memory of him.)

Olbricht, Thomas H. 1980. *He Loves Forever: The Message of the Old Testament*. Austin, TX: Journey Books.

Simpson, Don. 1977. *The Book of Daniel*. Fort Worth, TX: Star Publishing.

Stalker, James. 1949. *The Life of Jesus Christ*. Old Tappan, NJ: Fleming H. Revell Company.

Tabor, James D. 2006. *The Jesus Dynasty*. New York, NY: Simon & Schuster.

Warren, Rick. 2002. *The Purpose Driven Church*. Grand Rapids, MI: Zondervan Publishing House.

Woods, Guy N. 1968. *A Commentary on the New Testament Epistles of Peter, John, and Jude*. Nashville, TN: The Gospel Advocate Company.

About the Author

Sarah Fallis is an old farm girl who got away from that farm in northeast Texas as fast as she could. She enrolled in East Texas State University at 17, majoring in math and English. In 1964, while still in college and 18 years old, she met and married Gary Fallis. Gary was an English teacher, but decided preaching the gospel was his first love.

When Tonya was born in 1969, Sarah couldn't let someone else take care of this precious gift from God, so she quit teaching and became a full-time mom. Tonya prayed for a baby brother, and in 1975 Paden was born. When Paden was in second grade, Gary had an opportunity to attend graduate school at Abilene Christian University, so Sarah returned to the classroom to help support the family. In 1999, she was blessed to begin her dream job—mathematics professor at Tarrant County College.

Sarah holds a masters' degree in mathematics and education from Texas Woman's University and has done graduate work in Bible and counseling at Abilene Christian University. She has taught Bible classes for children, teenage girls, and women and has spoken at Bible workshops and lectureships in Texas, Colorado, Oklahoma, and Virginia. She has also taught at numerous ladies' days and retreats, including The European Christian Women's Retreat in Speyer, Germany, in 2007. She works with Gary in Tanzania, Ukraine, and other mission areas each summer, speaking for various ladies' programs and conducting personal Bible studies.

Gary and Sarah are members of the Bridgewood Church of Christ in Fort Worth where she teaches the Ladies' Bible Class. She recently retired to write and to travel more with Gary.

CPSIA information can be obtained
at www.ICGtesting.com
Printed in the USA
LVHW110138051121
702487LV00003B/12